A Spirit Voice I seem to Hear,
Mourn not for me, my parents dear.
Epitaph on the grave of 13-year-old
Allen Marces, 1864

IN THE BONEYARD

History & Horrors of American Cemeteries

TROY TAYLOR

- An American Hauntings Ink Book -

© Copyright 2020 by Troy Taylor
and American Hauntings Ink
All Rights Reserved, including the right to copy or reproduce this book, or portions thereof, in any form, without express permission from the author and publisher.

Original Cover Artwork Designed by
© Copyright 2020 by April Slaughter & Troy Taylor

This Book is Published By:
American Hauntings Ink
Jacksonville, Illinois | 217.791.7859
Visit us on the Internet at
http://www.americanhauntingsink.com

First Edition - July 2020
ISBN: 978-1-7352706-0-9

Printed in the United States of America

Remember me as you pass by,
As you are now, so once was I.
As I am now, so you must be,
Prepare for death and follow me.
Early American Epitaph

To quote Benjamin Franklin, "In this world nothing can be said to be certain, except death and taxes." There is nothing very metaphysical about taxes. But death, on the other hand, is something that we have both feared and worshipped since the beginning of history. We avoid it, we dread it, and then we accept it because death is inevitable. Since man started walking upright, he began dreaming up rituals to deal with it and to try and understand it in some way.

But he has always failed to understand it because death is a mystery. It's the world's greatest mystery, and all of us, as Benjamin Franklin noted, have to face it eventually, whether we want to or not.

And that means that all of us have contemplated the mystery of death at one time or another. We all wonder - no matter our beliefs - what will happen to us after we die. Some believe we simply come to an end and that this life is our only existence. Many think we will be born again in a new body with an old soul, while others believe our spirits pass on to another place - or perhaps remain behind as ghosts.

Of course, none of us will truly know what happens next until our lives come to an end, and death must finally be confronted. Perhaps not knowing is what has caused us to construct so many rituals and practices to deal with death. We have immortalized it with cemeteries, grave markers, and of course, with dark and frightening legends and lore.

Hence, this book.

These are the stories of the most haunted cemeteries in America, filled with forgotten places, ghosts, vampires, and nightmarish tales that seem to be too good to be true - but aren't. These are not tales from fiction but real-life stories of phantoms, strange deaths, premature burial, and the true story of one of the most famous cemetery phantoms of all time - Resurrection Mary. It's here that you'll find the most complete account of the life of the woman who spawned this eerie tale, as well as the only photograph of her in existence.

But why cemeteries? Aside from the fact that their link to the rituals of death makes them "spooky" places, experts of the occult say that graveyards are not usually the best places to find ghosts. And this makes sense. Nearly every ghost enthusiast can tell you that a place becomes haunted after a traumatic event or an unexpected death that occurs at that place. History is filled with stories of houses that became haunted after a murder happened there, or after some horrible event occurred that echoes over the decades as a haunting. We can understand why a spirit might linger at home or other locations where they spend their life, but why a cemetery, which seems to be simply the last stop on the way from this world to the next?

Graveyard ghosts seem to be a different sort of spirit than you might find hanging around a haunted house. These ghosts seem to be connected to the cemetery in a way that has nothing to do with events that occurred during their lifetime. Spirits usually remain on earth because of some sort of unfinished business that occurred while they were living. This seems to rule out a cemetery as a place where a person might have left unfinished business.

But haunted cemeteries do exist, and the ghosts that haunt them seem to be connected to the burial grounds because of events that occurred *after* their deaths instead of before. They seem to be seeking eternal rest that eludes them at the graveyard where their physical bodies were placed. They become disturbed by things like grave robbery, desecration, unmarked or forgotten graves, natural disasters, or perhaps because the deceased was never properly buried.

In these pages, we'll explore these tragedies - and others - together and will perhaps reveal some of the mysteries of haunted cemeteries that may have eluded us until now.

So, take my hand, light a candle, and let's whistle as we walk past the cemetery tonight - and hope that nothing is waiting for us out there among the stones.

Troy Taylor
Summer 2020

1. THE AMERICAN WAY OF DEATH

"Before 1831, America had no cemeteries," writes Rebecca Greenfield. "It's not that Americans didn't bury their dead - just that large, modern graveyards did not exist."

Death was the next-door neighbor to our ancestors. There were so many ways to die in America's past that it's impressive that so many of the early settlers lived to what passed for old age at the time. They died from hardship, disease, starvation, accidents, and in childbirth. Doctors, ignorant of real medicine, often killed as many as they cured. Fires, floods, and natural disasters wiped out entire communities. Few adults could swim - even fewer children and thousands drowned in lakes and rivers. Crime and violence claimed others, as did the Indian massacres that occurred on the frontier. Wars dramatically raised the death toll, forcing Americans to face death on a massive scale. Our ancestors produced so many children because they knew that most of them would never become adults.

And with all this death, the settlers needed someplace to put the bodies of the deceased. The notion of burying the dead or preparing them in various ways dates to before recorded time when the Neanderthals would carefully arrange their dead below the ground. The people of the Mediterranean region created rock shelters for

The Puritans of New England wanted death to be a frightening thing, so their cemeteries were filled with the most terrifying images of the afterlife they could find.

graves, and the Neolithic people buried the dead beneath the floors of their homes. Ancient Egyptians built cities of the dead outside the cities of the living, and early Christians in Rome created underground chambers for the dead.

In modern times the term *cemetery* - from the ancient Greek word meaning "sleeping place" - is typically used to describe park-like land that is used explicitly as a place to bury the dead. Before the word - and those plots of land - came into use in the 1830s, the dead were buried in graveyards and churchyards, plots of ground associated with a house of worship.

The first graveyards in America were created by the Puritans in New England, who brought the traditions of Europe with them to the New World. They lived strict, somber lives, passing laws against colorful clothing, holidays, and even showing affection in public. Is it any wonder that their graveyards were harsh places, warning against "unspeakable terrors" and eternal damnation in hell?

To the Puritans, death was inevitable, and a punishment for man's original sin. Their graveyards were used to warn the living of the horror they faced if they were unfaithful to God. They decorated their gravestones with winged skulls, skeletons, grim reapers, and faces of death. It was a warning from beyond the grave - see how I am now? You do not want to die if you have not served God because terror awaits.

Among the other colonists of the region, death was not seen as the dismal end to life and the beginning of a grim afterlife - it was a rite of passage taking them to a better place.

Burial rites became more formal and extravagant. Wealthy merchants spent money on funeral services for their families and themselves. Burials became more ritualized and turned into lengthy social occasions with their own sets of rules. There were mourners and dinners, funeral notices, and printed broadsides that included the name and death date of the deceased and often a discourse on death and salvation.

On the day of the burial, a mourning carriage transported the coffin to the churchyard. The mourners followed, and once the coffin had been lowered into the ground, they meditated in silence. Later, the party usually gathered for a funeral dinner.

Even before that, families spent substantial amounts of money on the trappings, food, and liquor for funeral events with liquor accounting for the biggest bills of all. Gallons of rum, wine, and spirits would be consumed at a funeral along with copious amounts of food. Feasting and drinking would take place before the procession to the burying ground. Corpses were laid out at home in coffins, and prior to burial, guests arrived to view the body, and then drank and ate - only to do it all again after the service was over.

Buried Out Back

Things were simpler in other parts of early America. For farm families, the dead would often be buried in an open plot of land or, for the more religiously minded, in the local churchyard. But even rural families had their own traditions and rituals.

When an individual neared death, family and friends would gather to keep a continuous vigil by the ailing person's side. Known as the "death watch" or more commonly as "sitting up," loved ones would often travel for many miles to be near the dying in his or her final days. No one was left to face death alone.

Before doctors were common, family members were left to determine whether the moment of death had arrived. This was usually done in simple ways. A hand mirror was typically brought to the body and placed under the mouth and nose of the corpse for as long as an entire minute, checking for any fogging on the glass.

Once death had been determined, mirrors and photographs in the house were turned to face the wall so that there was no chance that the departing spirit would see his or her reflection and decide to stay behind. All clocks were stopped in the house, both as a method of marking the time of death and because when started again, it would mark a new period in the family's life. Shades and curtains were also drawn because there were superstitions that claimed the next person to die would be one the sun shined on next.

Rural funeral services were simple affairs with homemade coffins, cooling boards, and lots of food and liquor.

Family members - usually women - prepared the body for burial. They would be washed and dressed and then laid out for visitors to pay their respects. Embalming didn't exist at the time, so the final rituals usually happened very quickly, especially during the summer months. There was little time spent waiting for distant relatives to arrive.

The deceased would be laid out using two chairs that faced each other. A "cooling board" - a long panel that was usually about the size of two table extensions - would be placed between the two chair seats. The body was then taken from the death bed and placed on the cooling board, stripped, bathed, and dressed for viewing. Some were wrapped in shrouds, but most of the time, they were dressed in their best dress or suit of clothing.

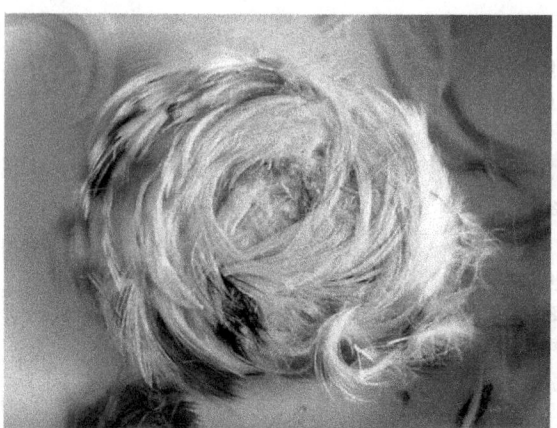

Feather death crowns sometimes formed in the pillow of the deceased. Tradition claimed they died in a state of grace.

A pillow - although not the one from the death bed - was then placed under the deceased's head. That pillow would later be opened, and the feathers removed. Tradition stated that if the person died in a state of grace, the feathers would form a crown inside of the pillow. When this occurred, the crowns were often framed and kept as a remembrance of the dead.

If a crown did not form, it was believed the person had died in sin, which many Appalachian families thought called for the presence of a "sin eater." This tradition, brought over from the Old World, called for a plate of food to be placed on the chest of the corpse for the sin eater to devour. It was believed that when he ate the food, he also "ate" the sins of the deceased and cleansed their spirit. Payment for this task had to be made with gold - even jewelry or a gold tooth would suffice.

Shoes were never placed on the corpse. They were draped with a quilt, and their hands were folded to make them look as though they were sleeping. The wrists were usually tied with a ribbon or a cord. Another band of cloth was tied under the chin and around the head to keep the mouth from falling open. Coins were placed on the eyes. An old tradition stated that the coins were used to pay the ferryman who transported the souls of the dead to the afterlife. But more practically, it hid the disturbing image of a corpse with its eyes open, staring at the mourners.

All of this had to be accomplished before rigor mortis occurred, or it would be nearly impossible to get the body into the coffin. Buckets of cold spring water would be kept close at hand during the wake to keep the body cool. Cold rags were often placed on the face to keep the skin from turning black.

After the wake, the body would be moved into the coffin, which was quite plain, unfinished, unlined, and usually made from poplar or pine. They were built by local carpenters and cabinetmakers and came with unhinged tops, rope handles, and the lid would be tacked in place once the body was inside. A wagon would be used to carry the deceased to the nearest burial ground.

The Rise of the Garden Cemetery

As time passed, customs changed, and so did the way the dead were buried. The churchyards and graveyards eventually became cemeteries, but that change did not begin in America. By the early nineteenth century in Europe, some churchyards had been in use for hundreds of years.

The wealthy had once preferred to be buried inside the church itself. Clerics, men with titles, and wealthy benefactors of the church regarded this kind of entombment as a right rather than a privilege, and within decades the buildings began to become very crowded. Officials tried to limit the number of the deceased buried within the church's walls but found offers of large sums of money too tempting to pass up. Soon the churches were packed with the dead. The health risks for the living finally forced the churches to stop this practice, and from that point on, only bishops, abbots, and "laymen of the first distinction" were interred within the church buildings.

Those who didn't make the cut were buried in the surrounding churchyard instead. Even there a person's social status depended on the section of the burial ground where you might spend eternity. The most favored sites were those on the east, closest to the church. This was the section that offered the best view of the rising sun on the Day of Judgement, and so they were sold for a premium. People of lesser distinction were buried on the south side, while the north corner of the graveyard was considered the Devil's domain. It was reserved for stillborn babies, bastards, and strangers unfortunate enough to die while passing through the local parish.

An overcrowded churchyard in the days before Garden Cemeteries were created

Suicides, if they were buried in consecrated ground at all, were usually deposited in the north end, although their corpses were not allowed to pass through the cemetery gates. They had to be passed over the top of the stone wall.

Centuries later, the churchyards were overflowing. As the population in towns and cities across Europe swelled in the eighteenth century, they simply ran out of space for the dead. Several different solutions were attempted. First, they started burying the coffins more closely together. After that, they tried stacking them atop one another and bringing in more soil to cover them. This caused churchyards to rise to more than 20 feet above the height of the church floor. Another solution was to grant only a short-term occupation of a gravesite. But it got to the point that the occupancy of a burial plot was being measured in only days - or even hours - before a coffin had to be moved so that another could take its place.

With so many bodies crammed into churchyards, protests began to arise from those who lived nearby. The decaying corpses and the vile stench coming from the graveyards were considered a considerable risk to local health, and doctors began issuing stern warnings about the unsanitary - and even frightening - conditions.

It had simply become impossible for the churchyards to hold the bodies of the dead. By the mid-1700s, the situation had reached a crisis in France. Dirt and stone walls had been added around graveyards to hold the burials in place, but they often collapsed, causing human remains to litter the streets of Paris. The government, forced into action, closed the churchyards for five years so that burial grounds could be established outside of the city.

But closing the city graveyards was not enough. In 1786, it was decided to remove bodies from the churchyards and transport the bones into the catacombs that had been carved beneath the southern part of the city. It was a massive undertaking. On the night of April 7, a long procession of funeral carts carrying the bones of tens of thousands of people made its way to the catacombs. The wagons were escorted by torchlight and were accompanied by the chanting of priests. There was no method by which to identify the individual remains, so it was decided to arrange the bones into rows of skulls, femurs, and so on. It has been estimated that the Paris catacombs contain the bodies of between 3 and 6 million people.

In addition to the catacombs, four cemeteries were built on the edges of the city - Montmartre, Vaugirard, Montparnasse, and Pere-Lachaise, the latter of which became known as the world's first "garden" cemetery. It was named after the confessor priest of Louis XIV and is probably the most celebrated burial ground in the world. As it was, the cemetery began in debt and caused a considerable amount of concern for the investors who created it. If Napoleon had been buried there, as he originally planned, the businessmen would have rested much easier. As it was, they were forced to mount a massive publicity campaign to persuade Parisians to be buried on the grounds. They even dug up the bones of famous Frenchmen who had been buried elsewhere and moved them to Pere-Lachaise.

Ironically, it was the burial of people who never

Pere-Lachaise Cemetery in Paris

lived at all that finally made the cemetery popular. The novelist Honore de Balzac began burying many of the fictional characters in his books at Pere-Lachaise. On Sunday afternoons, readers from all over Paris would come to the cemetery to see the tombs that Balzac described so eloquently in his novels.

Today the cemetery serves as the final resting place of artists and writers like Balzac, Victor Hugo, Colette, Marcel Proust, Chopin, Oscar Wilde, Sarah Bernhardt, and Jim Morrison of the Doors - if you believe he's dead, that is.

Pere-Lachaise became known around the world for its size and beauty. It covered hundreds of acres and was landscaped and fashioned with pathways for carriages. It reflected the new creative age where architecture and nature could combine to celebrate the lives of those buried there.

Paris seems always to set the standard for fashion, and others followed - even when it came to cemeteries. In London, risks to public health came not only from the dank confines of the graveyards but from the water people drank. In many cases, the drinking supply flowed right through the graveyards. By the early part of the nineteenth century, reformers were calling for the establishment of burials grounds away from London's population center.

In 1832, the London Cemetery Company opened the first public cemetery at Kensal Green. It was made up of 54 acres of open ground and was far from the noise and chaos of the city. From the very beginning, it was a fashionable place to be buried. In fact, it was so prestigious that it can still boast the highest number of royal burials outside of Windsor and Westminster Abbey. The dead here also include novelists Wilkie Collins, James Makepeace Thackery, and Anthony Trollope, among others.

But if Kensal Green is London's most fashionable cemetery, then Highgate is the most romantic - and the most legendary. It did not start as a cemetery; in fact, in the late 1600s, the grounds were part of an estate owned by Sir William Ashhurst, who had built his home on the outskirts of a small, isolated hilltop community called Highgate. By 1836, the mansion had been sold, demolished, and then replaced by a church. The grounds around it were consecrated in 1839, and the cemetery went on to hold the remains of Karl Marx, Sir Ralph Richardson, George Eliot, and several members of the Charles Dickens and Dante Rossetti families.

For years it was a fashionable and desirable place to be buried, but as the decades passed, hard times came to Highgate. The owners steadily lost money, and the monuments, statues, crypts, and markers soon became covered with undergrowth and began to fall into disrepair. By the end of World War II, which saw an occasional German bomb landing on the burial ground, the deterioration of the place was out of control. The ruined cemetery became the scene of many ghost stories, strange tales, and even the location of several horror films produced by legendary Hammer Films.

The cemetery has since been restored - somewhat - and has become a popular place to visit for tourists looking for the curious and the macabre.

Cemeteries Come to America

In America, the churchyard remained the most common place to bury the dead for more than a century. They closely resembled their European counterparts - they were cramped, overcrowded, and foul-smelling eyesores. In 1800, Timothy Dwight described the local burial ground as "an unkempt section of the town common where the graves and fallen markers were daily trampled upon by people and cattle." Years passed, and the criticisms of local graveyards intensified as social reformers began to regard them as a source of disease. In the years before the Civil War, many towns and cities started prohibiting burials from taking place within city limits.

The French style of "garden" cemeteries became popular in America. The first was Mount Auburn Cemetery in Cambridge, Massachusetts, which was started in 1831. Proposed by Dr. Jacob Bigelow and designed by Henry A.S. Dearborn, it was meant to be an oasis on the outskirts of the city. Other cemeteries followed - like Greenwood Cemetery in Brooklyn - imitating Mount Auburn's romantic winding paths and forest setting.

Mount Auburn Cemetery in Massachusetts was the first Garden Cemetery in America, but many others soon followed.

These new burial grounds were the exact opposite of crowded churchyards and became an immediate success. They began to appear outside of cities across America. In those days before most communities had public parks, the cemeteries were used as recreation areas and picnic grounds. Visitors enjoyed the shaded walkways and had lunch on weekend afternoons. Eventually, garden cemeteries inspired the American park movement and virtually created the field of landscape architecture.

As they continued to spread in popularity, many cities exhumed the dead buried years before and moved them to the new cemeteries. This allowed communities to expand and grow in ways they could not with a graveyard literally in the way of progress. It also allowed them to keep the bodies of those who died during the frequent epidemics of the nineteenth century segregated from their downtown business and residential areas.

In St. Louis, cholera epidemics created two garden cemeteries - Calvary and Bellefontaine - on what was the far north side of the city in the mid-nineteenth century. Bellefontaine, a secular cemetery, was created by Almerin Hotchkiss, a landscape architect and creator of Brooklyn's Greenwood Cemetery. Calvary, the adjoining Catholic burial ground, was started just a few years later. Both cities not only received the bodies of those who died during the epidemic but also many of the remains removed from other local burial grounds.

Both cemeteries hold the remains of local and national celebrities as well as authors, war heroes, and St. Louis brewers. Thomas Hart Benton, General William Clark, Sara Teasdale, William S. Burroughs, the infamous Lemp Family, Adolphus Busch, Dred Scott, William Tecumseh Sherman, Tennessee Williams, Kate Chopin, and many others are buried there.

In Chicago, one burial ground created several garden cemeteries, including Graceland and Rosehill. The graveyard had been the city's only burial place through the first five decades of its existence. It was located not far from the lakefront, at Clark Street and North Avenue, where Lincoln Park in Chicago is now located.

The graveyard was not used for long. Just a few years after it was established, it became the subject of many complaints. Not only was it overcrowded - largely thanks to cholera epidemics - but many felt the poorly managed burials that had occurred were creating health problems and contaminating the water supply. Additionally, both the city morgue and the local quarantine "pest" house were located on the graveyard's grounds. It was closed in 1870, and the remains were removed to new cemeteries - well, most of them were moved anyway.

We'll come back to that later in the book.

The two most notable cemeteries created from the closure of the graveyard were Graceland and Rosehill Cemeteries. Graceland, established on North Clark Street in 1860, was created by real estate developer Thomas B. Bryan. Two of the men primarily responsible for the beauty of the place were architects William Le Baron Jenney and Ossian Cole Simonds. Simonds became so fascinated with the site that he ended up turning his entire business to landscape design. It is filled with breathtaking monuments and buildings, including a cemetery chapel and the city's oldest crematorium.

Taking its name from a nearby tavern-keeper named Roe, Rosehill Cemetery began in 1859. The area around his saloon was known for some years as "Roe's Hill." The name was slightly altered when the cemetery was created after the closure of the dreary graveyard near the lake. Rosehill is the city's oldest and largest cemetery and is the final resting place for more than 1,500 Chicagoans, including Civil War generals, mayors, millionaires, authors, and city founders.

And our cemetery stories are far from over. Throughout these pages, we'll return to various burial grounds across the country - from garden cemeteries to rural churchyards to burial grounds secluded deep in the woods.

Embalming & Preservation

The significant changes began for the "American Way of Death" in the middle nineteenth century when the funeral industry was born. It was in the years following the Civil War that funeral customs would become a business that still prospers today. The local cabinet and furniture makers were no longer the merchants in the community who sold all the coffins - not after strict customs and embalming became essential elements of death in America.

Embalming, of one kind or another, has been around for centuries - probably longer. The ancient Egyptians had mummified their dead, giving those of royal birth an elaborate send-off to the other side. Brains and internal organs were removed from the dead and placed in separate jars. The corpses were purged and then soaked in chemicals for as long as 70 days. The empty cavity would then be stuffed with spices and resins before being sewed closed. Once the remains were mummified, they were wrapped in yards of cotton and linen and then placed in a tomb for what was assumed to be eternity.

The Greeks and Romans also embalmed the dead, although usually only those personages who needed to lie in state for an extended time. The Romans used wax masks to cover the decaying faces of the dead, making them appear more life-like - the same way modern embalmers use heavy make-up so that mourners can say "they look as if they are sleeping."

During the Middle Ages, those of noble birth were often pickled or crudely embalmed when their life came to an end. This usually involved boiling the corpse in chemicals so that only the bones and parchment-like skin remained. Bodies in this state were easily transported. The Crusaders and knights who traveled to the fight in foreign lands always took cauldrons along with them in case they were killed. They wanted their remains to be interred at home.

In 1618, doctors discovered the human circulatory system, which launched more advanced efforts to preserve corpses for medical research. A century later, Dr. William Hunter devised a method for arterial embalming in which the blood was drained from the body through a vein and replaced with a formalin-based fluid through an artery. The only problem with this method was that the removal of the blood drained all the color from the corpse, and the bodies then had to be painted with life-like colors before they could be put on display.

In America, the first patent for embalming was granted in 1856. It was still a crude yet complicated process that required a corpse to be injected with an arsenic and alcohol mixture, charged with electricity, washed with chemicals, covered with oils, and then sealed in a coffin that was filled with alcohol. The container could not be opened for viewing, but it did make it so that the dead could be transported to distant parts of the country without fear of decomposition. It wasn't popular, and it was rarely used.

The modern methods of embalming can trace their start to Thomas H. Holmes, who - thanks to his passion for dissecting corpses and leaving them in inappropriate places - was expelled from New York University's Medical School. During the Civil War, he received a commission in the Army Medical Corps and spent most of his time embalming soldiers who were killed in battle - at least 4,028 of them in four years. It became a common practice because families of officers -

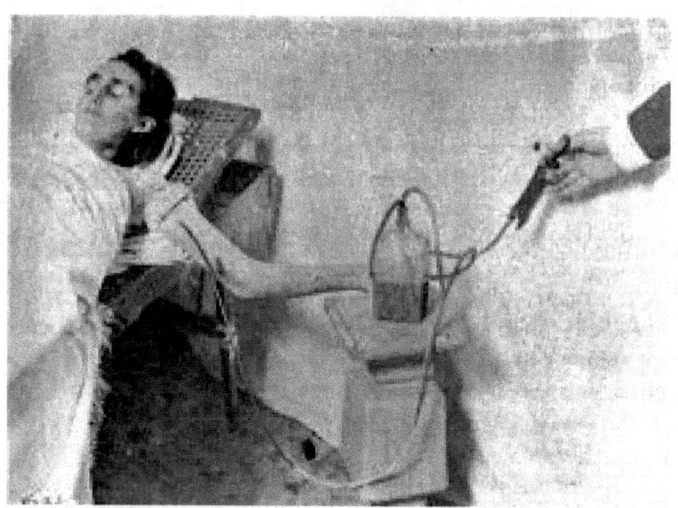
Embalming in the nineteenth century was a crude process, although it's not that different from the way it's still done today.

who could afford it - wanted their loved ones preserved and sent home for burial. Holmes charged the families $100 each for his services, and he ended the war an extraordinarily rich man. He never revealed the exact formula that he used to embalm the dead. Interestingly, he insisted that his own body not be embalmed when he died.

It makes you wonder just what sort of methods he used.

But Holmes was not the only man offering embalming services during the war. Many others set up tents in the wake of battles and offered their skills to whoever demanded them. Thanks to this, embalming came into its own during the early and middle 1860s. Military authorities permitted civilian embalmers to work within war zones, and it was not until the last year of the war that the Army required an examination that would prove their qualifications. It has been estimated that as many as 30,000 to 40,000 of the Civil War dead were embalmed. How well they were actually preserved remains in question, but at least the attempt was made.

In 1867, August Wilhelm von Hofman discovered a chemical called formaldehyde, the chemical basis for all modern embalming fluids. It would be several years before embalming came into common use, but by 1885 it was commonplace. By the end of the century, it was being used all over the country. In 1900, the Massachusetts College of

Embalming was started, and undertakers began advertising their services in newspapers.

Today the majority of people who die are embalmed, and the methods that are used are basically the same as they were during the Civil War. The chemicals and equipment may be improved, but basically, funeral home operators are still injecting three or four gallons of preservatives into the larger artery, while simultaneously removing blood from a large vein. They aren't mummifying the corpses anymore, but they are preparing them extensively - often repairing damage - so they can be viewed by their family and friends one last time.

The most significant difference between now and days gone by is that modern funeral directors don't have the worries of bad smells and leaking fluids from the bodies they put on display.

Undertakers, Burials & Funerals

The role of the person who would come to be known as an "undertaker" had been around for years prior to the Civil War, but it was during this period when the job began to be seen as a position of importance.

The term "undertaker" was actually in use as far back as 1698, and it originally meant the one who "undertook" to make funeral arrangements and to keep the body safe. The duties of this person have changed many times over the years, and today, the title of "undertaker" is disliked by modern practitioners of the industry. The term "funeral director" was first coined back in 1885, but it took well over a century to catch on - mostly because "funeral home" was not in everyday use. Through the nineteenth century, most funerals were still being conducted in the front parlor of the deceased. It would not be until the 1920s that the parlor of a home was renamed the "living room" to move it as far away as possible from what it had once been.

The undertaker's job began when the doctor's job ended. He performed tasks that, quite frankly, no one, especially the bereaved family, wanted to do. Of course, they had done it, mostly without complaint, for centuries, but when it became possible to hire someone to handle that grim task, most families readily did so.

An undertaker of the nineteenth century

The undertaker cleaned and took care of the corpse and prepared it for burial. Early undertakers usually combined their funeral business with other trades. It was not uncommon for them to be cabinetmakers or furniture makers who made coffins as a sideline. They usually stressed the "furniture" part of undertaking (the coffin) in their advertising, as this was their primary source of income. Businesses that combined furniture sales and funeral directing were common in America through the early twentieth century. However, undertakers in post-Civil War America were the first to rely on specialized coffin manufacturers.

The term "coffin" generally refers to the six-sided burial container, which was wide at the shoulders and narrow at the feet. A "casket" is rectangular-shaped and was first introduced in the 1840s and started to be in widespread use by the 1860s. In most writings on the subject - including this one - the terms are used interchangeably.

Caskets were initially custom-made to fit the specifications of the corpse but began to be mass-produced in the latter part of the nineteenth century. Metal coffins also came into fashion, and casket

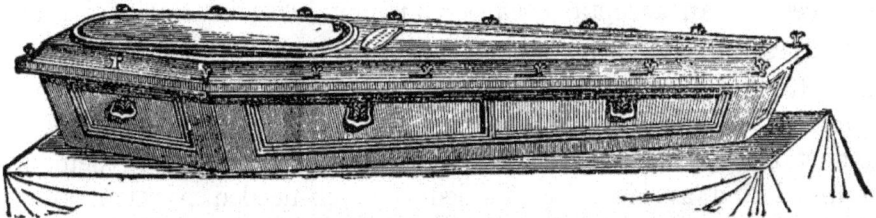

shops opened around the same time. A family could choose a casket from an undertaker's catalog or display room and have it immediately available. Coffins have since been made from a variety of materials, including wood, cloth, aluminum, terra-cotta, and even papier-mâché. The use of underground vaults as a protective receptacle for the coffin was not widespread until the early twentieth century. Even then, it was mostly just the wealthy who could afford them.

By the early 1910s, the industry had grown further. Many others had joined the ranks as undertakers. Retired carpenters, grave diggers, and the owners of horse carts saw undertaking as an excellent way to make a living. Owners of livery stables also realized increasing amounts of business with the rental of wagons, carriages, and coaches that could be used for funerals. The mass production of hearses - previously only used for the burials of important or wealthy people - also became a booming business.

Undertakers gradually began to incorporate embalming into their work, taking over the job from surgeons. The trade later organized as the Undertaker's Mutual Protection Association in Philadelphia in 1864 and, by 1881, had organized across the country. By 1900 undertaking had become an acceptable career, and by 1920 the National Funeral Directors Association had nearly 10,000 members.

It took some time for the work to be accepted in many communities, though. For years, a social stigma surrounded the local undertaker. While active in the community, many of them were shunned and avoided. They filled a much-needed position, and yet because of their constant contact with the dead, they were somehow seen as "unclean." This began to change by the 1910s when undertaking began to be accepted as a true vocation. By that time, more and more bodies were being prepared for burial, and funeral parlors, and fewer people were dying at home, spending their final hours in hospitals.

Caring for the dead moved into modern times. Gone were the days of the embalmer bringing his own "cooling board" to the deceased's home and draining the dead man's fluids down the kitchen sink. Times were changing, and the job of the funeral director started to be perceived as a dignified vocation.

Funeral customs also began to change. The tradition of sitting with and viewing the deceased - known by various names like "the wake" or "visitation" - is still practiced today, although it's different than it was in the past. Before funeral parlors, these events always took place in the homes of the dead. In the days before houses were equipped with screens, bugs and flying insects were unwelcome visitors at wakes, as were rats, dogs, cats, and even small children. Round-the-clock vigils needed to take place to protect the corpse from these nuisances.

This made the wake both a practical and a social ritual. The social aspects of the wake varied by culture and ethnic group. Perhaps the most festive wakes were held in Irish households where there was always an indulgence of food and spirits. On some occasions, the deceased was propped up in the corner so that he could enjoy the party, too. Today the visitation, as the practice has come to be known, does not require the family to "sit up" with the corpse. However, it does still allow for friends and family to gather in a setting where the body can be viewed, and remembrances can be exchanged about the deceased.

A funeral at home in the late nineteenth century. This tradition continued for years, until funeral parlors came into regular use.

Most of these gatherings are held at the local funeral home, however, which tends to cut down on the more festive aspects of the old ritual.

Funerals themselves have also changed. In early America, most funeral services were held after the burial because there was no way to preserve the body adequately. There may or may not have been a member of the clergy to preside over the service, especially for those living in rural areas. If a person died in the winter, when the ground was frozen, it's also possible that the funeral and burial would be delayed until the spring thaw. In those cases, the body of the deceased would be stored in a temporary receiving vault or even in a barn or unheated room of a home.

In the nineteenth century, most funerals were by invitation only. In cities, a man dressed in black mourning coats hand-delivered funeral notices and invitations. It was very rude to attend a funeral to which you were not invited. Funeral invitations were written on black-bordered stationery and placed in black envelopes so that the recipient would immediately know that someone had died. Later, when newspaper obituaries began to appear, and telephones made it much simpler to spread the word about a loved one's death, written invitations to funerals fell out of fashion.

Funeral services, like wakes, were social occasions and were held in the home of the deceased and later in the church or the funeral parlor. The odor of the decomposing body could be ghastly during a funeral service, and this created the custom of having floral arrangements surrounding the coffin. Flowers added color and life to a grim setting but, most importantly, masked the smell of the corpse. Funeral wreaths were hung on the family's door to not only identify the house to visiting mourners but also to warn away unwanted visitors, like traveling salesmen.

After the service, a funeral assistant stayed behind to put the family's home back in order while the mourners followed in a procession to the cemetery. The procession was led by the clergy, followed by the flower carriage, then the pallbearers, the hearse, the immediate family, the relatives, and then finally, friends and acquaintances. Before the use of hearses became common under bearers carried the coffin, while pallbearers - relatives or men of dignity - held the corners of the pall, a cloth that was laid over the coffin, to keep it from dragging on the ground. Palls were usually black, while children's coffins were draped in white, as were coffins of women who died in childbirth. If the distance to the cemetery were long, there would be a change in under bearers along the way, or they would be allowed to stop and rest. Over time the tradition of the pall faded away, and only one set of bearers remained.

In the late nineteenth century, when undertakers began taking over the management of death, they established "funeral parlors" or "funeral homes" to symbolize the parlor or home-like quality that people were familiar with. The undertaker handled the entire affair from planning the funeral to contacting the clergy, arranging the music, selecting flowers, and preparing the body and casket. He also secured a burial permit from the town or city and arranged to have the death certificate filed with the city clerk.

The undertaker's carriage transported the deceased with mourners following behind. Motorized hearses replaced horse-drawn carriages in the 1910s and have since gone through many changes over the years. Early on the plume that was atop the horse-drawn hearse was used to indicate the status of the deceased. If there were no feathered plumes, the deceased was poor, and if there were more than seven or eight of them, it meant that the occupant was a wealthy one. All other areas of financial status fell in between.

At the cemetery, there was a brief graveside service that focused on giving the body back to the earth - ashes to ashes, dust to dust, etc. - and the coffin would be placed on planks over the open grave. On occasion, the coffin would be opened one last time at the cemetery so that family and friends could place personal items inside with their loved ones. Also, if any precious jewelry was going to be removed from the body, this was done at the graveside. The casket was then lowered into the ground, and handfuls of dirt, or sometimes flowers, were dropped onto the casket to symbolize the return to the earth.

The earliest burials were simple. The body was wrapped in cloth and then placed on its back in the grave. Later, coffins, or caskets, came into common use, even though various types of enclosures for the body has been used for centuries. In early America, though, the old adage of being buried "six feet under" was out of necessity. The odor of the decaying body had to be suppressed to keep animals from digging up the remains.

Before cemeteries were plotted and gravesites accurately recorded, gravediggers had to rely on someone's memory to make sure they weren't about to dig a grave where someone else was already buried. If no one knew for sure, then a dowser would be brought in to determine where the graves were located. Just like looking for water, a dowser can also find an unmarked grave.

Another method to search for graves was to hit the ground with a hammer or to stomp on it with heavy boots. A grave would have a hollow sound to it since the ground never settled back as solidly as it had been. A metal rod could also be plunged into the ground at regular intervals, and where it slipped in the most easily, a grave could usually be found.

In many cemeteries, the graves were laid out on an east-west axis, with the feet to the east and the head to the west. In some cultures, this was done so that the deceased faced the rising sun. For Christians, it was done with the belief that on Judgment Day, Christ would return in the eastern sky and so the bodies would be positioned to rise in the proper direction. This wasn't foolproof, but it was a common tradition.

Husbands and wives also have certain positions in the grave. Just as the bride stands to the groom's left during a wedding ceremony, she will also be buried to the left at the time of death. The custom came from the belief that Eve was created from the left side (rib) of Adam.

Women and their infants who died in childbirth, or shortly after, were often buried in the same grave - a custom started because of the belief that a mother's ghost will not rest if she doesn't know what happened to her child.

The Victorian Celebration of Death

In America, simple burials were common until the Civil War when the country was faced with numbers of the dead like nothing they had seen before.

But it was an event in 1865 that changed the way America looked at death forever - the assassination of President Abraham Lincoln. The outpouring of grief over the president's death was not only the feeling of loss for a beloved leader, but it was also a public representation of mourning for all the dead who perished during the war. Many husbands, fathers, sons, uncles, and cousins left to fight in the war, were killed on the battlefield and were never returned home. After the president was murdered, many Americans expressed their heartache as mourning for the fallen president.

The traditions that were created to mourn the fallen president were greatly influenced by the mourning rituals introduced by England's Queen Victoria after the death of her husband, Prince Albert, who died of typhoid in 1861. For the next 40 years, she mourned his death. She even commanded her court to dress in mourning clothes for the first three years after Albert's death. Because of her extreme

The "Victorian Celebration of Death" was a period marked by lavish cemetery artwork, oversized mausoleums, expensive tombstones, and the periods of extended grief and mourning.

actions, the Victorians, in both England and America, imitated her actions and adopted them into their mourning rituals. Lincoln's death was the first public event to occur in what came to be known as the "Victorian Celebration of Death" - a romantic period of funereal excess.

From the end of the Civil war until World War I, the macabre celebration swept the country. During this period, elaborate monuments and funerary art joined expensive mourning clothes, caskets, and accouterments in periods of extended grieving and protracted ritual. It became a time that would lead to vast amounts of money being spent on funerals and cemeteries all over America. The entire funeral industry was transformed during those years and would never be the same again.

Death - and the funerals that occurred because of it - became a social event and a morbid way of life. Huge amounts of money were spent on funerals and mausoleums and monuments. Most of the ornate and breathtaking artwork that can be found in cemeteries across America was designed and purchased during this era. Many regarded the massive tombs, the statuary, and lavish designs as ridiculous. Author Ambrose Bierce called them the "folly of the rich" and pondered how the wealthy planned to enjoy such structures after death. For families that could afford them, they became commonplace during this period along with scores of customs and rituals - many of which survive in various forms even today.

Wearing Black

While even the early settlers considered death and funerals a somber occasion, they did not have any typical style of clothing that was set aside for mourning. The custom of wearing black became popular in America during the Victorian period. Black was believed to make the living less visible to the spirits that hovered around the body of the deceased. Widows were always encouraged to wear a black dress - which became known as "widow's weeds" - so that her husband's ghost would not return to bother her. Most of the etiquette involving the wearing of black clothing was directed toward women, but men would often sport black armbands and were encouraged to wear dark and conservative suits and black ties.

Widows were expected to wear black dresses for at least two years after the deaths of their husbands. After a year and a half, a widow could add some trim to her clothing but only in colors of gray, lavender, or white. Widows were expected to not attend any festive occasions during this time, such as weddings or parties. These two years were considered a suitable mourning time for a woman, and if a second marriage occurred during this time, it was frowned upon.

The mourning period for men was much shorter - as was the permissible timeframe in which they could remarry. Men with children were expected to remarry much sooner because they needed someone to care for their families.

If a woman were mourning the death of a parent or a child, she would wear black for one year. For the loss of a grandparent, sibling, or close friend, a mourning dress was to be worn for six months. If an aunt, niece, or nephew died, then three months was an appropriate length of time. Women who had large families - especially those not blessed with longevity - might be stuck wearing black dresses for a good part of every year.

Household Decorations

When funeral services were held in the home, it was common for all the mirrors in the house to be covered, for shades to be drawn, and for clocks to be stopped at the time of death. These traditions gained strength during the Victorian era but hearkened back to an earlier time when it was believed that the spirits of the dead could be distracted by their reflections in mirrors or glass and might remain behind the haunt the house.

During this period it was common to hang a funeral wreath on the front door of the house, but many families also covered the doorbell or the knocker in crepe paper so that knocks from visiting mourners would be more quiet and subdued. Various colors were used to designate who had died in the house - black for an adult, white for a child, and black with a white rosette and ribbon for a young adult.

Mourning Gifts

During the Celebration of Death, it was also common for funeral gifts - almost like party favors - to be given to those who attended funerals and wakes. The most popular items that were given out were rings, broaches, and scarves. Gloves were also a popular gift and were also sometimes given out with an invitation to a funeral. Even the poorest of funerals gave out some token to those who came to pay their respects.

During this era, rings, lockets, and brooches were mass-produced and immensely popular among the middle class. These jewelry items might contain a miniature portrait of the deceased and perhaps even a lock of their hair. There were also chains, bracelets, and necklaces that were braided from the hair of the deceased, and sometimes the dead person's hair was woven into wreaths of elaborate design and then framed. The jewelry items were made from black enamel, onyx, jet, and other dark-colored materials, then decorated with symbols that were likely to be found in cemeteries like weeping willows, broken columns, and urns. Each was usually inscribed with the name or initials of the deceased and their date of death.

Such macabre souvenirs remained popular for many years.

Memorial Pictures

Before photography was common, many mourners had paintings, lithographs, or needlework memorials stitched in honor of their loved ones. They were usually then hung in parlors or bedrooms as a tribute to those who were lost. The portraits were mainly an upper society trend, and most typically showed the deceased in bed, as if asleep. The middle class had their own posthumous portraits. However, in most of these, the deceased was portrayed as being alive.

Many of these portraits contained hidden clues to show that the subject was deceased when the painting was commissioned. For instance, there may be clouds surrounding the person, a willow tree in the background, or even a timepiece or a wilted flower in their hand. They remained popular through the middle nineteenth century but fell out of fashion after photography became more common.

Needlepoint portraits and memorials were also popular. Patterns for mourning samplers appeared in women's magazines of the day and usually contained tombs, willows, urns, and black-garbed people in mourning. For the most part, these samplers went out of style after the Civil War.

Another oddity of the middle 1800s was the mass-produced Currier & Ives lithographs that came with a blank space for the deceased's name and dates of birth and death. They resembled a needlework pattern and usually had a stone or monument in the center that had an inscription that began "Sacred to the Memory of..." and then space where mourners could write in the name of the loved one. The lithographs went out of fashion by the 1870s and were replaced mainly by memorial cards that families could send to relatives or save in a book.

Postmortem Photographs

Perhaps the most misunderstood tradition to come from the Victorian era was the creation of postmortem photographs - literally photos that were taken of the deceased in their finest clothing and then treasured by the family members after the burial. Today many consider such photographs to be morbid or grotesque, but to the people of the era, they certainly weren't thought of that way.

Before the wake and funeral services, families of all classes often had photographs taken of the deceased, especially when infants and children died. The resulting images were supposed to help the family through the grieving process and to remember their loved ones. It was not uncommon for the mourners to want to see the face of the deceased just one last time, and with such a photograph they could. These images also served as something to share with family and friends who lived far away and who could not be present for the funeral. Another reason for the popularity of these photos, especially those of children and babies, was that thanks to the high mortality rate, many children did not live long enough to have their photographs taken otherwise. Also, in many cases, a family might not be able to afford to have a professional photograph taken under normal circumstances - in those days hardly anyone but a professional photographer owned a camera or knew how to use one - and so having a photograph taken

Postmortem photographs, especially of children, were never meant to be morbid or strange, but were a way to hang onto memories of loved ones in the only way people knew at the time.

after death would be the only chance to capture the likeness of a loved one.

Because of this, families of the era treated postmortem photographs the same as they did photographs of the living. They could be found hanging on the walls of homes, on fireplace mantels, in photograph albums, and even attached to tombstones.

Photographing the dead dated back to the 1840s but reached its height of popularity in the late nineteenth century. Photographers routinely advertised in newspapers that they were able to take photographs of the deceased with only an hour's notice. Since the wake, funeral, and burial might all take place within 24 hours, the photographers had no time to waste, especially if they wanted to be there before rigor mortis began to affect the body. Most postmortem photos were created in the home of the deceased, and charges for the "sitting" ranged from $10 to $15.

Between 1840 and 1880, the most common style of postmortem photograph was one that denied death. This was known as the "last sleep" and was intended to make the subject look as if he or she was merely sleeping and not dead. Most of them showed only the upper half of the body. The photographer - with help from the family - would place the corpse on a sofa or bed, or for children in a cradle or a buggy. Often flowers, a book, or a Bible might be placed in their hands. Because the photograph tried to create the illusion that the subject was asleep, they were never posed in a coffin.

Starting in the 1880s and continuing into the 1910s, it became more common to photograph the entire body of the deceased, often in a casket. This change coincided with changes in the funeral industry like the widespread use of embalming techniques, lined and lavish caskets, and elaborate floral arrangements.

A popular type of postmortem photograph was to show the deceased with living family members. While this seems a little odd to us today, it was common to see photographs of mothers and fathers cradling dead infants, children with deceased siblings, or a husband or wife cradling their departed spouse, who might be stretched out next to them on the bed. Because funerals were not just a time to grieve for the departed but a social occasion as well, it was not unusual to see an entire group clustered around a casket for a family portrait of both the living and the dead.

I guess you can't have a "funeral" without the "fun."

While photographs are still taken of the dead at funerals and visitations today, the custom of postmortem photographs died out in the early part of the twentieth century. While most people who have taken such photographs today are more likely to hide them away than to put them on display, they were (probably) unknowingly carrying on a tradition practiced by their ancestors. In a coffin is the last way that I would want to remember them.

The "Celebration" Comes to an End

By the end of the nineteenth century, the Victorian's "Celebration of Death" was coming to an end. It hung on for a few more years, but with the arrival of the Great War, the world was faced with the wholesale slaughter of its young men. Death no longer seemed like something that should be celebrated.

It was now something to be feared.

The war - followed by the Great Depression a decade later - largely brought about an end to the kind of excess that had been celebrated death in homes and cemeteries across America. By the middle part of the twentieth century, hospitals, funeral homes, and traditional cemeteries began following uniform procedures to distance the dead from the living. The mourning customs and garden cemeteries of yesterday had become relics of the past.

The living had moved on, and the dead became the easily forgotten reminders of the past.

Or did they?

2. THE DARK SIDE OF DEATH

Why Would a Cemetery be Haunted?

Man has always had a fear of the unknown. And what greater unknown exists than death? No one truly knows what waits for us when we leave this world and continue on to the next. It's that fear that also conjures up man's fear of ghosts.

Fear of death is human nature. Not so long ago, our ancestor's lives were short, and death came early. A mother in the Victorian era might give birth to sixth children so that three of them would live to be adults. Our lives are different today. We live longer, and death is now remote and sanitized. Most Americans under the age of 40 have never even seen a corpse. When death comes for us, it's usually in the clinical and sterile setting of a hospital. The face of death is hidden from us, and yet we are still afraid.

Death is just as mysterious now as it was centuries ago. Death may find us in other ways, but the result is the same. It's what comes next that is the real mystery.

What happens when we die?
Is there a life beyond this world?

And thus, our fear of ghosts is born.

What rational person wants to return from the grave to wander the earth for eternity? Who would want to spend their final existence wandering the corridors of the house where they once lived, doomed to loneliness, isolation, and despair? Even worse, who would desire to remain trapped for all-time among the crypts, gravestones, and monuments of a cemetery?

In the opening pages of this book, I asked a question - do haunted graveyards really exist? And if so, why do spirits linger in them? As mentioned, the ghosts found among the tombstones of haunted cemeteries seem to stay behind because of events that occur *after* their deaths.

That our bodies might endure some sort of indignity is a horror that has remained with us since the days of the "body snatchers." Society endows on a lifeless corpse the capacity for feeling pain and the expectation of respect. All forms of defilement of the dead - especially thefts and the desecration of corpses - are considered not only distasteful but almost unholy.

And perhaps this belief has some merit. The majority of graveyard ghost stories stem from terrible events that have occurred within the confines of the burial ground long after the deaths of the restless spirits. Cemeteries gain a reputation for being haunted for reasons that include premature burial, the desecration of corpses, grave robbery, unmarked graves, natural disasters that disturb resting places, and more. It seems these kinds of events literally create the ghosts that haunt these pages.

The chapter ahead is not for the faint of heart - or the weak of stomach - so read on with that warning in mind.

BURIED ALIVE

To be buried alive is, beyond question, the most terrific of these extremes which has ever fallen to the lot of mere mortality... the boundaries which divide Life from Death, are at best shadowy and vague. Who shall say when one ends and the other begins?

Those words came from Edgar Allan Poe, and they were part of his macabre short story, "The Premature Burial." In the tale, Poe refers to being buried alive as something "too entirely horrible for the purposes of legitimate fiction." The narrator in Poe's story had reason to be afraid of that happening to him because he suffered from catalepsy. This neurological condition could produce episodes of extreme paralysis, mimicking, and being mistaken for death. Poe didn't suffer from the condition, but he did have a morbid fear of death - and he was not alone.

During the nineteenth century, *Taphophobia* - the fear of being buried alive - was quite common, and it was tragically justified given the state of the medical field at the time. Far too many people lived with an abiding fear of being mistaken for dead and then waking up trapped in a coffin, six feet below the ground.

It was simply too much for them to think about.

An obsession with premature burial in America emerged at the same that so many people became obsessed with death itself - the Victorian era. However, stories about being accidentally buried alive dated back centuries. In 1308, a man named Johannes Duns Scotus was mistakenly thought to be dead and was interred in his tomb. When the crypt was later re-opened, Scotus was found outside of his coffin. His hands were torn and covered in crusted blood - evidence that he had made a futile attempt to escape from the grave.

The anxiety over premature burial has its roots in 1742 when a distinguished French doctor named Jacques Benigne Winslow wrote *The Uncertainty of the Signs of Death*. The book examined the way that medical professionals were often mistaking the ailments of their patients and pronouncing them dead too early. Winslow's inspiration for the book? He had been declared dead and had been placed in a coffin himself on two occasions.

Stories from writers like Edgar Allan Poe fed the frenzy in the mid-nineteenth century. Fascinated and terrified by the prospect of being buried alive, Poe even wrote a true account about a Baltimore

L'Inhumation Precipitee or "The Premature Burial" by Belgian artist Antoine Wiertz

woman who was entombed alive. She was the wife an important city official and, after falling sick, appeared to have died. She was placed in the family's crypt and was left undisturbed for three years when the crypt was opened again to admit the body of a relative who had died. When the door was opened, the skeleton of the woman still dressed in her burial clothes tumbled out. Apparently, she had revived soon after her funeral and had succeeded in escaping her casket but had been unable to open the door of the tomb. She died there, her screams unheard by those outside.

While medical professionals were quick to disregard the claims of "rampant" premature burials, it is difficult to ignore the accounts, claims, and evidence that emerged in the wake of public interest. One physician, Franz Hartmann, published a book called *Premature Burial* in 1895. He collected over 750 cases of people being buried alive. He was universally condemned by other doctors who didn't want the public to know about their mistakes - mistakes that sometimes had people waking from trances to find themselves in a coffin.

But such stories fueled the public imagination and made for both scandalous and spine-tingling reading.

In 1849, a severe cholera epidemic killed 199 people. An older woman who oversaw the cholera wards stated that as soon as patients died, they were placed into wooden coffins, and the lids screwed down. They were then moved outside into a small shed so that they would be out of the way. "Sometimes," she coldly told authors William Tebb and Edward Vollum, "they'd come to afterwards, and we'd hear them kicking in their coffins, but we never unscrewed them, because we knew they had to die."

A particularly gruesome case was recounted in the *Undertaker's Journal and Funeral Directors' Review* for July 1889. A portion of the article recalled a New York case from 1854 in which a baker placed the coffin of his deceased daughter in a temporary vault so that the girl's older sister to come to New York from St. Louis for the funeral. This was possible, testified the undertaker who performed the services, because the death occurred in the winter and the outdoor temperature prevented severe decomposition. When the sister finally arrived, the vault was opened for the funeral. When the lid of the coffin was removed, they discovered that the girl had been placed in the casket alive. Her grave clothes had been torn to shreds, and according to the report, the ends of several of her fingers were gone. They had been torn away as she tried to claw her way out of the wooden coffin.

Another account, from *Eddowe's Journal* of August 1844, tells of a child who was accidentally buried alive. While the sexton was filling in the grave, he was startled to hear the boy calling for help. He quickly uncovered the coffin, and the boy was rescued. He later made a full recovery, and while this tale had a happy ending, the account ended with a somber postscript. "Not long ago, in making a grave in the same cemetery, a coffin was broken into, and it was found that the occupant had revived after burial, and had gnawed the flesh of both wrists before life was finally extinguished."

In the 1979 book *Buried Alive*, author Dr. Peron-Autret and his colleague Dr. Louis Claude-Vincent interviewed more than 60 gravediggers who had been working in Paris cemeteries for many years. He asked them if they had ever seen evidence of people buried alive, and to the author's surprise, all of them had. Most commonly, the coffins had marks of scratching and scraping on the inside of the lids. One gravedigger even described fingernails that had become embedded in the wood - all signs of a desperate need to escape.

In his book *The Lazarus Syndrome*, author Rodney Davies tells of a London cemetery that was damaged by a German bomb during World War II. The explosion unearthed many coffins and bodies. The gravediggers that were summoned to replace the corpses in the ground noticed that many of the cadavers exhibited signs of having been buried alive. Not only was skin torn away from the hands and the knees, but fingernails were split, broken, and ripped away. Fists of the dead clutched fabric from the coffins' linings and bodies were found with broken fingers and toes. The grim discoveries were kept from the public, but one of the gravediggers leaked the story to a local policeman named William Repton, and his daughter passed the story along to Davies. Repton was so unnerved by the story that he made his wife and daughter promise that they would have him cremated at the time of his death, rather than buried.

Today, it is difficult to know how fearful the Victorians needed to be about being buried alive. There were plenty of stories - not only about bodies that looked as though they tried to escape from the grave but also about "near miss" incidents when someone was almost buried alive - but how many of the stories were true and how many were the work of the popular press? Tales of death, ghosts, vampires, and terror were starting to find a huge audience in those days, and, of course, how much more frightening is a story that might actually happen to you?

The fear of premature burial created a cottage industry, not only for devices that would prevent being buried alive, but an entire litany of tests and measures were supposed to occur before a person was placed in the ground. As mentioned already, the medical field was not exactly sophisticated at that time, so methods and devices were implemented to soothe - and taken advantage of - a fear that many people had of being placed in their grave by mistake.

It was accepted that actual corpses felt no pain. Do something that would be excruciating to the living, it was suggested, and if a person is dead, he won't wake up. A doctor named Josat invented a pair of sharp forceps that were used to pinch the nipples of someone thought to be dead viciously. Dr. J.V. Laborde claimed to have revived a woman believed to be dead by applying forceps to her tongue and pulling at it until she woke up. Another idea was to thrust long needles under the fingernails or toenails. Some doctors also held a person's hand over a flame, poured boiling water on the body, or amputated a small body part like a finger or a toe.

All that I can say is that I really hope I am truly dead if anyone decides to bring back any of these methods.

Other physicians believed the tongue was the key. One suggested that an undead body could be stimulated by applying certain reactive substances on the tongue, such as bitter lemon, sour vinegar, or alcohol.

A scientist named Luigi Galvani was a bit ahead of his time. As early as 1780, he was applying electricity to animal corpses - as sort of a precursor to the modern defibrillator - and making them move about. He theorized this might bring the dead back to life, but we don't know if he ever tried it in real life. He did in fiction, though. Galvani was one of Mary Shelley's inspirations for *Frankenstein*.

Doctors also began experimenting with temperature to determine if someone was dead. Touching a cold corpse was not accurate, so "necrometers" were invented in the late nineteenth century. They were devices that worked with three settings - alive, probably dead, and dead. You can perhaps guess that they were not precisely accurate.

Using a mirror was considered to be a "foolproof" method to check for signs of life for many years. The glass would be placed beneath the nose of the allegedly deceased to see if their breath fogged it up. Based on the number of people who were mistaken for dead using such an "accurate" method, it's not one we can consider to be reliable.

But what in the world were people suffering from in the Victorian era that would cause so many doctors to think people were dead when they weren't?

Catalepsy was probably the most common sickness to mimic death in the nineteenth century. It is a nervous condition that is characterized by muscular rigidity and a decreased sensitivity to pain. During a trance state, a victim's limbs would have a wax-like flexibility that caused them to twist into odd positions, where they might remain indefinitely. Doctors stated that it often occurred during periods of hysteria and was a common side effect to schizophrenia before anyone knew what schizophrenia was and that it could be treated with drugs. When a person suffering from catalepsy entered a trance, it could seem as though they had died, and their bodies had stiffened. Because of their lack of sensitivity to pain, even the harshest tests could make it seem as though they were dead.

In a time of more limited medical knowledge, a coma might also be mistaken for death. The fate of the comatose patient in those days often depended on the patience and the vigilance of doctors and relatives and the legal time limits placed on the interval between death and burial. If you didn't wake up in time after being pronounced dead, well, you could be in serious trouble.

Many of those who awoke from trances just in time to escape the grave were able to give accounts of having been fully aware of what was going on around them. In every case, though, they were unable to react. Miss Eleanor Markham wrote of her experience in *Banner of Light* in 1894, recalling, "I was conscious all the time you were making preparations to bury me, and the horror of my situation was altogether beyond description. I could hear everything that was going on, even a whisper outside the door, and although I exerted all my will power, and made a supreme physical effort to cry out, I was powerless."

The horror of such talks continued to feed the public frenzy, and Victorians began to search for ways to prevent such incidents from occurring. Perhaps the surest way to avoid being buried alive was to obtain the services of a doctor who could be trusted to view and examine the possible corpse thoroughly. Many instances of premature burial occurred because of misdiagnosis by relatives or because of absentee doctors who, acting in perfect accordance with the law, were not required actually to see a body to pronounce the person dead. A certificate of death only needed to state that the doctor had been told they were dead. The obvious answer to this problem was to leave explicit instructions about what should happen if you were thought to be dead. That way, friends and relatives would have no lingering doubts.

Author Wilkie Collins always carried a letter with him detailing the elaborate precautions that his family should take to prevent his premature burial. Others had codicils added to their wills stating that no family member could claim their inheritance unless death were absolutely determined.

Others went as far as to leave substantial sums in their estate for friends who would sever their heads or pierce their veins to make sure they were not buried alive. A woman named Francis Power Cobbe had a last request that was designed to prevent her from reawakening in the grave. She wrote that a doctor should "perform on my body the operation of completely and thoroughly severing the arteries of my neck and windpipe, nearly severing my head altogether, so as to make any revival in the grave absolutely impossible."

The Undertaker and Funeral Director's Journal in 1889 told of a family in Virginia that had developed a curious custom. It had started a century before when a member of the family was discovered to have been accidentally buried alive. After that, when anyone in the family died, they were stabbed in the heart by the head of the household. They continued the tradition until 1850, when, after the death of a daughter, the knife was plunged into her heart, and she let out a terrible scream. She wasn't dead - but she certainly was after her father stabbed her.

Lady Isabel, wife of famous British explorer Sir Francis Burton, would have felt the girl was lucky. She wrote that it would be "infinitely preferable to be killed outright by the embalmer's needle than to regain consciousness below the ground."

Needles, mirrors, and forceps were used on those believed to be dead, but many felt those things didn't go far enough. What if those tests failed, and some people were still buried alive?

Those writing about the subject agreed that putrefaction - the decaying of the body - was the surest sign of irreversible death. Unfortunately, there were also a lot of disadvantages to keeping a loved one around until they had time to rot. So, for a price, "waiting mortuaries" began to appear so that families would have a place to store the bodies until they started to decay.

These mortuaries first became popular after several cholera epidemics in the late 1860s. Cholera had a habit of inducing a trance-like state that imitated death, and there had been too many close calls for many people's comfort. Now, a short time after death was presumed, the bodies could be taken to the nearest mortuary. On arrival, they were washed and placed in a zinc tub that was filled with antiseptic fluid. The tub was then surrounded with flowers, for both aesthetic and sensory reasons, and the family could come for final photographs with the deceased. The bodies would remain exposed for up to 72 hours, or less if signs of decay appeared earlier.

As an early alert system, an intricate tangle of cords and pulleys was attached to the corpse so that if the person moved at all, an alarm bell would ring, and attendants would be summoned. Staff members remained on duty 24-hours-a-day and made frequent inspections of the bodies. They rarely had time to get bored. The bell system was so sensitive that false alarms were numerous, usually caused by air drafts or the post-mortem movement of muscles.

It had to be a pretty unnerving place to work.

There is no doubt that the worst possible experience of premature burial would be awakening while trapped inside of a coffin, below six feet of earth. No matter how loudly you screamed or clawed at the lid of the coffin, there was little chance for escape.

Count Karnice-Karnicki, chamberlain to the Tsar of Russia, could only imagine the nightmare that might be faced by someone accidentally buried alive and was determined to prevent it. In 1896, he invented a clever device that would allow someone in the grave to call for help. The apparatus was a tube that traveled upward from the lid of the coffin to an airtight box above the level of the ground. Resting on the chest of the deceased was a glass sphere that was attached to a spring running the entire length of the tube. It connected to a mechanism inside of the box. The slightest movement of the chest would move the sphere in a way that the spring would cause the lid of

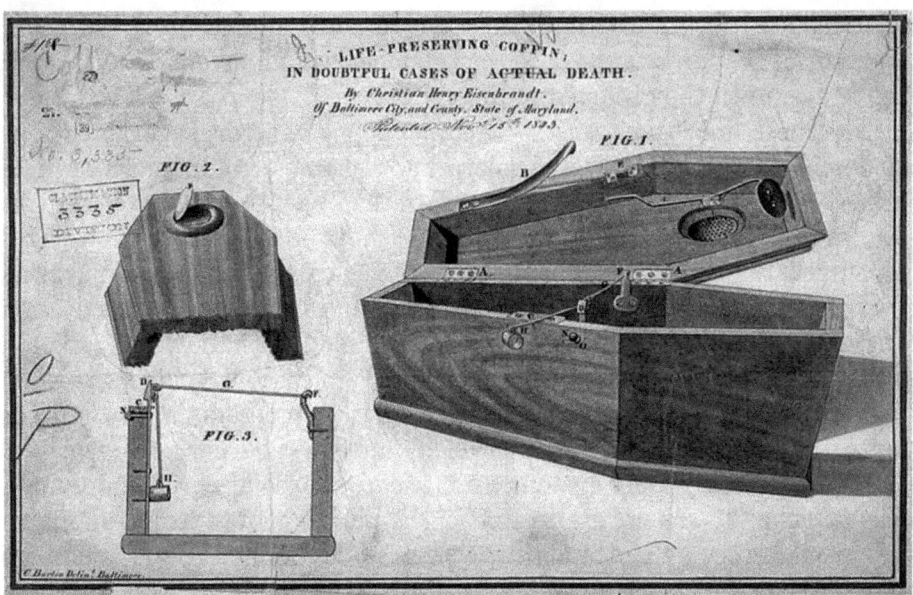

(Above) A safety-coffin model by Christian Eisenbrandt, meant to prevent being trapped in a coffin.

(Right) A coffin designed so that someone buried alive can get air and raise an alarm.

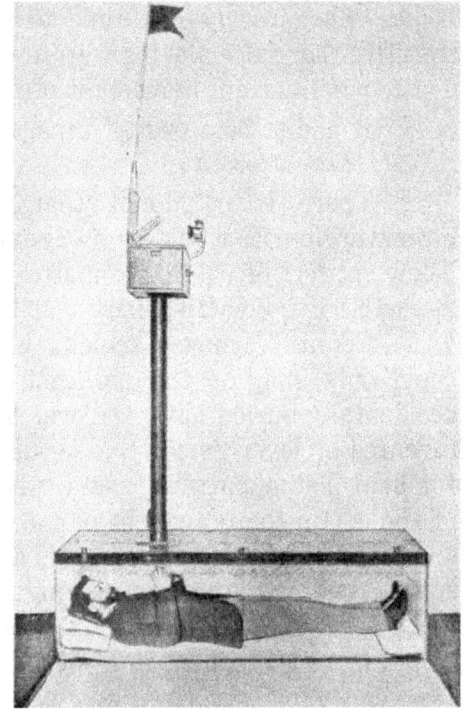

the box above to fly open and admit air and light. The spring also activated a flag, a light, and a loud bell to attract the attention of anyone who might be in the cemetery. The device could be rented for a small amount of money, and after a length of time went by - and there was no chance for revival - the tube could be pulled up and used in another coffin.

Almost immediately after this device was invented, a score of imitators began offering similar mechanisms that rang bells, sounded alarms, waved flags, and automatically unlocked caskets that might be placed in a crypt. There is no record of the success rate for these devices, but I can imagine that they gave many Victorians no small amount of comfort.

Others looked for a more direct solution to notify their families that they were alive. One man, John Wilmer, was buried in the back garden of his home. His family placed a switch in his hand that was connected to an alarm in the house. If he awakened from any sort of trance, he could immediately summon help. Fearing a mechanical failure, though, he had it written into his will that his relatives had to carry out an annual inspection of the wire. No one thought to ask Wilmar just how long he planned to remain alive in his grave.

Long Distance Call

Martin Sheets was a wealthy businessman who lived in Terre Haute, Indiana, in the early 1900s. One of his greatest fears was that he might accidentally be buried alive. He often dreamt of being awake, but unable to move, when the doctor pronounced him dead, only to regain his strength while trapped in a coffin below the ground. Sheets decided to fight his fears by investing some of his money in making sure that he would never be prematurely buried.

He purchased an expensive casket that was custom designed with latches on the inside. If he were ever placed inside prematurely, he would be able to open the coffin and escape. He also began construction on a mausoleum so that when he died - or was thought to have died - he would not be imprisoned under six feet of dirt. The mausoleum was well-built and attractive, but Sheets

Martin Sheets and his wife, Susan

realized that even if he did manage to escape from his casket, he would still be trapped inside of a stone prison.

That was when he came up with another clever idea. He installed a telephone inside of the tomb with a direct line to his home. If he were ever trapped inside, he could summon help by simply lifting the receiver. The line was fitted with an automatic indicator light so that even if no words were spoken, the light would come on, and help would soon be on the way.

On a side note, he was also buried with a bottle of whiskey. He said it was so that he could have a something to drink while he waited for someone to let him out of his tomb.

Death came for Martin Sheets in 1910, and he was entombed in the mausoleum. I would imagine that for several days afterward, his family kept a close eye on the telephone indicator light that was connected to the tomb. Years passed, though, and the old telephone line was largely forgotten. It became a dusty relic in the Sheets home, although one that was still operational. Thanks to specific instructions in Martin's will, funds had been set aside to keep the line active and connected.

Years after Martin's death, his wife, Susan, also passed away. She was discovered one day with the old telephone clutched in her hand. She held the receiver so tightly it was said that it had to be pried from her fingers. She had suffered a severe stroke, and family members assumed that she had been trying to call an ambulance when she finally died but had grabbed the old telephone to the crypt by mistake, thinking it was the standard line.

A service was held for her, and after a quiet memorial, she was taken to the family mausoleum where she was to be interred next to her husband.

The door to the tomb was unlocked, and family members stepped inside, where they received a shock. There was one chilling thing inside the tomb that had been disturbed. Martin Sheets' telephone, locked away for all those years, was hanging from the wall, just as it was supposed to be - but its receiver inexplicably off the hook.

The Girl Who Turned Her Back on Pikeville

There is a story that has been connected to the town of Pikeville, Kentucky, since the end of the nineteenth century. It has become such a part of the lore of the town that students in the local schools can tell at least a dozen different versions of how the main character in the story died and how her spirit makes herself known in the graveyard where she was buried. Such tales are regional legend and lore and have little resemblance to history.

The true story is much more frightening.

And it reveals the horrifying death of Octavia Hatcher, who has never rested in peace.

Pike County, Kentucky, is nestled in the hills that rise to meet the Appalachian Mountains. It is a secluded region in the extreme southeastern corner of Kentucky. It is rich in coal, hardwood timber, and history. It is in this area where the infamous feud between the Hatfields and McCoys took place and where the Hatcher family made their mark.

James Hatcher was a wealthy landowner and prominent business figure in the Pikeville region. He was one of nine children born in September 1859 to A.J. and Mary C. Layne Hatcher at the mouth of Beaver Creek in Floyd County. He moved to Pikeville early in life and attended school there.

Hatcher started his first business in Pikeville at the age of 18 when he opened a warehouse for goods brought in on the river. At one time, he handled nearly all the merchandise that was shipped via steamer to the city. Hatcher became associated with several other businessmen in building a steamboat called *Mountain Girl* and went into the construction business. He gained the contract for the building of the country courthouse in Pikeville in 1886.

Before coal, the most significant business in the region was cutting timber, and Hatcher became the first to make a fortune in the trade. He used hundreds of rafts to float lumber down the Big Sandy River to the Ohio River and then on to markets in Cincinnati, Louisville, and Evansville. He invested his profits in real estate, and he became one of the largest individual landowners in the valley. When coal was discovered, he started the James Hatcher Coal Co. and amassed another fortune. He also became a prominent figure in Democratic political circles, served a term as the Clerk of the Pike County Court, and in 1932 was elected railroad commissioner for the district.

In 1931, he opened the Hotel Hatcher on Main Street in Pikeville, and it became known as one of the showplaces of the Big Sandy river region. The spacious lobby included a museum that displayed ox-yokes, ancient hand-made furniture, antique weapons, and utensils used by the early settlers. The lobby also boasted a huge fireplace, and the walls were covered with historical photos, illustrations, maps, and information about Pike and Floyd Counties.

James Hatcher died in his home next to the Hotel Hatcher in October 1939. He had been ill for several weeks, having just celebrated his 80th birthday. The funeral was held at the hotel, and scores of his friends and relatives were in attendance, as was Kentucky Governor A.B. Chandler, Lieutenant Governor Keen Johnson, and many other state officials.

Hatcher was buried in the family plot at Pikeville Cemetery, in a casket that he had specially constructed for him. There is no indication as to what specifications the coffin had been designed with. Still, one has to wonder if it might have had some sort of safety release that would allow the person inside to escape in the event of premature burial.

You see, James Hatcher had an incredibly good reason to be afraid that being buried alive might happen to him.

The grave of Octavia Hatcher

Years before his death, in 1889, James had married a young woman named Octavia Smith. She was the daughter of another Pikeville founder and businessman, Jacob Smith. James and Octavia had only two years together. During their brief time together, they had one son, Jacob, who only lived for a few days. The death of her baby had a terrible effect on Octavia's mental and physical health. Deeply depressed, she grew progressively worse with each passing day. She slipped into a coma in April 1891. Doctors were unable to determine its cause, and when she died on May 2, her cause of death was listed as an "unknown illness."

Funeral services quickly followed. It was an unseasonably hot spring and so no time was wasted in placing Octavia in her grave at the Hatcher family plot in Pikeville Cemetery.

James Hatcher had just suffered a terrible double tragedy - but his grief was not over yet.

In the days that followed Octavia's death, several other people in town got sick and fell into comas. They remained in that state and then mysteriously recovered. Years later, it would be discovered that this illness was some sort of sleeping sickness that was caused by a particular fly. No one knew the cause at the time, though, they only knew that illness struck, and the patient recovered a few days later.

When news of the illness began to spread, James Hatcher - along with members of his family, several of whom were doctors - began to believe that Octavia had suffered from the same illness. Their belief turned to fear, and then to panic - Octavia may have been buried alive!

An emergency exhumation took place, and Octavia's casket was opened. Her body was in a horrific state. She had not been dead after all. In fact, she survived for at least a few days. The lining on the inside lid of the coffin had been torn and shredded by the young woman's bloody nails. Her face was scratched and contorted into a rictus of terror. She must have awakened and found herself trapped in the coffin. Unable to escape, she had died there, trapped and alone.

Octavia was returned to her grave, but James's heart was broken. He had an expensive monument erected over his wife's grave, a tall stone with a likeness of Octavia standing atop it. The statue had a baby in her arms, but it would later be destroyed by vandals.

The statue remained above the gravesite, looking out over the town of Pikeville for decades, a marble memory of a young woman who had been buried alive.

With a story as horrifying as this one, it became inevitable that legends would make the tale even stranger and more frightening. Students from the nearby high school and local college made the trek to the cemetery to drink and scare one another. They began to claim that the statue of Octavia Hatcher would come to life some nights and chase the trespassers from the graveyard. They heard her voice, some claimed, crying and weeping, or heard the sound of her baby crying.

Pranksters even went to the trouble of climbing onto the monument to disturb the statue of Octavia - creating another legend. In this version of her story, Octavia's spirit was angry at the people of Pikeville for allowing her to be buried alive. Because of this, she literally turned her back on the city on the anniversary of her death. On May 2, each year, the statue rotated on its pedestal and faced in the opposite direction. And it was true; it happened - with a little help from some clever college students.

But even though Octavia's spirit didn't turn its back on Pikeville, the stories about the cemetery being haunted didn't stop. People who visited the site, along with those who lived on the hill where the graveyard was located, often spoke of hearing strange cries in the darkness and reported seeing a misty apparition in the vicinity of Octavia's grave.

Finally, in the 1990s, the Hatcher family placed a stone in the cemetery that contained accurate information about Octavia's death and set her statue on a new marble base. They also enclosed the area with a fence, hoping to keep out the trespassers and vandals.

It worked but still didn't stop the stories. They have continued to be told, and many refuse to come into the cemetery at night, believing that the ghost of Octavia Hatcher still walks here.

Is her spirit still restless, or is this merely an urban legend that was spawned by a tragic event? According to many witnesses, inexplicable happenings still occur around Octavia's grave. She is, they believe, still searching for peace.

"RESURRECTIONISTS"

Beyond the fear of death itself, perhaps the greatest concern that most of us have is what happens to our bodies after our spirits have departed. The fear of something terrible happening to our corpse was the main reason why so many people invested in expensive private crypts and even chose cremation over burial during a time when cremation was forbidden by the Church.

The fear of their body being defiled was a very real one. During the eighteenth and nineteenth centuries, the chance of your body being dug up and removed from your coffin was much greater than your likelihood of being buried alive.

Grave robbery had existed for centuries prior to the European Renaissance. It dated as far back as the ancient Egyptians when thieves invaded the tombs of pharaohs, and likely before that. It soon

became something of a necessity, not desire. Scholars eventually realized that the dissection of human bodies was essential for furthering medical knowledge and that merely relying on medical texts was not sufficient.

But human bodies were not easy to come by. Volunteers were few, and medical schools faced a severe shortage of specimens. Occasionally, their cadavers had to come from someplace closer to home than most would have liked. To become seasoned anatomists, surgeons of the time had to be able to suppress normal emotional responses to their experiments. For example, the English physician William Harvey, famous for furthering the knowledge of blood circulation, participated in the dissections of both his sister and his father.

As the appetite for fresh corpses became even greater in the early 1800s, anatomists were forced to collaborate with "body snatchers" and "resurrectionists" to provide their specimens. The only corpses that could be legally used for dissection were the bodies of executed murderers, so there simply weren't enough to go around. Grave robbers would exhume fresh cadavers from cemeteries and then sell them to surgeons for medical experimentation and teaching.

Even though this was obviously done in secret, word spread of empty graves and vanished corpses. The general population abhorred body snatchers and the doctors who employed them. They went to great lengths to keep their loved ones from ending up on a dissecting table. Devices called "coffin collars" were invented to thwart the efforts of grave robbers. The collars were fixed around the neck of a corpse and then bolted to the bottom of the coffin, making it nearly impossible to move the body.

"Cemetery guns" were also used to keep the body snatchers away. They were set up at the foot of a grave with three tripwires strung up around its position. Those unlucky enough to approach a protected grave in the dark were likely to end up either dead or wounded.

As ingenious as these devices were, they only protected the graves of those whose families were wealthy enough to purchase them. So, naturally, most of the bodies that ended up in the hands of surgeons were those of the poor. The Anatomy Act of 1832 gave British physicians legal access to unclaimed corpses - also usually the poor - and those who died in the workhouses. The act was motivated by the growing anger at "resurrectionists" and by the 1828 murders in Scotland that had been committed by William Burke and William Hare, who strangled at least 16 victims before selling their corpses to anatomists.

The new law didn't do much to pacify the public, though. They felt it was unfair to the poor whose corpses were being used without their consent. Before 1832, dissection was considered a punishment for murderers, and now the law seemed to be punishing people for their poverty. After the act passed, riots broke out, and some medical school buildings were damaged, but the lucrative trade of the resurrectionists was effectively ended - in England anyway.

In America, the need to steal bodies for medical schools continued into the 1840s and 1850s. In St. Louis, the brilliant but eccentric Dr. Joseph McDowell started the first medical school west of the Mississippi River. When he needed fresh cadavers, he and his students took it upon themselves to raid the local burial grounds, usually stealing the corpses of poor immigrants. This led to a public outcry and even several armed raids against the medical school. But McDowell was prepared - he kept a cannon on the roof and more than 100 rifles to repel any attacks.

Grave robbery in America seemed to be less about procuring medical specimens and more about stealing valuables that had been buried with the dead. It was not uncommon in the nineteenth and early twentieth centuries for cemetery caretakers to discover coffins unearthed and rings, jewelry, and even gold teeth taken from corpses.

Undoubtedly worse than the removal of valuables from the grave was the violation of the corpse itself. And by that, I don't mean cutting them up on a dissection table - this is much, much worse. Necrophilia, the most reviled of all sexual perversions, is pleasure derived from sexual intercourse with a corpse. It represents a posthumous indignity of the most twisted sort.

Necrophilia - like anything else to do with sex - is nothing new. It has been described since ancient times. Legend says that King Herod continued to have sex with his wife, Marianne, for seven years after he killed her. In a case that was prosecuted in the 1760s, Sir John Pryce embalmed his first wife when she died and kept her in bed with him, even after he married a second time. When his second wife died, she was also embalmed and placed in the same bed. His third wife, however, wanted no part of his gruesome hobbies.

Necrophilia was a frequent theme in the writings of the Marquis de Sade. In 1886, a criminal named Henri Blot was arrested for raping several disinterred corpses. A gravedigger who was also arrested for this offense justified his perversion by saying that he could find no live woman to yield to his desires, so he saw no harm in giving his affections to dead women instead.

History often mistakenly identifies these types of individuals as harmless eccentrics, dismissing them "because they're not hurting anyone." This is a bad idea. There is a much darker and more dangerous pathology in most instances of necrophilia. We haven't been identifying serial killers for what they are until about 50 years ago, but they have always been with us. Many even speculate that the legends of monsters, werewolves, and vampires were created because of serial killers, necrophiles, and mass murderers. It was impossible in those days for the populace to comprehend the brutal and twisted acts that man was capable of. They created the monsters of myth and folklore to explain the horror.

This may be especially true when it comes to necrophilia. It has been called the most monstrous of all perversions, so we should not be surprised to learn that it is common among the most monstrous of our killers and criminals. Many infamous psychopaths - from Edmund Kemper to Jeffrey Dahmer, Ed Gein, and Ted Bundy - raped the bodies of their freshly slain victims. They were acting on a malevolent desire to dominate and violate their victims, even after death.

"Strange Love"

Key West, Florida, has always home to some of America's great eccentrics. It's a place that, far removed from the mainland of America, serves as sort of the last outpost for writers, dreamers, musicians, and weirdos. But in 1940, news spread around the island that something very strange was taking place in "Dr. von Cosel's" local laboratory and when details were revealed about what it was - it finally realized just what was "too much" even for Key West folks to handle.

Maria Elena Milagro de Hoyos

Maria Elena Milagro de Hoyos was born on July 31, 1909, the daughter of a Key West cigar maker named Francisco "Pancho" Hoyos and his wife, Aurora. Maria Elena had a bit of a tragic life. She had a sister who died from tuberculosis and a brother-in-law who was electrocuted on a construction site. Not long after she was married, she miscarried her child and her husband abandoned her and moved to Miami. To make matters worse, Maria Elena also contracted tuberculosis, a typically fatal disease at the time. She sought treatment at the United States Marine Hospital in Key West, and that's when her story takes a very strange turn.

While at the hospital, she met a German-born radiologic technologist named Carl Tanzler - or as he liked to refer to himself, "Carl von Cosel." Tanzler actually had many names. He was born Karl Tanzler, or George Karl Tänzler, on February 8, 1877, in Dresden, Germany. Little is known about his real background because his

Carl von Cosel - also known as Karl Tanzler, George Tanzler - who fell in love with Elena Hoyos

invented one was so confusing and changed often. He grew up in Germany, but claimed to have traveled to India and Australia where he did electrical work, bought boats, purchased a South Seas island, and began building a trans-ocean flying plane around the time of World War I. When the war broke out, he claimed that he was jailed by British authorities for "safe-keeping" and was released at war's end. We do know that he emigrated to the United States in 1926, via Cuba. From Cuba, he settled in Zephyrhills, Florida, which is where his sister lived. In 1927, he took a job at the U.S. Marine Hospital using the name Carl von Cosel.

It was at the hospital that he met Elena Hoyos, and he immediately fell in love with her. He later claimed that, as a child, he was visited by visions of a dead ancestor, Countess Anna Constantia von Cosel, who revealed to him the face of his true love, an exotic dark-haired woman. He was convinced the vision had been of Elena. Tanzler, with his self-professed medical knowledge, attempted to treat and cure her tuberculosis with a variety of medicines, as well as x-ray and electrical equipment that was brought to Maria's home. He showered her with gifts of jewelry and clothing and frequently professed his love to her. There is nothing to say that Elena ever reciprocated his affections. She was likely baffled by the attention being given to her by the strange little man.

Despite Tanzler's best efforts, Elena died from tuberculosis at her parents' home in on October 25, 1931. Tanzler paid for her funeral, and with the permission of her family, he then commissioned the construction of an above-ground mausoleum in the Key West Cemetery, which he visited almost every night. No one knows what finally pushed Tanzler over the edge, but it's believed that he "heard" Elena calling to him from her grave, asking him to free her from her stone prison. He later stated that Elena's spirit appeared to him when he sat next to her tomb and serenaded her with her favorite song.

So, one night in April 1933, Tanzler crept into the cemetery and removed Elena's body from the mausoleum, carting it out of the graveyard in a toy wagon. He took her home with him - and that's when things got even stranger.

Tanzler wired Elena's bones together with wire and coat hangers and inserted glass eyes into her head. As her skin began to decompose, he replaced it with silk cloth that had been soaked in wax and plaster. When her hair fell out, he fashioned a wig from hair that had been given to him by Elena's mother soon after her funeral in 1931. He filled her cadaver with rags so that she could keep her original form, and he dressed Elena in her clothing, stockings, jewelry, and gloves. Tanzler also used copious amounts of perfume, disinfectants, and preserving agents to mask the odor and slow the decomposition of the body.

He had to do this because he kept Elena's body in his bed.

In October 1940, Elena's sister, Florinda, heard rumors about Tanzler sleeping with the disinterred body of her sister and confronted Tanzler at his home, where Elena's body was discovered. Tanzler was arrested and detained - but only for desecrating Elena's tomb. Stealing her corpse was not illegal at the time. Tanzler was examined by psychiatrists, but they found him mentally competent to stand trial. After a preliminary hearing, though, the charges had to be dismissed. The statute of limitations for the crime had expired.

The case drew the attention of South Florida newspapers, and it created a sensation among the public, both regionally and across the country. Believe it or not, the public mood toward Tanzler was generally sympathetic. Many viewed the eccentric German as "romantic." There was no conclusive evidence at the time that Carl had sexual relations with Elena's corpse, but later examinations suggested that it was possible.

During the furor over the story, Elena's body was examined by pathologists and then put on public display at the Dean-Lopez Funeral Home in Key West, where it was seen by nearly 7,000 people. Elena's corpse was eventually returned to the Key West Cemetery and was reburied in an unmarked grave, in a secret location, to prevent any further tampering.

In the aftermath of the discovery, Tanzler left Key West, but he didn't do so in shame. He returned to Zephyrhills, Florida, and wrote an autobiography that appeared in the pulp magazine, *Fantastic Adventures,* in 1947. He became a U.S. citizen in Tampa in 1950.

He never got over his obsession with Elena Hoyos. Still longing for his lost love, he created a "death mask" of her as the basis for a life-sized dummy, which he kept in his bed until his death on July 3, 1952. Some accounts of Tanzler's death claim his body was found in the arms of the dummy, but this is merely wishful thinking by those of morbid sensibilities. According to his obituary, he died on the floor of his home.

It was noted, though, that overlooking his corpse was a "waxen image, wrapped in silken cloth and a robe." It seems that his replacement Elena was with him to the very end.

The story of "Count Von Cosel" is undoubtedly a tale of grave robbery and necrophilia, but there's no way to know if the ghost of

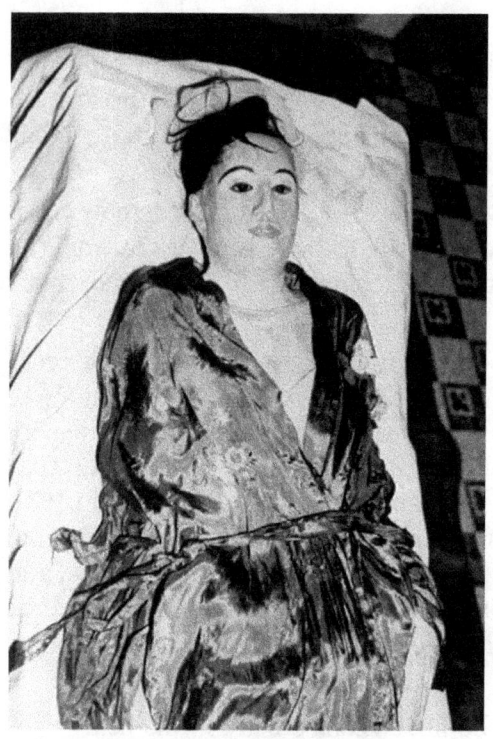

The doll that von Cosel created from Elena's body by wiring her bones and remaining flesh together. He slept with it in his bed every night.

Elena that appeared to him was real or merely the product of his twisted mind.

There are several other hauntings connected to grave robberies and one case that is linked to necrophilia, too. It was certainly not recognized as such in nineteenth-century Utah, but today it's evident that the story of Jean Baptiste has some pretty strange sexual undertones. There seems to be little doubt that this unusual gravedigger was helping himself to more than just the clothing of the corpses.

The Ghost of the Great Salt Lake

Utah's Great Salt Lake covers more than 2,300 square miles in the northern part of Utah and is one of the world's saltiest bodies of water. It is also a very shallow lake for its size, plunging to depths of only 27 feet in its deepest parts.

But even those shallow depths hold secrets.

In the late nineteenth century, a Salt Lake City gravedigger was exiled to an island on the lake because of the ghoulish crimes he had committed. Years later, he vanished without a trace, but the legends say he left a lingering spirit behind.

Salt Lake City was founded by the Church of Jesus Christ of the Latter-Day Saints - the Mormons - in 1847. They settled in the valley after a long trek west from Illinois, where their original prophet, Joseph Smith, had been murdered. Led by Brigham Young, they built homes, church buildings, official meeting places, roads, bridges, and became first a territory of the United States and later, a full-fledged state. After putting aside their practice of polygamy, that is.

Jean Baptiste was one of the first gravediggers ever employed in Salt Lake City. He lived in a two-room house with a lean-to at the corner of K Street and Temple, and he was believed to be well-off and lived comfortably. He was regarded as a hard-worker, upstanding and punctual man who always carried out his appointed duties at the city cemetery without complaint. He was a quiet fellow, though, and had few friends, so most people never paid much attention to him as he went about his work.

In the third year of his employment for the city, Baptiste buried a man who had recently died. There was nothing out of the ordinary about this. He had done his job hundreds of times already - but this time would be different. A few weeks after the burial, the brother of the dead man came to Utah from the east. He had been unhappy with his brother's conversion to Mormonism and wished to have his sibling returned east to be buried in their family plot. He obtained permission to have the body exhumed, and workers opened the grave. But when they removed the lid of the coffin, they found the corpse to be completely naked and lying in the coffin facedown, as if he had been dumped there. The clothing of the dead man was nowhere to be found.

His brother was outraged and demanded an immediate investigation. City officials agreed and questioned Jean Baptiste. He denied any knowledge of the disturbance, but the police weren't convinced by his story. They began to keep him under surveillance.

When the next burial was set to occur at the cemetery, Baptiste dug the grave but didn't immediately fill it in after the services were over. Later that evening, he was seen in the cemetery pushing a wheelbarrow toward the new grave. When the authorities rushed to the scene, they found that the corpse had been removed from the grave, his clothing had been taken off, and Baptiste was moving the body in the wheelbarrow to a more "private location" in the graveyard.

Baptiste was arrested, and his home was searched. Officers found that his home was filled with clothing. He had used it for drapes, for furniture covers, carpets, blankets, and towels. In the cellar, he kept a large vat where the clothing could be boiled before he began using it.

News of the discovery spread, and local citizens rushed to the cemetery to check on their loved ones. It was soon realized that he had stolen the clothing of at least 350 corpses - and apparently had violated them, too.

The clothing from the house was taken to City Hall to be identified by family members, and officers learned that Baptiste had sold thousands of dollars in jewelry that was also taken from the graves.

Baptiste was tried and convicted of grave robbery, branded with a hot iron, and exiled to Antelope Island, which was located on the Great Salt Lake. He wasn't allowed to ever return to Salt Lake City again.

A few weeks after his banishment, police officers returned to the island to bring supplies. A search discovered the remains of a fire and a small shelter, but Baptiste was gone. Some believe that he killed himself, while others maintain that he built a raft and escaped from his prison. Either way, he was never heard from again.

Or was he?

Stories say that Baptiste still haunts the island today. He has been reported many times walking along the edge of the water, looking out toward the city, with a bundle of wet and rotted clothing in his hands.

Stealing Mr. Lincoln

After President Abraham Lincoln was assassinated in April 1865, his body traveled west from Washington, spending several weeks visiting towns and cities along a route that was the reverse of the trip he took when elected president in 1860. His funeral service in Springfield, Illinois, did not take place until May 4, and it followed a parade route from the former Lincoln home to Oak Ridge Cemetery, on the far edge of the city. But it would be many years before Lincoln was allowed to rest in peace. His tomb has long been a place of mystery, intrigue, speculation, bizarre history, and some say a haunting.

But if Abraham Lincoln's tomb is haunted, it's likely not by the president's spirit but rather from an event that occurred at the tomb in 1876 that began a bizarre series of events that have left many questions behind.

The Civil War changed the way Americans looked at death. Never before had they seen death on such a massive scale, and the war introduced Americans to the creation of national cemeteries, embalming, and other customs.

Then a death after the war created the way that we mourn for the dead - it was the assassination of President Abraham Lincoln. The outpouring of American grief over the president's death was not only

Abraham Lincoln

the feeling of loss for a beloved leader, but it was also a public representation of American grief for all those who perished during the war.

After a massive public funeral service in Washington, D.C., Lincoln's body was taken by train to Illinois, stopping at various northern cities along the route. At each stop, tens of thousands of people gathered to view his body and pay their last respects. People wailed, cried, fainted, and became hysterical at the sight of his corpse or even because the train was passing through their town. Homes and buildings were draped in black crepe, funeral cards were printed, badges were worn, and everyone dressed in black. Lincoln's death would create a standard for American mourning traditions for the remainder of the nineteenth century.

The city of Springfield had been stunned by the news of Lincoln's assassination and had lobbied the president's oldest son, Robert, to have Lincoln buried there in a city he'd loved. Robert had to deal with his mother - through her locked bedroom door - because she had the final decision. Mary was torn between the fact that she had quarreled with just about all of her old friends and her family in Springfield and never wanted to set foot there again, and the sincere desire to choose a burial place that would have been her husband's choice.

At the time of the Washington funeral, she insisted that Chicago was her first choice for Lincoln's tomb. Her husband had promised her that after he left the Presidency, they would make a tour of Europe and then retire in Chicago, so she favored a quiet burial place near Lake Michigan.

But Mary also looked back at her last days with Lincoln and realized that he had a foreshadowing of his death - something that had occurred several times in their years together. "You will see Europe, but I never shall," he told her. She also remembered her husband's dream to live once more in Springfield and recalled his saying, just a few weeks before his death, that he wanted to be buried in "some quiet place." He had told her in 1860 that the new Springfield cemetery, Oak Ridge, was one of the most beautiful spots that he had ever seen.

After agonizing over her decision, Mary finally decided that Oak Ridge was the "quiet place" that Lincoln would have wanted and directed that his coffin be placed in the public receiving tomb there until a proper site could be chosen for his monument.

Her decision was telegraphed to Springfield, and days and nights of frantic preparation were made. Mary wanted Lincoln to be buried at Oak Ridge - but the city of Springfield had other plans.

When the body of President Lincoln arrived in Springfield, he had two different graves waiting for him. One of the graves was a temporary vault at remote and wooded Oak Ridge, which Springfield officials believed was no place to bury a fallen hero, and the other was a small hill located in the heart of the city. This spot was called Mather's Hill, and it had been the site of the magnificent stone house that was owned by Thomas Mather. Builders were employed to work around the clock and convert the house into a tomb, complete with a handsome vault and stone urns on either side of the entrance.

Mary learned of the downtown tomb and sent a telegram stating that her husband absolutely was to be buried at Oak Ridge. Springfield officials nervously telegraphed Edwin Stanton and told him that her wishes would be respected - but continued the work at the Mather tomb anyway. They simply could not believe that Mary would want her husband buried out in the woods, and even if she did, they were sure that they could change her mind when she arrived in Springfield.

Even after Lincoln was entombed in the temporary crypt at Oak Ridge, Springfield's leaders had no intention of leaving him there. They marched ahead with plans to place the president in the Mather tomb. In fact, plans had already been started for a huge ceremony to mark the occasion.

Lincoln's first tomb at Oak Ridge Cemetery

Mary was furious when she read in the newspapers of Springfield's intentions. Immediately, she sent word and threatened to remove Lincoln's body from the city if a monument was not built at Oak Ridge.

In the summer of 1865, Mary moved to Chicago, and a delegation from Springfield went up to plead with her again. She refused to see them, and at last, they surrendered to her wishes.

A temporary vault was built for Lincoln at Oak Ridge, and in seven months on December 21, he was placed inside. Six of Lincoln's friends wanted to be sure the body was safe, so a plumber's assistant named Leon P. Hopkins made an opening in the lead box for them to peer inside. All was well, and Lincoln was allowed a temporary rest. Hopkins stated in a newspaper story at the time, "I was the last man to look upon the face of Abraham Lincoln."

Of course, he had no idea at the time just how many others would look upon the president's face in the years to come.

Construction on a permanent tomb for Lincoln lasted more than five years, and on September 19, 1871, the caskets of Lincoln and the sons that preceded him in death - Eddie and Willie - were removed from the hillside crypt and taken to the catacomb of the new tomb. The plumber, Leon P. Hopkins, opened the coffin once more, and the same six friends peered again at the president's face. Several crypts were waiting for Lincoln and his sons, although one of them had already been filled. Tad Lincoln had died in Chicago a short time before, and his body had already been placed in the nearly finished monument.

The dead president was laid to rest again, for another three years, while the workmen toiled away outside.

It was during this time that strange things began to be reported in the vicinity of Lincoln's resting place. A short time before the bodies were moved into the new monument, Springfield residents and curiosity-seekers began to tell of a spectral image that was seen near the crypt. It was believed to be Lincoln himself, investigating the construction site where he and his sons were to be laid to rest.

Lincoln's Monument and Tomb

Even after the move was completed, the eerie stories continued. Inside of the monument, strange sobbing noises and what sounded like footsteps also began to be reported. Many of the locals believed that the ghost of President Lincoln was haunting Oak Ridge Cemetery and the new tomb. This was the first ghost story connected to Abraham Lincoln that was ever told. It would certainly not be the last.

On October 9, 1874, Lincoln was moved again. This time his body was placed inside a marble sarcophagus, which was in the center of the semi-circular catacomb. A few days later, the monument was finally dedicated. Now Lincoln - after being taken by train across the country and moved three times - could finally rest in peace.

But that peace ended in 1876.

The strangest events connected to Lincoln's tomb began when Captain Patrick Tyrell of the Chicago office of the U. S Secret Service arrested a counterfeiter named Benjamin Boyd and sent him to the Joliet Penitentiary for ten years. In those days, the Secret Service only investigated counterfeiting, which was a huge problem in America in the nineteenth century. They were not yet in charge of protecting the president or government officials - but in this case, they would - well, sort of.

Shortly after Boyd's arrest, events were set into motion in Lincoln, Illinois - a town ironically named for the president. The city was a staging point for a successful gang of counterfeiters run by James "Big Jim" Kneally. It was an ideal refuge for Kneally's "shovers," pleasant-looking fellows who traveled around the country and passed, or "shoved," bogus money to merchants.

Following Boyd's arrest, business took a downturn for the Kneally Gang. With their master engraver in prison, the gang's supply of money was dwindling fast. Things were looking desperate when Kneally came up with a plan. He would have his men kidnap a famous person and for a ransom negotiate for the release of Benjamin Boyd from Joliet prison.

Kneally even had the perfect candidate as his kidnapping victim: Abraham Lincoln, or at least his famous corpse.

The plan was pretty elaborate, and it involved opening a tavern and dance hall in Springfield as a cover. The gang made frequent visits to the Lincoln Tomb at Oak Ridge, where they found the custodian, John C. Power, more than happy to answer questions about the building. On one occasion, he innocently let slip that there was no guard at the tomb during the night. They made plans to steal Lincoln's body on July 3, 1876 - which was nearly a month away.

The problem was that this left the gang several weeks to hang around in Springfield and drink free liquor at the bar they had created as a front. One night, one of the men spilled the details of the plan to a prostitute - telling her to look for a little extra excitement in the city on Independence Day. He and his buddies planned to steal Lincoln's body while the rest of the city was celebrating the holiday. The story was too good to keep to herself, and the woman passed it along to several other people, including the city's Chief of Police - although no record exists how these two knew one another. The story spread rapidly, and Kneally's men disappeared.

Kneally didn't give up on the plan, however. He simply went looking for more competent help. He moved his base of operations to a tavern called the Hub at 294 West Madison in Chicago. Kneally's man there was named Terence Mullen, and he operated a secret headquarters for the gang in the back room of the tavern.

One of Kneally's operatives, Jack Hughes, came into the Hub in August and learned that a big job was in the works. Kneally wanted to steal Lincoln's corpse as soon as possible. Hughes and Mullen had no desire to do this by themselves, so they brought another man into the mix. His name was Jim Morrissey, and he had a reputation for being one of the most skilled grave robbers in Chicago. They decided he would be perfect for the job.

Unknown to the gang, "Morrissey" was a Secret Service operative named Lewis Swegles. When he heard what was happening with the counterfeit gang, he posed as a grave robber.

Swegles, pretending to be "Jim Morrissey," came into the Hub and discussed the methods of grave robbery with the other two men. The three of them quickly devised a plan. They would approach the Lincoln monument under cover of night and pry open the marble sarcophagus. They would then place the casket in a wagon and drive away. The plan was for this to happen on Election Day when most of Springfield would be distracted by other things.

Swegles, being the most experienced of the group, agreed to everything about the plan except for the number of men needed. He believed the actual theft would be harder than they thought and wanted to bring in a famous criminal friend of his to help them. The man's name was Billy Brown, and he could handle the wagon while the others pillaged the tomb. The other two men readily agreed - not knowing that Brown was also a Secret Service agent.

The gang took a train from Chicago to Springfield, sharing it with at least six other Secret Service agents, Pinkerton detectives hired by Robert Lincoln, and Elmer Washburne, one of Robert's law partners.

The plan was for Swegles to accompany the grave robbers to Springfield and, while assisting in the robbery, would signal the detectives, who would be hiding in another part of the monument. They would then capture Mullen and Hughes in the act.

When they arrived in Springfield, Tyrell contacted John Todd Stuart, Robert's cousin, and the head of the new Lincoln National Monument Association, which cared for the tomb. He advised Stuart of the plan, and together, they contacted the custodian of the site. The detectives would hide in the museum side of the monument with the custodian. This area was called Memorial Hall, and it was located on the opposite side of the structure from the catacomb. They would wait there for the signal from Swegles, and then they would in forward and capture the robbers.

The first Pinkerton agent arrived just after nightfall. He carried with him a note for John Power, the custodian, which instructed him to put out the lights and wait for the others to arrive. The two men crouched in the darkness until the other men came inside. Tyrell and his men explored the place with their flashlights. Behind the Memorial Hall was a damp, dark labyrinth that wound through the foundations of the monument to a rear wall of the catacomb, where Lincoln was entombed. Against this wall, Tyrell stationed a detective to wait and listen for the sounds of the grave robbers. Tyrell then returned to the Museum Room to wait with the others. Their wait was over as darkness fell outside.

A lantern flashed outside the door, and sounds could be heard as the grave robbers worked at the lock. Once inside, they saw the marble sarcophagus of President Lincoln. Now, all they had to do was to remove the lid and carry away the coffin, which turned out to be much harder than they had anticipated. The stone was too heavy to move, so using an ax, they broke open the top, then moved the lid aside and looked into the vault.

Swegles was given the lantern and was stationed nearby to illuminate the work area. Left with no other option, he complied, although he was supposed to light a match at the door to alert the

Secret Service agents that it was time to act. Meanwhile, Mullen and Hughes lifted out the heavy casket. Once this was completed, Mullen told Swegles to go and have the wagon moved around. He had assured Mullen and Hughes that Billy Brown had it waiting in a ravine below the hill.

Swegles raced around to Memorial Hall, gave the signal to the detectives, and then ran outside. Tyrell whispered to his men, and, with drawn revolvers, they rushed out and around the monument to the catacomb. When they arrived, they found the lid to the sarcophagus was moved aside, and Lincoln's casket was on the floor - but the grave robbers were gone.

The detectives instantly searched the place. Tyrell ran outside and around the base of the monument, where he saw two men near one of the statues. He whipped up his pistol and fired at them. A shot was returned, and they fought it out in a hail of gunfire, dodging around the monument. Suddenly, one of the men at whom he was shooting called out Tyrell's name - he was firing at his own agents.

Mullen and Hughes had casually walked away from the tomb to await the return of Swegles, Brown, and the wagon. They never suspected the whole thing had been a trap. They had only wanted to get some air and moved into the shadows where they wouldn't be seen in case someone wandered by. After a few minutes, they saw movement at the door to the tomb and had started back, thinking that Swegles had returned. Then they heard the pistol shots and saw men around the monument. They took off running past the ravine and vanished into the night. Assuming that Swegles had been captured, they fled to Chicago, only to be elated when they found him waiting for them at the Hub tavern. He had returned with the horses, he told them but found the gang gone. Not knowing what else to do, he had come back to Chicago to find them.

Meanwhile, the story of the attempted grave robbery began to circulate after the election - but no one believed it. Only one paper, the *Chicago Tribune*, would even print the story because every other newspaper in the state was sure that it was not true. Most people believed it was a hoax created for some bizarre political agenda. They refused to believe that the Secret Service and a group of Pinkerton agents would be stupid enough to have gathered all in one room where they could see and hear nothing, and then wait for the criminals to act.

But the doubters became believers on November 18, when Mullen and Hughes were captured. The newspapers printed the story the following day, and America realized it was true. People were outraged, and punishment for the two men would have been severe - If the law had allowed it. Grave robbery was not against the law in Illinois at the time, and all they could be charged with was petty larceny. And that was not for trying to steal Lincoln's body - it was for trying to steal his coffin. They each received a one-year, all expenses paid stay at Joliet Penitentiary.

And Abraham Lincoln was once more left to rest peacefully in his grave, but only for a little while.

The story of the Lincoln grave robbery became a hot topic at the tomb, which saw thousands of visitors every year. The custodians of the site simply decided that it was something they did not wish to talk about, even though people asked about it every day.

From 1876 to 1878, custodian John C. Power gave rather evasive answers to anyone who prodded him for details about the grave robbery. He was terrified of one question in particular, and it seemed to be the one most often asked: was he sure that Lincoln's body had been returned safely to the sarcophagus after the grave robbers took it out?

Power was terrified of that question for one reason because, at that time, Lincoln's sarcophagus was completely empty.

Immediately after the attempted robbery, Power and John Todd Stuart became convinced that someone else might attempt to hide the body, so they decided to hide it in the passages that were between the Memorial Hall and the catacomb.

They hid the casket near some construction materials left over from building the tomb and Power began digging a grave in the dirt floor. It was slow work, because it had to be done between visitors to the site, and he also had a problem with water seeping into the hole. Finally, he gave up and simply covered the coffin with the leftover boards and wood.

For the next two years, Lincoln lay beneath a pile of debris in the walls, while visitors from all over the world wept and mourned over the sarcophagus at the other end of the monument. And the suspicious questions continued to be asked.

In the summer and fall of 1877, the story took another turn. Workers arrived at the monument to erect the naval and infantry groups of statuary on the corners of the upper deck. Their work would take them into the labyrinth, where Power feared they would discover the coffin. The scandal would be incredible, so Power made a quick decision. He called the workmen together and swearing them to secrecy, showed them the coffin. They promised to keep the secret, but within days everyone in Springfield seemed to know that Lincoln's body was not where it was supposed to be. Soon, the story was spreading all over the country.

Power was now in a panic. The body had to be more securely hidden; to do that, he needed more help. Power contacted two of his friends, Major Gustavas Dana and General Jasper Reece, and explained the situation. These men brought three others, Edward Johnson, Joseph Lindley, and James McNeill, to meet with Power.

On the night of November 18, the six men began digging another grave for Lincoln at the far end of the labyrinth. These men, sobered by the responsibility that faced them, decided to form a brotherhood to guard the secret of the tomb. They brought in three younger men, Noble Wiggins, Horace Chapin, and Clinton Conkling, to help in the task. They called themselves the Lincoln Guard of Honor and had badges made for their lapels.

After the funeral of Mary Lincoln, John Todd Stuart told the Guard of Honor that Robert Lincoln wanted to have his mother's body hidden away with his father's. So, late on the night of July 21, the men slipped into the monument and moved Mary's double-leaded casket, burying it in the labyrinth next to Lincoln's.

Finally, in 1886, the Lincoln National Monument Association decided that it was time to provide a new tomb for Lincoln in the catacomb. A new and stronger crypt of brick and mortar was designed and made ready.

The press was kept outside as the Guard of Honor, and others who shared the secret of the tomb brought the Lincoln caskets out of the labyrinth. A group of 18 people, all who had known Lincoln in life, filed past the casket, looking into a square hole that had been cut into the lead coffin.

Strangely, Lincoln had changed extraordinarily little. The last man to identify the corpse was Leon P. Hopkins - the same man who had closed the casket years before. He soldered the square back over the hole, thinking once again that he would be the last person to ever look upon the face of Abraham Lincoln.

The Guard of Honor lifted Lincoln's casket and placed it next to Mary's. The two of them were taken into the catacomb and lowered into the new brick and mortar vault.

There, they would sleep for all time.

"All time" lasted for about thirteen more years. In 1899, Illinois legislators decided the monument was to be torn down and a new one built from the foundations. It seemed that the present structure was settling unevenly, cracking around the "eternal" vault of the president.

There was once again the question of what to do with the bodies of the Lincoln family. The Guard of Honor came up with a clever plan. During the 15 months needed for construction, the Lincolns would be secretly buried in multiple graves a few feet away from the foundations of the tomb. As the old structure was torn down, tons of stone and dirt would be heaped onto the gravesite both to disguise and protect it. When the new monument was finished, the grave would be uncovered again, and the bodies would be moved back into the building.

In 1901, the placement of Lincoln's body in the new tomb was personally supervised by Robert Lincoln, and he paid for all the latest security measures of the era, including an electric burglar alarm that rang into the caretaker's house. As up to date as this device was, it still did not quench the fears of Robert Lincoln, who was sure that his father's body would be snatched again if care were not taken. He stayed in constant contact with the Guard of Honor, who was still working to ensure the safety of the Lincoln remains and made a trip to Springfield every month or so as the new monument was being completed. Something just wasn't right. Even though the alarm worked

Work was started on a new tomb for Lincoln in 1899 and was completed two years later. During the construction, the entire Lincoln family was hidden under construction materials.

perfectly, he could not give up the idea that the robbery might be repeated.

He journeyed to Springfield and brought with him his own set of security plans. He met with officials and gave them explicit directions on what he wanted to be done. The construction company was to break a hole in the tile floor of the monument and place his father's casket at a depth of 10 feet. The coffin would then be encased in a cage of steel bars, and the hole would be filled with concrete, making the president's final resting place into a solid and impenetrable block.

On September 26, 1901, a group assembled to make the final arrangements for Lincoln's last burial. A discussion quickly turned into a heated debate. The question that concerned them was whether Lincoln's coffin should be opened, and the body viewed one last time. Most felt this would be a wise precaution, especially in light of the continuing stories about Lincoln not being in the tomb. In the end, practicality won out, and Leon P. Hopkins was sent to chisel out an opening in the lead coffin.

There was no question, according to those present, that Abraham Lincoln was in his casket. After the entire group studied the slain

After the interior of the tomb was completed, the bodies of the Lincolns were moved inside, and Lincoln's body was placed in a vault under the floor and encased in concrete.

president's face, Leon P. Hopkins sealed the casket. He made real his claim of many years before. Hopkins indeed was the last person to look upon the face of Lincoln.

The casket was then lowered down into the cage of steel, and two tons of cement was poured over it, securing it forever.

That should have been the end of it, but as with all lingering mysteries, a few questions remain. The strangest are perhaps these: does the body of Abraham Lincoln really lie beneath the concrete in the catacomb? Or was the last visit from Robert Lincoln part of some elaborate ruse to throw off any further attempts to steal the president's body? And did, as some rumors have suggested, Robert arrange with the Guard of Honor to have his father's body hidden in a different location entirely?

Most mainstream historians would agree that Lincoln's body is safely encased in the concrete of the crypt, but let's look at this with a conspiratorial eye for a moment. Whose word do we have for the fact that Lincoln's body is where it is said to be? We only have the statement of Lincoln's son, Robert, his friends, and of course, the Guard of Honor. But weren't these the same individuals who allowed visitors to the monument to grieve before an empty sarcophagus at the same time the president's body was hidden in the labyrinth beneath a few inches of dirt? It's interesting to consider, but it's likely that we will never know, one way or another.

And what of the stories that claim that Lincoln's ghost still walks the tomb?

Many have reported that he, or some other spirit here, does not rest in peace. Many tourists, staff members, and historians have had some unsettling encounters in the dimly lit monument that aren't easily laughed away. Usually, these encounters have been reported as the sound of ceaseless pacing, tapping footsteps on the tile floors, whispers, and quiet voices, and the sounds of someone crying or weeping in the corridors.

Is it Abraham Lincoln? Most likely, it's not. In fact, it's unlikely that the tomb is even "haunted" in the traditional sense of what we think of when we consider a place to be haunted by ghosts. If strange things are occurring here, it's most likely that they are "echoes" of events from the past that are still making themselves known today.

Could the weeping sounds simply be "memories" of the millions of grief-stricken people who have visited this site? Could the voices, banging sounds, and the restless tapping be a "residue" of the dark events that occurred here in 1876? Yes, I think events may be what has made this tomb haunted, not the people whose bodies remain behind.

These aren't what we think of as ghosts. They are the lingering energy of more than a century and a half of grief and pain experienced by millions of mourners, the fear and excitement of the grave robbers, and the paranoia of the men who were sworn to protect the president's remains at all costs.

"NO MAN KNOWS MY GRAVE"

One of the causes of haunted cemeteries is obviously "disturbance." As you have likely noticed from the preceding pages, it's a central theme here. We often find that graves that are purposely - or accidentally - left unmarked can also cause burial places to become haunted. I think this is mostly because unmarked graves often lead to resting places becoming disturbed since no one knew the dead were buried there.

There are other, more tragic stories, too. It seems in some cases; the spirits are reaching out from the other side looking for recognition or remembrance. They want someone to know where their bodies were laid to rest - rest they have been unable to find.

For instance, there was an event that occurred in 1995 in Rosehill Cemetery in Chicago that illustrates this point. In October of that year, a groundskeeper at the cemetery reported that he had seen a woman wandering about in the graveyard at night. She had been standing next to a tree, not far from the wall that separates the cemetery from Peterson Avenue. The staff member stopped his truck and got out. The cemetery was closed for the night, and he was going to tell the woman that she had to leave and offer to escort her to the gate. When he approached her, he realized that the woman - dressed in some sort of flowing white garment - was floating above the ground. Before his eyes, she turned into a mist and slowly vanished. Not surprisingly, the groundskeeper wasted no time in rushing to the cemetery office to report the weird incident.

Yes, this story does get stranger.

The following day, a woman from suburban Des Plaines, Illinois, called the office and requested that a marker be placed on the grave of her aunt, Carrie Kalbas, who had died in 1933. The family had been unable to afford a stone at the time Carrie died, and her grave had always been unmarked.

Why wait 60 years to mark the grave? The previous night, the woman claimed that her aunt had appeared to her in a dream. She asked her niece to be sure that her burial place was marked because she wanted to be remembered.

The woman offered the location of the grave - in an old family plot - and staff members went to the site to verify the location and determine what kind of marker could be used. They were astonished to discover that the unmarked grave was in the exact spot where the apparition had been seen the night before.

The grave marker was ordered, and the ghost was never seen again.

Unmarked graves and disturbed burial grounds can lead to hauntings, and sites don't even have to be official cemeteries to become haunted. Even the graves of settlers killed in a massacre in 1812 have managed to cause a haunting that will be forever part of Chicago's mysterious history.

Massacre at Fort Dearborn

It may not have been a cold morning in April 1803, when Captain John Whistler climbed a sand dune around which the sluggish Chicago River tried to reach Lake Michigan - but chances are, it was. A chilling wind would have been a characteristic greeting from the landscape that Whistler had come to change. His orders had been to take six soldiers from the 1st U.S. Infantry, survey a road from Detroit to the mouth of the river, and draw up plans for a fort at this location. Whistler managed to beat the British to the site. The British had also planned to build a fort at the entrance to the Chicago River, and one has to wonder how the city might be different today if they had managed to show up first.

After claiming the site, Captain Whistler returned to Detroit to get his garrison and his family. He was 45 years old, and neither his poor Army pay, nor the dangers of the frontier stopped him from living a full and domesticated life. Eventually, he fathered 15 children.

Captain Whistler's family was spared the arduous trek over erratic Indian trails to the Chicago River. While the troops marched on foot, the captain and his brood boarded the U.S. schooner *Tracy*, which also carried artillery and camp equipment. It sailed to the mouth of the

St. Joseph River, where it met the troops. The Whistler family took one of the *Tracy's* rowboats to the Chicago River, while the troops marched around the lake.

There were 69 officers and men in the contingent that had the task of building Fort Dearborn, which was named in honor of Secretary of War Henry Dearborn, a man who would go on to be considered one of the most inept leaders in American history. During the War of 1812, he became infamous for failing to find Canada.

The hill on which Fort Dearborn was built was eight feet above the river using logs that had been cut by soldiers along the north bank. It was a simple stockade made from digging holes in the ground, inserting poles, and then sharpening them at the end. The outer stockade was a solid wall with an entrance in the southern section that was blocked with heavy gates. Another exit, this one underground, was located on the north side. As time went on, they built barracks, officers' quarters, a guardhouse, and a small powder magazine made from brick. West of the fort, they constructed a two-story log building, with split-oak siding, to serve as an Indian agency, and between this structure and the fort, they placed root cellars. South of the fort, the land was enclosed for a garden. Blockhouses were added at two corners of the fort, and three pieces of light artillery were mounted at the walls. The fort offered substantial protection for the soldiers garrisoned there, but they would later learn that it was not protection enough.

Soon, a settlement began to grow around the fort. The self-appointed civilian leader of the group was a trader named John Kinzie, a troublesome man who bickered so often with Captain Whistler that he was eventually banned from the fort itself. Kinzie became known for his crooked dealing with the Potawatomi Indians, trading liquor for furs, which caused tension among the other settlers.

Kinzie had his wife, Eleanor, had four children, and while many called him "a very decent man and a good companion," not everyone agreed. One of them was Jean Lalime, who was briefly Kinzie's partner in the trading post. The two men became bitter enemies after Lalime sided with the Captain Whistler and the officers at the fort when they demanded that Kinzie stop giving liquor to the Native American populace. Eventually, the animosity between the two men boiled over into violence, and Lalime was stabbed to death. Kinzie claimed the murder had been self-defense but fled the settlement for a short time. When he returned, he found that military officers who had been friends with Lalime had buried the dead man in Kinzie's yard.

In 1810, Captain Nathan Heald replaced Whistler at Fort Dearborn. Heald brought with him Lieutenant Linus T. Helm, an officer, like Heald, who was experienced in the ways of the frontier. Not long after arriving, Helm met and married the stepdaughter of John Kinzie. In addition to Captain Heald's wife, there were also several other women at the fort, all wives of the men stationed there. More families arrived and, within two years, there were 12 women and 20 children at Fort Dearborn.

At the start of the War of 1812, tensions in the wilderness began to rise. British troops came to the American frontier, spreading liquor and discontent among the Indian tribes, especially the Potawatomi, the Wyandot, and the Winnebago - all of whom lived near Fort Dearborn. In April, an Indian raid occurred on a nearby farm, and two men were killed. The fort became a refuge for many of the settlers and a growing cause of unrest for the local tribes. When war was declared that summer - and the British captured the American garrison at Mackinac - it was decided that Fort Dearborn could not be held and that the fort should be evacuated.

General William Hull, the American commander in the Northwest, issued orders to Captain Nathan Heald through Indian agent officers. He was told that the fort was to be abandoned, that arms and ammunition were to be destroyed, and that all remaining trade goods were to be distributed to friendly natives. Hull also sent a message to Fort Wayne, ordering Captain William Wells and a contingent of allied Miami Indians to Fort Dearborn to assist with the evacuation.

There is no dispute about whether or not General Hull gave the order, nor that Captain Heald received it, but some have wondered if perhaps his instruction, or his handwriting, was not clear because Heald waited eight days before acting on it. During that time, Heald argued with his officers, with John Kinzie, who opposed the evacuation, and with local Indians. One of whom fired off a rifle in the commanding officer's quarters.

The delay managed to give hostile Indians time to gather outside the fort. They assembled there in an almost siege-like state, and Heald realized that he was going to have to bargain with them if the occupants of Fort Dearborn were going to reach Fort Wayne safely. On August 13, all the blankets, trading items, and calico cloth were given out, and Heald held several councils with Indian leaders, which his junior officers refused to attend.

Eventually, an agreement was reached that had the Potawatomi providing safe-conduct for the soldiers and settlers to Fort Wayne in Indiana. Part of the agreement was that Heald would leave behind all the surplus arms and ammunition, but his officers disagreed. They questioned the wisdom of handing out guns and ammunition that could easily be turned against them. Heald reluctantly went along with them, and the extra weapons and ammunition were broken apart and dumped into an abandoned well. Only 25 rounds of ammunition were saved for each man. As an added bit of insurance, all of the liquor barrels were smashed, and the contents were poured into the river during the night.

On August 14, Captain William Wells and his Miami allies arrived at the fort. Wells was a frontier legend to the soldiers and settlers in the Illinois territory. He was also the uncle of Captain Heald's wife, Rebekah, and after receiving the request for assistance from General Hull, he headed straight to Fort Dearborn to aid in the evacuation. But even the arrival of the frontiersman and his Miami warriors would not save the lives of those trapped inside Fort Dearborn.

Throughout the night of August 14, wagons were loaded for travel, and the reserve ammunition was distributed. Early the next morning, the procession of soldiers, civilians, women, and children left the fort. The infantry soldiers led the way, followed by a caravan of wagons and mounted men. A portion of the Miami who had accompanied Wells guarded the rear of the column. It was reported that musicians played the "dead march," a slow, solemn funeral march that would be a foreboding of the disaster that followed.

The column of soldiers and settlers was escorted by nearly 500 of the Potawatomi. As they marched southward and into a low range

The massacre of the soldiers and settlers from Fort Dearborn

of sandhills that separated the beaches of Lake Michigan from the prairie, the Potawatomi moved silently to the right, placing an elevation of sand between themselves and the column. The act was carried out with such subtlety that no one noticed it as the soldiers and settlers trudged along the shoreline.

The column traveled to an area where present-day 16th Street and Indiana Avenue are located. There was sudden milling about of the scouts at the front of the line, and suddenly a shout came back from Captain Wells that the Indians were attacking. A line of Potawatomi appeared over the edge of the ridge and fired down at the column. Surprised, the officers nevertheless managed to rally the men into a battle line, but it was of little use. Soldiers fell immediately, and the line collapsed. The Indians overwhelmed them with sheer numbers, flanking the line, and snatching the wagons and horses.

What followed was butchery. Officers were slain with tomahawks, and the fort's surgeon was cut down by gunfire and then literally chopped into pieces. Rebekah Heald was wounded by gunfire but was spared when she was captured by a sympathetic Indian chief. The wife of one soldier fought so bravely and savagely that she was hacked into pieces before she fell. In the end - reduced to less than half their original number - the garrison surrendered under the promise of safe conduct. In all, 148 members of the column were killed, with 86 adults and 12 children slaughtered in the initial attack. The children who died had been loaded onto a single wagon for safety.

Captain Wells managed to kill eight men with his bare hands before he was felled and pinned down by his horse. Warriors clubbed him to death, then cut out his heart and ate it, hoping to ingest some of his ferocious bravery.

Captain Heald was wounded twice in the fighting. Rebekah was wounded seven times. Both survived and were later released. A St. Joseph Indian named Chaudonaire took them to Mackinac, where they were turned over to the British commander there. He sent them to Detroit, where they were exchanged with the American authorities.

The surrender that was arranged by Captain Heald did not apply to the wounded, and it is said that the Indians tortured them throughout the night and then left their bodies on the sand next to those who had already fallen.

Even the survivors suffered terribly. One man was hacked to pieces when he could not keep pace with the rest of the group being marched away from the massacre site. A baby who cried too much during the march was tied to a tree and left to starve. Mrs. Isabella Cooper was scalped before being rescued by an Indian woman. She had a small bald spot on her head for the rest of her life. Another man froze to death that winter, while Mrs. John Simmons and her daughter were forced to run the gauntlet, which both survived. In fact, the girl turned out to be the last survivor of the massacre, dying in 1900.

John Kinzie and his family were spared in the slaughter. He and his family were supposed to travel by boat to a trading post on the St. Joseph River, but because of the attack, they never departed. Appealing to the Potawatomi chiefs, they were taken away from the massacre site and returned to the Kinzie cabin. There they were joined by Mrs. Helm, the wife of Lieutenant Helm, and Mrs. Kinzie's daughter from her previous marriage. She had been shot, and Kinzie removed the bullet with a penknife. After presenting gifts to the Indians, the Kinzies later escaped.

But the war ruined Kinzie. He was now deeply in debt and had lost a fortune during the attack on Fort Dearborn. Though in no danger from the Indians, he was captured by the British and accused of high treason since he was a British subject. He was placed in irons and held on a prison ship off Quebec for seven weeks. He was freed in 1814 and rejoined his family. Two years later, he returned to Chicago but found that much had changed. He failed in re-starting his business, thanks to a bad loan, and soon was working for his largest competitor, the American Fur Company. In time, the fur trade ended, and Kinzie worked as a trader and Indian interpreter until he died in 1828. Thirty years later, his daughter-in-law would write a book that named Kinzie as the founding settler of Chicago. The book would overlook Kinzie's questionable business practices and the murder of Jean Lalime and would be accepted as fact for many years. Later, it would be realized as evidence of Juliette Kinzie's affinity for social climbing and her need to be part of a Chicago dynasty - not actual history.

After the carnage, the victorious Indians burned Fort Dearborn to the ground, and the bodies of the massacre victims were left where they had fallen, scattered to decay on the sand dunes of Lake Michigan. When replacement troops arrived at the site a year later, they were greeted with not only the burned-out shell of the fort but also the grinning skeletons of their predecessors. The bodies were buried, and the fort was rebuilt in 1816, only to be abandoned again two decades later, when the city was able to fend for itself.

It would be those bodies - unceremoniously buried where they had fallen along the lakefront - that spawned the ghostly tales of Fort Dearborn.

The massacre site was quiet for many years, long after Chicago grew into a sizable city. However, construction in the early 1980s unearthed dozens of human bones around 16th Street and Indiana Avenue. First thought to be victims of a cholera epidemic in the 1840s, the remains were later dated more closely to the early 1800s. Thanks to their location, it was realized that they were the bones of the massacre victims.

The remains were reburied elsewhere, but within a few weeks, people began to report the semi-transparent figures of people wearing pioneer clothing and outdated military uniforms wandering around an empty lot that was just north of 16th Street. The apparitions reportedly ran about in terror, silently screaming. The most frequent witnesses to these nocturnal wanderings were bus drivers who returned their vehicles to a garage that was located nearby, prompting rumors and stories to spread throughout the city.

In recent times, the area has mainly been filled with new homes and condominiums, and the once empty lot where the remains were discovered is no longer vacant. But this does not seem to keep the victims of the massacre in their graves.

Eerie reports from this part of the city still tell of specters dressed in period clothing, providing proof that the unlucky settlers of early Chicago do not rest here in peace.

The Black Hope Horror

One of the strangest, but often overlooked, cases of cemetery disturbance took place in the town of Crosby, Texas, in the early 1980s. That was at about the same time that the film *Poltergeist* was playing in movie theaters across the country. In the movie, spirits and strange activity besiege a family because their home was inadvertently built on the top of a cemetery.

In Crosby, Texas, these same events were taking place, except this was no movie - these events were happening in real life.

The macabre story began in 1981 when Ben and Jean Williams moved into their brand-new home on Poppets Way in the Newport subdivision in Crosby. Within a few years, the Williams' and seven out of eight of the families who lived close to them would move away from the area. All of them did so at great expense, including the loss of their mortgages, but why?

They said it was because of the ghosts.

Shortly after Ben and Jean moved into the house, they noticed something odd about the place. At first, it was an oppressive feeling that seemed to permeate the place, but soon it was other things, too. They were all little things, but when combined, each of the events formed a more terrifying picture. Hundreds of ants began invading the

This quiet neighborhood in the Newport subdivision of Crosby, Texas, had some secrets hidden under the ground

house, followed by snakes that acted uncharacteristically hostile. Plants died for no reason, and pets began acting very strangely.

Perhaps most odd were the sinkholes that began to appear in the yard. Located out near an oak tree that bore some peculiar markings, the depressions slowly widened and collapsed. Even when dirt was added to them, they refused to fill. No one noticed at the time how eerily the holes resembled open graves.

Then, more mysterious and frightening events began to occur. The toilets in the house flushed on their own. Lights turned on and off without explanation, and the garage door started opening and closing itself. Ben and Jean separately began to hear footsteps pacing back and forth through the house. Both assumed that it was the other, but when they went to check, they found no one there. Tapping and knocking sounds were sometimes heard by not only Ben and Jean but by neighbors and visitors to the house. Several people reported seeing shadowy shapes and figures that looked like people in the yard.

Was the house haunted? If so, how could it be? The house had only been completed a short time before the family moved into it. There was no strange history associated with the house, and certainly, no one had died in it. But what Ben, Jean, and other families in the neighborhood were about to discover was what had been located at the property before the subdivision was built.

In 1983, neighbor Sam Haney contracted for a swimming pool to be built in his back yard. The excavation came to a halt when workers unearthed human remains in the yard - the bodies of an African American man and woman.

But those two bodies turned out to be just the beginning. It turned out there were dozens of sets of remains buried beneath the entire neighborhood. The subdivision was located on land that had once belonged to the McKinney family, wealthy landowners, and farmers who had owned slaves before the Civil War. One section of their property had been used by the slaves - and by their descendants - as a burial ground, they called Black Hope Cemetery. That section of land, the Williams family discovered, had been located beneath the houses on Poppets Way.

As Ben tried to track down information about the cemetery, he received help from a man named Will Freeman, who claimed to have helped with burials at the site. He said that the graveyard had been disorganized but that they always tried to bury the dead on higher ground to avoid rocks and boggy low spots. The homes of the Williams and Haney families were on this "higher ground."

Freeman also told them that no one could afford tombstones in those days, but when he had buried his two sisters, he had used a nearby oak tree as a sort-of marker. This was the tree that Ben and Jean had discovered in their backyard.

Following the discovery of the bodies in his yard, Sam Haney filed suit against the Purcell Corporation, the developers of the subdivision. The Williams family was urged to join the expensive suit, but as it dragged on, they were tempted to simply sell their house. However, the attorney told them that if they listed it, they would have to disclose the fact that it had been built on top of Black Hope Cemetery. They decided to wait and see what happened with the Haney lawsuit, which didn't make it a courtroom until 1987.

They couldn't afford to wait and tried unsuccessfully to sell the house. Their attorney tried also tried pressuring the title and realty companies, ensnaring the property in mountains of red tape and legal hassles. What it boiled down to was that the house was impossible to sell - and it was also impossible to prove the graveyard was really on the property since no official record of it existed. The only way to prove it was to dig for more human remains, which was illegal under Texas law.

Meanwhile, the strange events in the house continued. The unexplainable sounds and incidents kept occurring, and apparitions were spotted both inside and outside the house. The entire family was plagued by nightmares, and several of the family pets mysteriously died.

Finally, Jean could stand it no more, and she took a shovel from the garage and went out into the yard. She found the tree that had been marked so many years ago by Will Freeman, and she started digging. Jean later claimed that she was only able to dig down a short distance before a terrible piercing pain stabbed through her back. She was forced to stop. Later that afternoon, her daughter, Tina, suddenly died. She had been in remission from cancer for some time, but her health had improved. Tina's death was completely unexpected, and her doctors were unable to explain it.

Their nerves shattered, the Williams family fled the house and moved to Hamilton, Montana, where they owned a vacation home. They were convinced that if they stayed in the house on Poppets Way, their lives would be destroyed. In the end, they lost an $18,000 down payment, seven years of mortgage payments, and ruined their credit rating - but they were glad to be out. Later, a paperback book would be published about their ordeal - which was made into an awful television movie - so at least some of their losses were recouped.

In May 1987, the Haney family lost their lawsuit against the Purcell Corporation. The jury initially awarded them $142,000 in damages, but the judge nullified the verdict and left them with nothing. Purcell executives had testified that they knew nothing of a graveyard in the area, and the judge ruled that Purcell had not been intentionally negligent - even though rumors had placed the graveyard on the site for years before the development began. The Haneys, along with several other families, also moved out of the neighborhood.

Today, the Crosby neighborhood that was built on the old Black Hope graveyard seems peaceful - at least on the surface.

Tom Hunt, who lives in the former Haney house, has stated, "I still believe that there are two graves buried in my front yard, but nothing weird has ever happened in our home. If there are spirits, they are good spirits, and they like us."

Walter Wintjes lives a few houses down from the Williams' original house, has also never experienced anything eerie in his home. Still, his wife, Linda, said in an interview, "Seriously, I've never noticed anything out of the ordinary. Except the lamp comes on and off without warning, but it's one of those touch lamps, and I think it may be a circuit problem or something."

Joe Clark, the neighbors directly east of Tom Hunt, said, "One time my mother, friend Jeff Griffith and I were in the house, and the bedroom door slammed shut. I told them it was a draft or just the wind. I don't think it's anything, but to this day, my mother won't stay here past dark."

"The only thing that ever happened to me over the years," said Clark's wife, Kim, "is that one time I felt the definite presence of a hand on my shoulder, but there was no one there."

Clark's mother, Jan, who reported an incident where she and her grandson, Shelby, saw a black shape floating in the room and across the television set, said, "I don't tell stories unless they're true. When that door slammed shut, there was no wind, no fan, and the window wasn't open," she said.

Jan also said that her 3-year-old granddaughter, Taylor, told her mother that a "brown man" saw her and tried to pick her up. "There is something to this," she said. "Some people won't talk about it because they don't want to be considered crazy, or they just don't care to know the truth."

Another neighbor, Venay Luna, who also lives on the old graveyard, reported coming home one-night several weeks after moving into her house. She said that she found it strange that both her husband and dog were looking straight ahead at the television and would not acknowledge her presence. Two weeks later, her husband told her what had happened. He had come home and found the dog cowering in the corner of the living room. Venay recalled, "When he went to check on the dog, he bent over to pick up his slippers, and they flew from his hands across the room. He said the reason they hadn't looked at me is because they were both still afraid."

To this day, Black Hope Cemetery has still not been officially acknowledged, and the dead still lay restlessly beneath the soil of the subdivision, perhaps waiting to be able to rest in peace finally.

Rest in Peace?

Denver's Cheesman Park seems to be a place of peace and tranquility. The rolling lawns and stately trees offer an oasis of shade and quiet among the busy streets of the city. It's a spacious area of relaxing green that was once a former cemetery.

It is technically still a cemetery.

Cheesman Park has a long and unsettling history. There is no ignoring the fact that it has been considered haunted for many years - and for reasons that most readers will understand. This beautifully landscaped park was built over the top of the 320-acre Mount Prospect Cemetery. It was not done by accident. This was not a case of a few buildings constructed over an old burial site. This was a scandal that rocked the city government, outraged the public, and filled the newspapers with lurid accounts.

It's no surprise that Cheesman Park and the surrounding neighborhood is believed to be infested with ghosts.

In 1858, when General William Larimer founded the city of Denver, Colorado, he set aside 320 acres of ground that were to be used as a cemetery for the soon-to-be thriving city. The graveyard, which he called Mount Prospect, would be segregated by religion, ethnicity, and wealth. The rich and influential were to be buried on the crest of the hill. Paupers and criminals were buried in the southwest corner, and ordinary folks would be planted somewhere in the middle. Chinese immigrants, Catholics, and Jews had their sections.

There is some debate as to who the first person was buried in the cemetery. One story claims that it was a man named Abraham Kay who died from a lung infection in 1859.

Another story claims that it was a Hungarian immigrant named John Stoefel who had come to Denver to settle a dispute with his brother-in-law and murdered him. After a short trial, Stoefel was dragged away by a mob and hanged from a cottonwood tree. He and his brother-in-law were then taken to Mount Prospect, and their bodies were unceremoniously dumped into the same grave.

Unfortunately, the increasing numbers of murder victims, criminals, undesirables, and those killed in accidents being buried in the cemetery caused the name Mount Prospect to fall out of use. Most people simply referred to it as "Boot Hill" or the "Old Boneyard." It certainly no longer had the respect and reverence that William Larimer intended for it to have.

Around it, the city of Denver grew and flourished. Fortunes were being made in mining and real estate, and the local cemetery had become something of an embarrassment. City leaders decided to rename the burial ground the City Cemetery in 1873. But changing the name couldn't hide the fact that it had become an eyesore. The cemetery was in terrible disrepair. Headstones had fallen over, prairie dogs had burrowed into the hills, and cattle grazed among the graves.

In 1881, a "pest house" for smallpox and typhus victims was built where the community gardens section of the Denver Botanic Gardens now stands. The hospital also housed the elderly and the terminally ill, who went there to die.

A few years before, wealthy Denver families had started burying their loved ones at the newer Riverside and Fairlawn Cemeteries and left the City Cemetery to paupers, criminals, transients, and unclaimed smallpox and typhus victims, who were buried in mass graves behind the pest house.

Meanwhile, ownership of the cemetery passed from the Larimer estate to a cabinetmaker named John J. Walley, who soon went into the undertaking business. He did little to improve the situation in the cemetery, and with new homes and mansions being built nearby, the city government was pressured to do something about the cemetery. Thanks to some tricky legal maneuvering, it was suddenly announced that the U.S. government had discovered that the cemetery was on land that was part of a treaty with the Arapahoe nation that dated back to

The poor condition of the City Cemetery before it was removed to make way for Cheesman Park in Denver

before 1860. This made the United States the legitimate owner of the property, and in 1890, they sold it to the city of Denver for $200.

The city began working to turn the property into a public park. City Cemetery was promptly renamed Congress Park, and families were notified that they had only 90 days to move their loved one's remains to another cemetery. Some were reburied by concerned family members, but more than 5,000 of the dead were forgotten and went unclaimed - likely because many were criminals, transients, and the unknown.

In the early spring of 1893, preparation began to remove the bodies of the unclaimed. At that time, Denver's mayor, Platt Rogers, who worried about the health hazards of opening the graves, was out of town. Ordinances were passed on releasing funds for the removal, and an unscrupulous undertaker named E.F. McGovern was awarded the contract. He specified that each body would be dug up and then placed in a new box at the site, but the box was only to be 3 1/2 feet long and one foot wide. Upon delivery of these boxes to Riverside Cemetery, McGovern would be paid $1.90 each.

In March, McGovern's men went to work. Curiosity-seekers and reporters came out to watch, and at first, things were orderly, but it didn't take long for the work to become careless. According to one legend, an older woman came down to speak to the men and told them that they should whisper a prayer over each body that was unearthed - or the dead would return. The workmen laughed at her, but they had a hard time concealing their obvious unease. Their haste also allowed souvenir hunters and onlookers to help themselves to items from the caskets. The bodies that had not decayed sufficiently enough to fit into the small wooden boxes were broken apart and shoveled from the coffin to the box that awaited the bones.

Some of the workmen were not only uneasy about the job - they were downright scared. One man, Jim Astor, claimed that he felt a ghost land atop his shoulders. He was so frightened that he threw down a stack of brass nameplates that he had looted from old coffins and ran for his life. He did not return to the site the following day.

People who lived in nearby homes began to report spectral manifestations in their houses and confused spirits who knocked on their doors and windows throughout the night. In the darkness, low moaning sounds could be heard over the field of open graves - a sound that many say can still sometimes be heard today.

By the time that Mayor Rogers returned to town, the local newspapers were running front-page stories about the atrocities being committed at the cemetery and the general state of corruption at City Hall. On March 10, 1893, the *Denver Republican* ran the headline, "The Work of Ghouls!" In the story, it was noted:

The line of desecrated graves at the southern boundary of the cemetery sickened and horrified everybody. Around their edges were piled broken coffins, rent, and tattered shrouds and fragments of clothing that had been torn from dead bodies. All were trampled into the ground by the footsteps of the gravediggers like rejected junk.

The stories went on to reveal there were discrepancies between the number of re-burials being charged to the city and the actual number of boxes being delivered to Riverside Cemetery. The matter became a full-blown scandal, and with the help of the health commissioner, the mayor brought the project to a halt.

The Cheesman Memorial in the park, named for railroad and water baron Walter S. Cheesman

McGovern's contract was terminated after the city's Health Commissioner investigated the matter, and the city put up a wooden fence around the cemetery, leaving the gaping holes in the ground unfilled. In 1894, work was started on the park, even though the rest of the bodies were never removed. They were eventually forgotten. The park was finally finished in 1907, leaving as many as 2,000 remains beneath the park and gardens.

When work was completed, it became Cheesman Park. It was named in honor of Walter S. Cheesman, railroad builder, water baron, and prominent citizen of Denver.

Many years have passed since then, but the macabre history of the park has never really gone away. The spirits of those who were buried on the land have returned - or perhaps they have never really gone away. Many people who come to the park - even those unaware of its past - speak of feelings of oppression and sadness, despite their peaceful surroundings. Others claim to occasionally see misty figures, strange shadows, and apparitions of the dead. The ghostly images

The excellent film *The Changeling*, starring George C. Scott is said to be based on a house that was near Cheesman Park in Denver

wander in confusion, perhaps wondering what has become of their final resting place.

And some of the ghostly stories of the neighborhood are not confined to the park. At the time of the exhumations, those who lived near the graveyard also began to report strange happenings. At least one house was so haunted that it inspired the 1980 classic film, *The Changeling*.

In the film, George C. Scott plays a composer who loses his wife and child in a terrible car accident. Looking for a fresh start, he moves into an old house that he quickly discovers is haunted. Those who have seen it will vividly recall its many chilling scenes - like the séance and an incident involving a red rubber ball - and agree with me that it ranks as one of the best haunted house movies of all time.

But this film has a basis in true events - or at least as true as most "based on a true story" horror films seem to be.

In 1968, a composer named Russell Hunter moved from New York into the Henry Treat Rogers Mansion, located near Cheesman Park. According to his account, he rented the sprawling old home for a mere $200 a month "because no one else wanted to live there."

After only a few months, Hunter began noticing some strange things in the house. It started with a banging sounds that he heard each morning, which stopped whenever he got out of bed. Doors opened and closed by themselves, faucets turned on and off, and sometimes pictures shook so violently that they flew off the walls.

Looking for a source for the weird happenings, Hunter later stated that he discovered a hidden staircase in the back of an upstairs closet. It led to a small room that contained the belongings of a young boy, including a journal of his secret life. After reading through the journal - and holding seances in the house - it was learned that the resident ghost was a sickly child who had once lived in the house and had been the heir to a fortune left to him by his grandmother. The boy died when he was young, and his parents were so worried that the inheritance might be passed on to another family member that they buried him in an unmarked grave. Soon after, they adopted a boy from an orphanage to pose as their child. He kept the secret, received the family fortune, and went on to great wealth and success.

Hunter claimed that the ghost of the sickly boy directed him to the location of his unmarked grave, which was now beneath a house on South Dahlia Street in Denver. The spirit reportedly threatened the family living in the house if Hunter could not convince them to let him dig up the boy's body. The family agreed, and Hunter and some friends managed to unearth a set of human remains - along with a gold medallion that was inscribed with the dead child's name.

The haunting should have been over, but it wasn't. Things got worse. The activity in the mansion became violent. Objects were thrown, a wall collapsed behind Hunter's bed, and one night, a set of glass doors exploded, severely cutting him. Afraid for his life, he finally fled the house. He moved into a new place on Kearney Street, but the haunting followed him. Eventually, a minister from the Epiphany Episcopal Church cleansed the house, and the activity came to an end.

Hunter's story is remarkably close to the story told in the movie. Even the red rubber ball makes an appearance in his account since it was the sickly boy's favorite toy.

Over time, Hunter's story has been called into question. His ghostly claims were fact-checked, and no record was found that said that he ever lived in the Henry Treat Williams mansion, although he did reside in Denver in the late 1960s, when he was helping his parents manage the Three Birches Lodge in Boulder. It's possible that his residence in the house was "off the books" - just as he claimed - for a low price because no one wanted to live in the house.

There's also no record of the boy who supposedly haunted house, but there are some curious facts about the family who built the mansion - including that they owned the farmland where the child's unmarked grave was said to be located. It's improbable that Hunter could have known this or had access to the records that proved this information when he lived in the mansion.

No, the story may not have anything to do with the old cemetery. Still, its location is interesting, nevertheless, mainly because the haunting at Cheesman Park has never really gone away. As recently as just a few years ago, workers in the park unearthed a few sets of skeletal remains.

And that means the questions remain - will the dead in Denver's Cheesman Park ever truly rest in peace?

DESECRATION OF THE DEAD

Some of the disturbances that occur in what become haunted graveyards go beyond unmarked graves, reburials, and exhumations. In some cases, natural disasters play a role in unearthing bodies and destroying gravesites. Another kind of disturbance is caused by "progress" - as new building sites are laid out for structures and homes with little thought as to what once existed on the land. As with the Black Hope Cemetery, construction crews often make pretty gruesome discoveries.

Perhaps the worst kind of disturbance, though, occurs because of the malicious activity of vandals and of alleged "cultists" who practice what they consider dark rituals in isolated or abandoned cemeteries. While there are claims that occult activities can draw negative energy to a location, I believe that even worse than that is the physical destruction of the grounds - knocking over tombstones, digging up graves, and destroying cemetery artwork.

This still leaves the question as to how - or why - such a disturbance causes a burial ground to become haunted. Is it because of natural or supernatural reasons? It seems that many spirits linger behind because their remains are disturbed, and they are unable to find rest, and that might explain why desecrated cemeteries gain a reputation as haunted.

But could there be a natural explanation for the activity that occurs in a vandalized graveyard? What if the disturbance of graves and human remains releases energy that might account for the bizarre happenings reported in these cemeteries? Could that energy have caused what our ancestors believed was a haunting? Science states that all matter is energy and since energy can't be destroyed, only changed, it might react in ways that seem like ghosts.

So, perhaps there is a rational explanation for the activity that occurs in vandalized cemeteries, but let's talk about the spooky stuff for a moment.

The other type of disturbance we're discussing here is what some have called "ritual desecration." Some believe that a few cemeteries have become haunted because of cult rituals and "black magic" practiced within them. They believe that this kind of activity draws negative spirits and energy to the place. It's also been suggested that occultists seek out locations where the energy already exists and make things worse by performing rituals there.

Whatever the reasoning behind it, it has become common to hear about desecrated cemeteries where dark rituals occur, causing the graveyards to become malevolent places. When researching these theories, though, I've found that most so-called "Satanists" are merely confused, lonely teenagers looking for a thrill or pretending to be "witches."

Although not in every case, which is the disturbing part.

But whether genuine occultists or high school witches, we still must wonder if the rituals that they perform might be enough to attract negative energy to these graveyards. Is that why such places are nearly always regarded as haunted?

The Graveyard in Rubio Woods

Located near the southwest suburb of Midlothian, Illinois is the Rubio Woods Forest Preserve, an island of trees and shadows nestled in the urban sprawl of the Chicago area. The rambling refuge creates an illusion that it is secluded from the crowded city that threatens its borders, and perhaps it is. On the edge of the forest is a small graveyard that many believe may be the most haunted place in the region. The name of this cemetery is Bachelor's Grove, and this ramshackle burial ground may be infested with more ghosts than most can imagine. Over the years, the place has been cursed with more than 100 documented reports of paranormal phenomena, from actual apparitions to glowing balls of light.

There have been no new burials here for many years, and it likely doesn't provide much peace for the departed buried within its borders. It is a place that has seen chaos, destruction, midnight trespassers - and an unusually large number of spirits.

The history of Bachelor's Grove is a confusing one, but most historians believe that it was started at some point in the 1830s. The name - sometimes spelled "Batchelor" - originally seems to have come from a settlement near the future cemetery, which was founded in the 1820s. It consisted of mostly German immigrants who had moved west from New York, Vermont, and Connecticut. The village remained Batchelor's Grove for some years, but then in 1850, its name was changed to "Bremen" by postmaster Samuel Everden, in honor of the city in Germany. In 1855, it was changed back by Postmaster Robert Patrick, but the post office closed just three years later.

The cemetery itself has a much stranger history - or at least a more mysterious one. The land was purchased from the government by the Everden family in 1835, but some reports claim that the section that would soon become an official cemetery already had burials on it when the Everdens bought the property. Whether this is true or not, the land was designated as a burial ground in 1844, and the first recorded burial was that of Eliza (Mrs. Leonard H.) Scott.

The old sign that once marked the entrance to the cemetery - it vanished decades ago.

At that time, it was known as Everden Cemetery after the family that owned the property. Years later, the last burials to take place in the cemetery was that of Laura H. McGhee in 1965 and Robert E. Shields, whose ashes were buried in a family plot in 1989.

The last caretaker of the cemetery was a man named Clarence Fulton, whose family were early settlers in the township. By that time, the nearby settlements were gone. The land where homes and businesses had stood was now part of the Cook County Forest Preserve - and so was the cemetery and the nearby quarry pond. The quarry had been started by Christ Boehm in 1909, and it operated until the 1920s when it was closed by forest preserve district. By the time the forest preserve took over the area, there were very few people living nearby.

Even so, it was a popular recreation area. The Midlothian Country Club was a short distance away, and in the 1930s it was a common practice for young people to meet at a local dance hall and picnic area and walk over to the cemetery to "get scared." At that time, Bachelor's Grove was described as "serene" and "undisturbed." And that was even after the attention that the graveyard gained in April 1934, when readers of Robert L. Ripley's "Believe It or Not" newspaper column featured Bachelor's Grove for its name and the ironic fact that women were still buried there.

The vandalized confines of Bachelor's Grove

But the peaceful atmosphere of the cemetery was soon to come to an end. By the early 1950s, the first problems began to be reported. Just a few years before, the nearby turnpike had been scheduled to be abandoned, leading to fewer people who passed by the graveyard regularly. Its isolated setting helped the gravel drive that passed the cemetery become a popular "lover's lane." Vandals followed.

On September 11, 1952, the first newspaper reports of vandalism at Bachelor's Grove noted that "at least 10 granite monument headstones" had been knocked over by vandals. Things became so bad that police officers had to make daily visits to the cemetery to keep visitors away.

More damage was reported in April 1958, when several smaller tombstones were pulled out of the ground. In 1965, coffins were unearthed, and at least one was burned. More tombstones were knocked over, sprayed with paint, broken apart, and even stolen. In 1973, another coffin was exhumed, although the vandals were captured by the police.

Year after year, reports appeared in the newspapers that included shocking photos of desecrated stones, opened graves, bones that are strewn about, and of course, ghosts. The 1970s marked the first time that Bachelor's Grove was being designated as "one of the most haunted places in America." Though ghost stories had been told locally about the burial ground for at least two decades by the time of the first publicized desecrations, they were now reaching a much wider audience.

Which came first - the destruction or the hauntings? There was no doubt that Bachelor's Grove was a spooky spot as early as the 1930s. If it hadn't been, it never would have become a so-called "lover's lane," and young men wouldn't have been taking their girlfriends there from the local dance hall to scare them.

But it seems that things became worse - and much more frightening - after the vandals began wreaking havoc on the cemetery grounds. It appeared that the vandalism had "stirred something up" at Bachelor's Grove, and most researchers have come to believe that this might be the source of the haunting activity.

But others will swear the cemetery is haunted for another reason. Starting in the late 1970s, forest rangers and cemetery visitors began making grim discoveries within the fence that surrounded the burial ground. It was not uncommon to stumble across the remains of chickens, cats, and other small animals that appeared to have been mutilated in a ritualistic fashion. Officers who have patrolled the surrounding woods at night have reported seeing evidence of black magic and occult rituals in and around the graveyard. In some cases, inscriptions and elaborate writings have been carved into and painted on trees, on grave markers, and the cemetery earth. This has led many to believe that the cemetery has been used for occult activities - which if they didn't cause the cemetery to become haunted, they believe, it has undoubtedly enhanced the activity.

A visit to Bachelor's Grove today does little to convince anyone that it was once a "peaceful and serene" place. It is overgrown with weeds and surrounded by a high, chain-link fence but is easily accessible, thanks to the holes that have been cut in it by trespassers. The cemetery sign that was once above the entrance has been gone for years.

The first thing that a visitor will notice is the destruction. Tombstones seem almost randomly placed, many no longer marking the resting places of those whose names are carved upon them. Many of the stones are missing, lost forever. The missing markers gave birth to legends about how the stones of the cemetery move about under their own power. They don't. They have simply been knocked over by vandals or carried away by thieves.

Even more disturbing than the missing and toppled stones are the unfinished exhumations of graves, where vandals have attempted to disturb the bodies of the dead.

Just past the back edge of the cemetery is the small, stagnant pond, left behind when the quarry closed in 1927. Years before, rumors claimed that gangsters from Chicago dumped the bodies of murder victims in the secluded pond. There are no news reports to substantiate the stories, but the violence of the era didn't leave the local vicinity untouched. Local newspapers were filled with stories of the explosion of homemade liquor stills, raids on the operators of the stills, and bullet-riddled bodies of rivals found dumped along desolate area roads.

On October 21, 1927, a local bootlegger named Fred Passini had been taken on a "one-way ride" and his body was tossed into a ditch just a few blocks away from Bachelor's Grove. He had been shot in the head nine times. The following summer, a farmer and his son found an identified man not far from the cemetery. He had been shot in the head and tossed from a moving car. With these murder victims found so nearby, it makes the chances that bodies were dumped in the quarry pond even greater. Perhaps their spirits have also lingered behind.

But those aren't the strangest things connected to the pond.

One night in the late 1970s, two Cook County Forest Preserve officers were on night patrol near the cemetery and claimed to see the apparition of a horse emerge from the waters of the pond. The animal appeared to be pulling a plow behind it that was steered by the ghost of an older man. The two apparitions crossed the road in front of the rangers' vehicle - were clearly visible for a moment in the glare of their headlights - and then vanished into the woods. The men simply stared in shock for a moment and then looked at one another to be sure that they had both seen the same thing. They later reported the incident - as would others in years to come.

The sightings of the farmer and his horse have given birth to a legend that may explain the encounters. The story goes that a farmer was plowing a nearby field in the 1870s, and his horse was spooked by something. The farmer became tangled in the reins and was dragged behind the horse into the pond. Unable to free himself, he was pulled down into the murky water by the weight of the horse and the plow, and he drowned.

Of course, you may have noticed a small problem with this legend since the pond didn't exist until it was dug by Christ Boehm's quarry operation, which didn't start until 1909. So, while the story may not be true, there is still no way to explain the credible sightings of the farmer and the horse. They remain yet another of the mysteries of Bachelor's Grove.

Crossing over the pond is the Midlothian Turnpike, which becomes West 143rd Street, and even the roadway is rumored to be haunted. It has become a place where people have seen what can only be described as "phantom" automobiles. There are no historical events to explain the encounters, and yet, mysterious older vehicles that disappear have been reported numerous times along this stretch of road over the years. Motorists traveling west along the road report seeing the taillights of another car in front of them, then the brake lights flare, and the car pulls off the road - and vanishes. Others have reported passing vintage automobiles coming from the opposite direction, only to see them suddenly disappear. Why do these automobiles "haunt" this road? Where do they come from, where do they go, and are they connected to the cemetery in some way?

It's just another part of the mystery of the cemetery in the woods.

If you go searching for Bachelor's Grove Cemetery, it's recommended that you don't go at night. There are more than ghosts lurking in the surrounding woods - like Forest Preserve officers who will write you a ticket for trespassing or may even take you to jail. The protection of the cemetery is taken very seriously.

But if you do go - during the daytime, of course - you'll find the cemetery by leaving the road and walking up an overgrown gravel path into the woods. The old road is blocked with concrete barriers to prevent anyone from driving on it, and a dented "no trespassing" sign hangs across it on a rusted chain. The burial ground lies about a half-mile or so beyond it in the woods.

And yes, even the trail is haunted.

It's from the trail where most of the reports of "ghost lights" come from. They've been seen by literally hundreds of people over the years and are white, flicking lights that are larger than fireflies and move very quickly and erratically. There is a report of a red, beacon-like light, too. It flies rapidly back and forth along the path to the cemetery. It's said to be so bright and so fast that it's impossible to tell what it looks like. Most witnesses state that they have seen a "red streak" that it has left in its wake.

The trail through the woods to Bachelor's Grove

It's along this deserted road where other strange events connected to the cemetery are reported. Perhaps the strangest is the numerous sightings of the "phantom house." It has been seen along the trail for several decades - appearing and disappearing - often by people who had no idea that no house was supposed to be there.

The house along the trail has been reported in all weather conditions, in the daytime and at night. There is no historical record of a house ever existing near the cemetery, but the descriptions of it rarely vary. Each person claims it to be an older two-story farmhouse, painted white, with wooden posts, a porch swing, and a welcoming light that burns softly in the window. No one has ever claimed to have set foot on that front porch - and perhaps that's for the best because it has a nasty habit of vanishing. It's merely there one moment - looking completely solid, stable, and life-like - and then it's gone as if it never existed at all.

To make matters more confusing, the house has been seen at dozens of different locations around the cemetery. Rarely is it reported in the same place twice. There's no explanation for it, and sightings of the house further add to the chilling ambiance of Bachelor's Grove.

There have been many sightings of ghosts and phantoms within the cemetery itself over the years. They run the gamut from reports of figures in dark robes to a man in a yellow suit, a tall, shadowy figure, women in mourning clothes, and much more. But there is no spirit encountered as frequently as the woman who has been called everything from the "Madonna of Bachelor's Grove" to the "White Lady" to the affectionate "Mrs. Rogers."

The stories say that she is the ghost of a woman who was buried in the cemetery next to the grave of her young child. She reportedly wanders the cemetery at night with an infant wrapped in her arms. She walks aimlessly, completely unaware of those who claim they have seen her.

There have been many reports from those who claim to have seen her, but no clear evidence as to who she might have been in life. There are several possible candidates. One of them is Amelia Patrick, the first wife of Senator John Humphrey. Their infant daughter, Libby May, died and was buried with Amelia's family at Bachelor's Grove, although Amelia was later buried elsewhere. Could her spirit have come to Bachelor's Grove to search for her child?

There are also two sisters-in-law who could be the "White Lady" - Katherine Fulton and Luella Rogers. Katherine, who married Luella's brother Bert Fulton, was heartbroken by the death of her daughter, Marci May, who died in infancy. The baby was buried at the Fulton family plot in Bachelor's Grove. Katherine, like Amelia Patrick, was buried elsewhere after she died, and it's suggested that perhaps her spirit could also be searching for her child.

Luella Rogers was killed by a hit-and-run driver in 1937 and buried at Bachelor's Grove, also in the Fulton family plot. Luella's baby sister, Emma, is buried with her in the same plot, but her grave marker was stolen long ago. It was later recovered, but it was not returned to the cemetery. Instead, it was placed in the care of the Tinley Park

The famous Bachelor's Grove phot o taken by Judi Huff-Felz in 1991. Is this the "Madonna" of the Cemetery?

Historical Society. Some believe that Luella's spirit is upset by her sister's missing stone, and that might be what she is looking for as she wanders the grounds of Bachelor's Grove.

No one knows for sure who the "Madonna" is or why she continues to linger at the cemetery, but, unlike most spirits, there is actual photographic proof that she exists - a photograph that has been examined, studied, and analyzed many times. No one has ever been able to explain it.

The photo was taken by a woman named Judi Huff-Felz in August 1991. She attended a daytime paranormal investigation at Bachelor's Grove Cemetery and, along with others in the group, she assisted with taking measurements and mapping out the burial ground. The investigators were then given maps of the cemetery and instructed to walk through and note any changes with the various kinds of equipment they were using. While the others were doing this, Judi and her sister, Mari, decided to follow their instincts and take infrared photographs in locations where they felt something unusual. Later, when the film was developed, Judi was surprised by one of the photographs she had taken.

In the image, she could see the semi-transparent form of a woman seated on the base of a tombstone that had been toppled over years before. There had been no one in that section of the cemetery at the time, and it certainly did not look like any of the investigators who were present. Was it one of the many ghosts of Bachelor's Grove? Debunkers immediately said "no," claiming that it was nothing more than a double exposure or an outright hoax.

But it wasn't. Experts, most of whom had no interest in ghosts and who would have liked to come up with a reason why the photo could not be authentic, were unable to debunk it. They ruled out the idea of double exposure and the theory that the woman was a real person who had been placed in the frame to look like a ghost. One skeptic claimed that the woman in the photo was casting a shadow, but according to the experts who analyzed the image, the "shadow" was nothing more than the natural shading of the landscape. Besides that, one of them asked if she is casting a shadow in that direction, then why isn't everything else in the photo doing the same?

I've had my own experiences with this cemetery over the years. I've interviewed countless people who have had experiences there which they cannot explain, I have visited dozens of times, and have spent the night there - with expensive permits - on several occasions.

In 2007, I was an executive producer for a short-lived web series - we were ahead of our time, I swear - called "Cringe," and we paid for a permit and spent the night at Bachelor's Grove. When the filming was concluded, it was discovered that almost all of the digital footage from the night was distorted and destroyed, something that a crew with many years of experience had never encountered before.

This is a very strange place. Is it as haunted as so many believe? And if so, is the haunting caused by the desecration that the burial ground has endured over the years? That's something you'll have to decide for yourself, but I believe that it's one of the most haunted places in the country.

MYSTERIES OF THE GRAVE

Premature burial. Grave robbery. Necrophilia. Desecration. All reasons why the dead don't rest in peace. Are the only reasons why cemeteries become haunted? Probably not. Since no one is an expert when it comes to ghosts and hauntings, there is no way that any of us can have all the answers as to why a place becomes haunted.

Perhaps it's just because something occurs at a cemetery that is so strange and bizarre that it leaves an impression - a reverberation, if you will - that echoes through time and refuses to remain quiet.

The "Italian Bride"

In Hillside, Illinois, just outside of Chicago, is Mount Carmel Cemetery. In addition to being the final resting place of Al Capone, Dion O'Banion, and other notorious Chicago mobsters, the cemetery is also the burial place of a woman named Julia Buccola Petta.

While her name may not spring to mind as a part of Chicago history, for those intrigued by the supernatural, she is better known as the "Italian Bride." Julia's grave is marked today by a life-sized statue of the unfortunate woman in her wedding dress, a stone reproduction of the wedding photo that is mounted on the front of her monument. While a beautiful monument, there is nothing about it to suggest that anything weird ever occurred in connection to it. However, once you know the history behind the site, it's soon realized that this is one of the weirdest tales in the annals of American graveyards.

Julia was born on June 6, 1891, in Italy. Her father, George, died in 1913, and her mother, Filomena, emigrated to the United States with her daughter. They traveled to the west side of Chicago, where three other Buccola children - Henry, Joseph, and Rosalia - were already settled. In June 1920, Julia married Matthew Petta at Holy Rosary Church on North Damen Avenue. Julia became pregnant soon after the wedding, but complications occurred, and on March 17, 1921, Julia died while giving birth to her son, Filippo. Because of the Italian tradition that dying in childbirth made the woman a type of martyr, Julia was

The grave of Julia Buccola Petta in Mount Carmel Cemetery in Hillside, Illinois.

buried in white, the martyrs' color. Her wedding dress also served as her burial gown, and with her dead infant tucked into her arms, the two were laid to rest in a single coffin at Mount Carmel Cemetery.

Filomena Buccola was inconsolable over her daughter's death. Shortly after Julia was buried, Filomena began to experience strange and terrifying dreams every night. In these nightmares, she envisioned Julia telling her that she was still alive and needed her help. For the next six years, the dreams plagued Filomena, and she began trying, without success, to have her daughter's grave opened, and her body exhumed. She was unable to explain why she needed to do this; she only knew that she should. Finally, through sheer persistence, her request was granted, and a sympathetic judge passed down an order for Julia's exhumation.

In 1927, six years after Julia's death, the casket was finally removed from the grave. When it was opened, Julia's body was found not to have decayed at all. It was said that her flesh was still as soft as it had been when she was alive. A photograph was taken at the time

The postmortem photograph ta ken during the exhumation - six years after Julia died - shows a body that hasn't decayed at all.

of the exhumation, and it shows Julia's "incorruptible" body in the casket. Filomena set out to raise money for a more elaborate tombstone. The finished work would be a grandiose tribute to her dead daughter-- a life-size sculpture of Julia on her wedding day.

Filomena - financed by prayer cards and donations - added the postmortem photo of Julia to the front of her grave monument. Below the image is the Italian phrase "Presa Dopo 6 Anni Morta," which roughly translates to "taken 6 years after death." A photo of Julia in her bridal gown, the inspiration for the statue, was also fastened to the stone.

The postmortem photograph shows a body that appears to be fresh, with no discoloration of the skin, even after six years. The rotted and decayed appearance of the coffin in the photo, however, bears witness to the fact that it had been underground for some time. Julia appears to be merely sleeping. Her family took the fact that she was found to be so well preserved as a sign from God, and so, after collecting money from other family members and neighbors, they created the impressive monument that stands over her grave today.

What mysterious secret rests at the grave of Julia Petta? How could her body have stayed in perfect condition after lying in the grave for six years?

Many devout Catholics in the neighborhood believed that Julia's "incorruptibility" meant that she was a saint. Skeptics scoffed at the idea, claiming that the postmortem photo must have been taken before she was originally buried - although this doesn't explain the condition of the casket or the decomposition of the infant that is nestled in her arms. Another explanation was attributed to *adipocere*, also known as "corpse wax" - "a waxy substance consisting chiefly of fatty acids and calcium soaps that is formed during the decomposition of dead body fat in moist or wet anaerobic conditions." In other words, the shape and state of Julia's body were preserved by a natural process.

Of course, these explanations did little to dispel the local belief that Julia's preserved body was proof of a miracle. But was it really? There were stories that have since been told about her mother, Filomena, questioning the reality of her dreams. Some claimed that she fabricated the entire story as retaliation for a marriage of which she did not approve. She never liked Matthew Petta, the stories say, and this claim is given some credence by the fact that Julia's married name does not appear on the grave monument - only Buccola.

But even if Filomena lied about her nightmares to gain sympathy from the community and to help finance the building of the elaborate monument, how does this explain the postmortem photograph? The photo of Julia in her casket - six years after her death - appears to be real. It has defied explanation for nearly a century.

And that's not the end of this odd story. Reports have been told over the years of a ghostly "woman in white" who has been seen wandering at the edge of the cemetery where she rests. Stories claim to have seen her in the daytime and at night, and many who know the story of Julia Petta believe that this is her restless spirit.

One eerie tale that was told involved a young boy who was accidentally left behind at the cemetery, not far from Julia's grave. When his family returned to Mount Carmel to look for him, they saw him holding the hand of a dark-haired young woman in a white dress. When the boy ran toward his parents, the woman in white disappeared.

Vampires in the American Graveyard

On the cold morning of March 17, 1892, a group of men marched down Purgatory Road in the town of Exeter, Rhode Island. They were walking to Chestnut Hill Cemetery. Their intention was not to witness the burial of a loved one, but rather to remove the coffins of the dead from the ground. But were those they sought truly dead? Or had they returned in some way to prey on the living? This is what they hoped to learn from their journey to the graveyard. In this case, the life of a young man named Edwin Brown - and perhaps the lives of the rest of his remaining family - might depend on it.

Edwin Brown, many believed, had become the prey of a vampire. His life had literally been drained away from him. In such danger that he fled to Colorado to escape; he had returned to Rhode Island when his health did not improve. He was now resigned to the fact that he would die among family and friends, but some believed he could be saved. If they could find the vampire that was stealing his life, he might recover.

It all depended on a macabre ritual - a "certain cure" for vampire victims that had been written about in 1784 by a Willington County, Connecticut resident named Moses Holmes. The "cure" required that the body of a dead relative be disinterred and that any part of the deceased that is not decomposed be burned and then consumed by the victim. In those days, it was believed that vampires did not prowl the night looking for victims among strangers - they drained the life from surviving family members instead. By searching the graves of Brown family members who had already died, Edwin's friends and family members believed that they might find the culprit that was leading the young man into his own early grave.

Edwin's father, George Brown, had buried his wife and his two daughters over nearly ten years, and now it looked as though his son was lost to him, as well. Nevertheless, George had initially put no stock in the ghoulish superstition that some claimed might save Edwin's life. As time passed, though, he was at last convinced to allow the ritual to proceed. He loved his son and planned to accompany him to the cemetery that morning, but at the last moment, he balked at the idea of exhuming the graves of the three women. If one of them truly was a vampire, he was unable to face it.

The group of would-be vampire hunters adjourned to the local cemetery, carrying with them a collection of picks and shovels for the grim work ahead. The body of Edwin's sister, Mercy, would be the easiest to obtain. She had died only two months earlier, on January 12, and her body had been placed inside of a stone receiving crypt on the cemetery grounds so that she could be buried when the ground began to thaw for the season.

The exhumation that occurred that day might have never come to public attention if the family did not seek out official sanction for their plan. They approached the district medical examiner, Dr. Harold Metcalf, to oversee the uncovering of the corpses. Metcalf, who "acted under protest, as it were being an unbeliever," stated a letter about the incident that appeared in a local newspaper, was an intelligent young man who didn't believe Edwin's illness had anything to do with a vampire. He did all that he could to discourage the exhumation, but since it was not technically against the law, there was little he could do. He watched in horror as the men opened the graves of Mary Brown and her eldest daughter, Mary Olive.

The two women had died nearly a decade earlier. Mrs. Brown, aged only 36, had died in December 1883, and her 19-year-old daughter had perished just six months later. The men worked hard to break through the cold and unforgiving late winter earth. Each of the caskets, now deteriorated with age, were pulled from the ground and broken open. Both corpses were found, after the passages of years, to be in states of advanced decomposition. There was no question that they had rested in peace during the past nine years. Neither of the two women could be the vampire that was draining the life from young Edwin.

But there was one coffin left - that of Mercy Brown.

The stone receiving crypt was located at the edge of the cemetery. It was a triangular-shaped building with a heavy wooden door that was usually kept locked. On this morning, one of the men had obtained the keys from the sexton, and the door was opened to reveal a dark, damp interior. The cool smell of earth rushed out at them as

The old stone receiving vault at Chestnut Hill Cemetery

they stood in the doorway, allowing their eyes to adjust to the darkness within. Mercy's casket was carried from the crypt and out into the sickly sunlight of the overcast morning. The hasp was broken, and the lid was raised.

    The bodies of her mother and sister had been decayed, but as the men looked down on Mercy, they saw a face and form that was still remarkably intact. This was not all that strange in that she had died just two months before, and it had been a cold winter, which would have preserved the body. What was strange, though, was that the corpse had turned onto her side. She had moved! This was not something that an ordinary corpse could do!

    Despite further protestations from Dr. Metcalf, one of the men cut open the body and found that her heart was still wet with blood. Dr. Metcalf insisted that this was not unusual and was, in fact, consistent with the amount of time that she had been dead, but the men weren't listening. They believed that they finally had all the evidence they needed to show that one of the Browns was indeed a vampire. It was Mercy, they were convinced, and only the prescribed ritual could save the life of her brother.

Throwing up his hands in frustration, Dr. Metcalf walked away from the cemetery and left the men to their gruesome work. Atop the nearby stone wall, the men made a fire and burned the heart of Mercy Brown. After it had been consumed by the flames, one of the men gathered the ashes and concocted the notorious mixture that was supposed to save Edwin's life. He drank the mixture with great reluctance.

But it was too late to save him. On May 2, he, like his mother and two sisters, died despite all the efforts to save him.

But perhaps it was not all for nothing. After Edwin's death - and perhaps because of the destruction of Mercy's heart - the vampire never troubled the Brown family again. The horror was finally over, and Mercy Brown had earned a place in history as the last of the New England vampires.

There is no supernatural creature that fascinates us as much as the vampire does. Although long considered to be nothing more than a myth, the vampire is still a strangely attractive and enticing being to the modern reader. We think of them as nothing more than the fanciful creation of folklore and literature, but this is not what our ancestors believed. They were convinced that vampires were very real creatures, destroying the living in ways that usually not recounted in popular literature. They were terrified of these creatures - and with good reason.

Few can really say what the traditional vampire is. Some believe that he is an evil spirit that wears the body of the newly dead, while others believe that he is a corpse, re-animated by his original soul. What everyone can agree on is what this creature must have to survive - blood. This vital bodily ingredient must be taken from the veins of a living person so that the vampire can survive.

In nearly every case, a vampire that is exhumed from his grave, or resting place, is always found to be ruddy of complexion, well-

nourished, and apparently in good health, even after having been dead for many years. His appearance is often marked by long, curving fingernails that have grown long in the grave, and blood smeared about the mouth. According to European legends, the only way to destroy one of these living corpses was to drive a stake through its heart. After that, the body would be burned.

The legends of vampires have their roots in traditional fears. In days past, it was not uncommon for people to be fearful about the dead returning from their grave, especially in cases of suicides or unfortunates buried without the last rites. Occasional deviants who practiced necrophilia or corpse-stealing often provided apparent "proof" that some of the dead could leave the graveyard. An empty coffin was not seen as evidence of theft, but evidence of vampirism instead.

Terrible and what seemed to be mysterious outbreaks of disease and plagues were sometimes thought to be caused by supernatural means. Another ailment thought to have created the vampire legend was a rare disorder called porphyria. This is a skin pigment disorder in which the body produces an excess of red blood cells. The result is an unbearable itching, redness, and bleeding cracks in the skin that appear after a brief exposure to sunlight. Sufferers naturally avoided coming out in the daylight and appeared only at night.

Probably the most common source of vampire legends came from premature burials. People suffering from catalepsy and other ailments sometimes found themselves buried alive. When later exhumed, the distorted state of the corpses led many to believe the dead had been coming and going from their coffins. In the eighteenth century, it was not uncommon for bodies to be dug up to see if they had become vampires, especially when it involved the death of a suicide, a murder victim, or someone who had died during a period of unexplained deaths. If a body was discovered to be out of the ordinary, it was burned to prevent it from leaving the grave again.

Vampire-like creatures have existed in the folklore of the world since almost the beginning of recorded history. But an authentic, traditional vampire was originally a Slavonic monster, bringing fear to the superstitious in Eastern Europe - Hungary, Czechoslovakia, Rumania, the Balkan countries, and their neighbors. Even the word "vampire" is an adaptation of the Magyar word *vampir*, which also had close ties to Bulgarian and Russian words that mean the same thing. It is believed that the vampire legend began to grow in notoriety around the sixteenth century. Within the next few decades, a considerable amount of vampire activity began to be reported, creating eerie tales and haunting stories throughout the region.

Soon after, the legend began to spread. A Greek writer, Leone Allacci, produced a small book about vampire belief, and other travelers started to pick up stories as they passed through Eastern Europe. Learned clergymen alluded to tales of vampires that were reported to them by parishioners, but in 1746, a Benedictine monk named Don Augustin Calmet published a full-length treatise on ghosts and vampires that firmly planted the legend within the lore of the western world.

The arrival of the vampire in Western Europe was achieved in part by the dissemination of Balkan folk tales, but the process was completed by another essential thread in the construction of the legend - pure fiction. The German romantics of the late eighteenth century found useful images in the horrors of folklore, and the use of the vampire motif in poems by Goethe spread the tales ever further. A vampire appeared in a poem by Lord Byron, and in another by Southey, early in the nineteenth century's English romantic tradition. Oddly, though, none of the earlier writers of Gothic horror fiction, like Horace Walpole, Ann Radcliffe, or Matthew Lewis, ever included vampires in their popular books.

What has been regarded as the first true vampire story was written in 1819 by Dr. John Polidori, and it was titled simply "The Vampyre." This short tale was written during the same fateful summer that Polidori spent with his friend Lord Byron, Percy Shelley, and Mary Shelley on the shores of Lake Geneva. A writing contest that summer spawned not only the first vampire story but Mary Shelley's *Frankenstein*, too. Polidori's short piece appeared in the *New Monthly Magazine*, a British literary journal, and delighted readers with its gloomy atmosphere and its depraved aristocratic vampire, Lord Ruthven, which had been modeled after Lord Byron. It was not one of the finest stories ever written, but it had the advantage of being the first about vampires and, thanks to this, Polidori has earned a place of honor in the annals of horror.

Decades passed, and the public gained a taste for blood - at least in a literary sense. In Paris, a play about vampires was one of the most popular theater attractions of the 1820s. Alexandre Dumas wrote a play about vampires in the 1850s, joining other productions that were all the rage across Europe. The French poet, Gautier, used the vampire theme in one of his poems, as did Baudelaire. Then, in 1847, one of the first major written works appeared on the subject in the form of a "penny dreadful" novel by Thomas Preskett Prest called *Varney, the Vampire*. Although it was more than 800 pages long - it appeared in a series of cheap, penny booklets - this simple, fast-moving horror story became a sensation with the masses. Vampires had come to stay.

One of the most exciting literary vampires of the nineteenth century appeared in an 1872 novella by Joseph Sheridan Le Fanu called *Carmilla*, but the book with the greatest impact on the vampire legend was released in 1897 by Irish author Bram Stoker. It was called *Dracula*, and the titular character became the most widely accepted symbol of the vampire. Almost everything we know about vampires was probably learned from the bits and pieces of authentic lore that Stoker included in the book.

Stoker studied Balkan folklore while working on his book and included several references to regional history. His title character was given the name of a historical figure, Transylvanian-born Vlad III Dracula of Wallachia. During the central years of his reign, between 1456 and 1462, "Vlad the Impaler" was said to have killed from 20,000 to 40,000 political rivals, criminals, and anyone else he considered "useless to humanity." His favorite method of death was impaling his victims on a sharp pole. The name Dracula means "Son of Dracul," a title that Vlad II gave to his son. Stoker came across the name "Dracula" in his reading on Romanian history and chose it to replace the name "Count Wampyr," which he originally intended to use for his villain.

But this is not the only bit of history that Stoker used to create his legendary book. While touring the United States as the manager of famed British actor Henry Irving, Stoker was hard at work writing and researching his book. As he reached a section of the book that dealt with the final death of the vampire Lucy Westerna, he discovered a newspaper clipping about a strange ritual that occurred in Rhode Island at the grave of a young woman named Mercy Brown. It would become an important part of the death of Lucy in his book.

Dracula set the standard for every piece of literary fiction about vampires that followed. The novel also had the unique role of changing the folklore about what vampires could and could not do. Stoker mixed in real Balkan folklore with his own imaginative elements, jumbling up the popular conception about what a vampire should be. In this way, folklore lent itself to fiction, which in turn, altered folklore.

Vampires were described as the "undead." They were lean and cadaverous like an old corpse. He had red lips and extended canine teeth. His skin was white, almost transparent, and his flesh was always cold - only warmed after a meal of blood. His eyes gleamed, sometimes flashing red, and his eyebrows were said to meet above his nose. His fingernails were curved like claws, his ears might be pointed, and his breath had the fetid, coppery smell of blood. He was also supernaturally strong, said to have the strength of a dozen or more men.

The vampire as a living corpse was permanently attached to its burial place, or at least to the soil in which he had been buried. One of the many rules that seemed to govern a vampire's behavior was his need to return to his coffin, grave, or tomb before sunrise each morning and sleep in it during the day. Although Hollywood suggested that sunlight could destroy a vampire, folklore said nothing of the kind, only relegated most of the vampire's activities to the nocturnal hours. Since they only prowled at night, Bram Stoker created the idea that a vampire must spend his days in his own coffin, very much at the mercy of the living vampire hunters.

Luckily, the vampire's weaknesses were overshadowed by its variety of supernatural powers - not the least of which was his ability, in many tales, to get in and out of a grave through six feet of soil. Hungarian tales gave the vampire the supernatural ability to change into a cloud or mist. Stoker also did this in *Dracula* and included the Balkan belief that vampires can control a variety of fearsome animals like wolves or bats.

Occasionally, a few tales would give the vampire himself the ability to change into an animal, like a wolf or a cat, but a few Romanian stories mentioned her could transform into a bat. Bats, of course, are nocturnal animals, often associated with dark and evil deeds, so it's not a surprise that it became part of the vampire legend. However, it was rarely mentioned until the nineteenth century, when European travelers first began to regularly visit South America - and return with tales about a bat that nourished itself solely on blood. It was promptly named after its human counterpart from folklore and was just as promptly incorporated into vampire stories.

Finally, one of the more useful of the vampire's talents was his hypnotic ability, which enabled him to mesmerize his victims and send them to sleep, so that he could feed on them without a struggle. A victim might wake up feeling tired and drained but would remember nothing of the previous night's visitor - perhaps until she saw the two small punctures on the side of her neck.

Perhaps it is another magical power, or perhaps just another rule in vampire lore, but the vampire seemed to have many ways to recruit new bloodsuckers to the ranks. In the most traditional sense, a person could become a vampire after being fed upon and then drinking some of the vampire's blood. This exchange of fluids seemed to be the most reliable method, although some stories claimed that a person who was drained of his blood would rise from the grave after three days as a vampire himself.

But according to the lore, this was, by no means, the only way that you might end up as one of the undead. The old tales stressed most frequently that anyone who died in a state of sin, without the blessings of the Church, risked becoming a vampire; so, did those who were exceedingly wicked, or who dabbled in black magic. Balkan legends added that people might return as vampires if they died after perjuring themselves, or were cursed by their parents, committed suicide, or - most prominently - after being excommunicated from the Church. In all these cases, the horror of becoming one of the undead was seen as a punishment for evildoers.

But a man could turn into a vampire through no fault of his own. If his corpse did not receive full funeral rites of the Church, if he died without being baptized or was murdered and his death was never avenged, he might become a vampire. Some were cursed, it was said, by something as simple as a cat jumping over a coffin that had not been buried. If anyone saw the cat perform this act, the transformation of a corpse into a vampire could be prevented with a little homemade magic. They simply had to place a piece of iron in the corpse's hand, put a piece of hawthorn in the coffin, or hang a wreath of garlic around the cadaver's neck.

Such remedies were expected to protect a person from a vampire, too. But folk magic was not the only thing that was believed to keep vampires away. In the past, vampire legends briefly overlapped with Christian demonology, so that many Church officials ascribed Balkan tales of vampires to the actions of various devils, who had reanimated corpses for nefarious purposes. And while later tales refuted this idea, claiming that vampires were not demons but the original person re-inhabiting his own body, some Christian elements were not entirely absent from vampire traditions. The most common Christian element was the protective nature of holy water, holy relics, and even communion wafers. But given the vampire's evil nature, the best protection was the crucifix, the most powerful symbol of good. Wearing a cross around one's neck was always a good insurance policy, as was clutching a piece of silver, which was universally feared by every kind of evil spirit.

If anyone suspected that a recently buried body might rise again as a vampire, and it was too late to place hawthorn or garlic in the coffin, Slavonic legend suggested thrusting iron skewers straight down into the grave, pinning the vampire into his coffin. It also might be possible to bury a person in question, such as a suicide, under running water to prevent his return as a vampire. Running water had always been considered a barrier to evil creatures and, in some cases, could even kill vampires if they fell into it.

If vampire activity broke out in some regions and no one knew where to find the monster, a few traditional tests could be applied in the local graveyard. Vampire hunters examined the graves for scatterings of small holes, through which a vampire could emerge as a mist. Or Hungarian tradition had it that a white stallion that had never been to stud could be taken to the cemetery, and he would refuse to cross over any grave that contained a vampire. If all the tests failed to reveal the monster, and the vampire's attacks continued unchecked, it was suggested that all the graves had to be opened and the corpses examined to find the one that had not decomposed. Such activity had to take place in the daylight when the vampire was dormant and could do no harm.

Once the body was disinterred, a wooden stake - preferably of hawthorn, aspen, or another sacred wood - was driven through the creature's heart. Usually, this was the end of the ritual, but some traditions called for the vampire's head to be cut off, the body burned, or the heart torn from its body.

In America, our colonial ancestors were aware of vampires as monsters, death-bringers, and things to be feared. An unsuspecting community that fell under the spell of one of these creatures could very well be destroyed. In historic America, vampires were not mythical creatures from books and folklore - they were unquestionably real.

The stories of vampires in America originated in colonial New England. The influx of various immigrants from Europe - British, Dutch, German, Romanian, and Polish - brought many old traditions to the American shores and created a place where many different beliefs could flourish, develop, and change. The German and Dutch settlers came to the New World with many supernatural creatures that translated to the undead being called back to life. Nearly all of them attacked the living and drank their blood. Such ghoulish traditions blended with American Indian myths of nameless creatures, which were halfway between some sort of monster and specter. Both the Wampanoag of Massachusetts and the Narragansett of Rhode Island told of a thing that had the form of a man but hid in the shadows of the forest. It would attack hunters and travelers unlucky enough to pass by. No weapon could kill it, and a man had only to speak its name to summon it from the dark woods. Precisely what this creature did with its victims was unknown, but it was unwise to cross its path. It's easy to see how belief in such a being could easily mix with some of the mythology brought to America by the new settlers.

Another element in American vampire mythology was religion. The stern Christianity of the Puritans shaped the lives of New England settlers, and the Devil was everywhere in those days. He was in the forests, the remote valleys, and the dark caves that were scattered around god-fearing settlements, ready to ensnare the unsuspecting. Their only protection from diabolical attacks was their faith and belief in God. From the earliest days of the Pilgrims in 1620, the colonists framed their world through religion and supernatural intervention. In 1692, when the Massachusetts colony was facing its most serious political and religious crises, their anxiety was expressed not by political activity, but through a witchcraft-inspired panic in the village of Salem. It was a perfect example of the way the American colonial world was heavily influenced by faith and the signs of evil that were all around them.

In the 1740s, a radical minster named George Whitefield traveled along the American coast, preaching to packed conversations at the start of what came to be called the First Great Awakening. From this period emerged groups with radical theories regarding salvation, sin, and the world. They were the strict Baptists, the Universalists - who denied the existence of Hell - Evangelical Calvinists, and many others.

Some faiths expressed views that were, let's say, a little strange. The early followers of the minister Edward Browne, for instance, believed the Devil was a woman and, consequently, no woman could enter heaven. Saintly women were turned into men at the time of death. Mother Anne Lee's Shakers, who had fled England in 1774, believed that lust was the Original Sin, so any contact between men and women was forbidden. A Perfectionist named Shadrack Ireland believed that the "second coming" of Christ was imminent, and he instructed his followers to place themselves on stone slabs in sealed underground chambers beneath the Massachusetts hills. That way, when the trumpet sounded that could walk out, whole, and ready to meet God.

For many of the faithful, sin and evil - and the avoidance of both - became serious preoccupations. Once a man had given his life to God, the Devil would stop at nothing to destroy him. The Devil's agents were everywhere. The Indians who lived in the woods were often described in the writings of ministers of the era as "worshippers of the Devil." When Indians attacked their settlements, it was unquestionably the work of Satan. And God permitted these atrocities to occur because of the sins of the colonists, whether real or imagined. Such raids were punishment for the colonists and a powerful reminder of the evil that lurked in the shadowy corners of the new land.

On May 19, 1780, a spectacular event occurred that shook New England to its core and galvanized many of the radical churches. It was already a time of religious fervor as itinerant preachers traveled among the people, preaching of sin and the presence of evil. Then, at mid-day on May 19, the sky suddenly went dark, and the sun disappeared, forcing lamps and candles to be lit. What caused the famous "New England's Dark Day" is unknown. It may have been a solar eclipse, heavy cloud cover, thick fog, or even smoke from forest fires, but it was terrifying. The total darkness blanketed Massachusetts and was also experienced in Pennsylvania and New Jersey. While undoubtedly some sort of strange, natural phenomenon, the religious felt there could only be one explanation - Judgement Day had arrived. The darkness lasted until around midnight, and when it finally dispersed, the stars could be seen shining above. The world had not come to an end.

The effect on New England's religious community, however, was electric. If the darkness was not a sign of Christ's return, then it had to be something else, perhaps even more dire. Many said that it was a warning from God that America was a place of sin. It was a hint of things to come if men did not mend their ways and follow the word of the Lord. In many places in New England, everything was treated as a sign from God or evidence of the Devil's work. Satan was stepping up his efforts to bring ruin and damnation to America and, as if to prove it, many local villages and towns experienced epidemics of typhoid fever and smallpox in the months that followed.

Fear, myth, rumor, and religion all combined to create the legends of American vampires, but perhaps the greatest element of the emerging mythology was disease. The conditions under which the settlers lived were poor and unsanitary. Many of them lived on the edges of lakes, bogs, and swamps, which were perfect breeding grounds for all sorts of ailments, most of them fatal. Epidemics of various kinds swept through the colonies, claiming the lives of the weak and vulnerable as they did so. Once again, thanks to the religious fervor of the time, epidemics were regarded as another sign of God's judgment upon a sinful people. Typhoid and tuberculosis, along with many forms of respiratory and lung infections, flourished through the colonies. It was not uncommon for entire families - even entire towns - to sometimes be lost to a single epidemic.

One of the first writers to connect the stories of vampires with disease was an anthropologist named George R. Stetson. He wrote an article called "The Animistic Vampire of New England" for the *American Anthropologist Journal* in January 1896. He wrote of many places in New England where, thanks to isolation and poverty, a belief in vampires still flourished. He made a connection between epidemics and the belief that vampires preyed on families.

Between about 1780 and the latter part of the 1800s, plagues of typhoid, smallpox, and tuberculosis claimed many lives in small communities already devastated by poverty and a decline in the agriculture that had once been the lifeblood of the town. Poor diet and harsh life often took their toll on the more vulnerable, making them easy victims for all sorts of contagions. Perhaps looking for some kind of explanation for the lives that were ruined, vampires were blamed. In

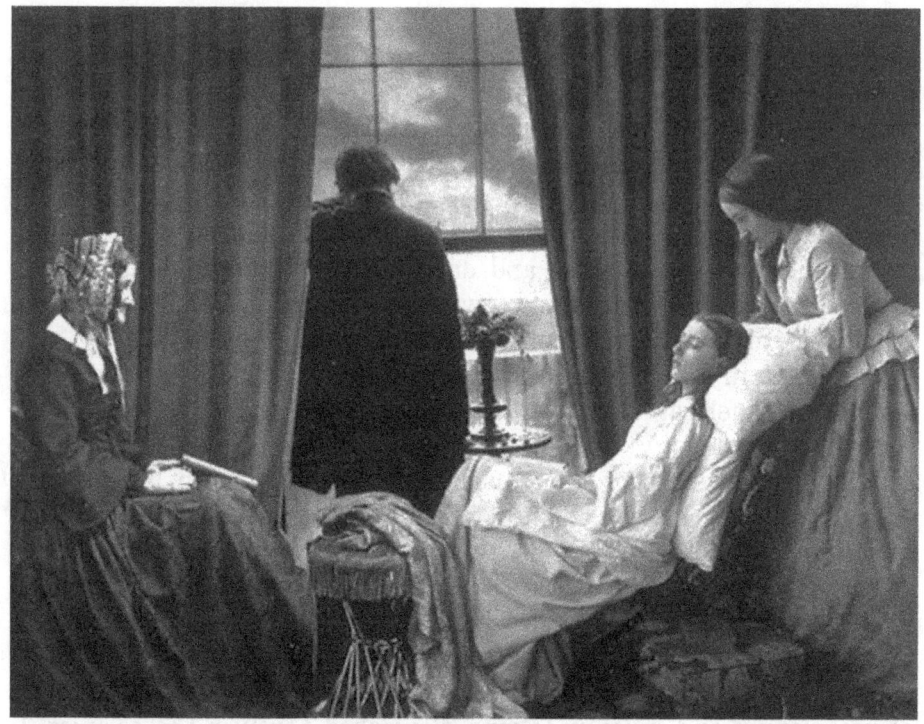

Tuberculosis, or "consumption" as it was often called, was the great plague of the nineteenth century, wiping out entire families and, sometimes, entire communities.

Stetson's writings, he mentioned a curious custom that had started to occur following the outbreaks of disease. Bodies of victims were exhumed and examined, and, in many cases, hearts and some internal organs were burned in an effort to prevent the corpse from coming back to claim the lives of other members of his or her family.

It's easy to understand how tuberculosis came to be connected to something that drained the lives from its victims. Consumption, as it was usually known then, was the great plague of the nineteenth century. In New England alone, death tolls were staggering. The illness was spread by everyday living conditions - large families, often poorly nourished, who shared living space for long periods of time. It was common for the disease to run through entire families. Highly contagious and generally fatal, tuberculosis was so lethal that doctors called it the first disease "to deter practitioners from attempting a cure."

As consumption claimed life after life, it began to be called the "White Death." It was a fitting nickname. As the disease progressed, the body was transformed from its previous ruddy complexion to the skin becoming stark white, almost ghostly, and translucently thin. A network of light blue veins became visible beneath the surface. Victims often ran fevers, which caused their cheeks to become reddened. They had difficulty breathing and developed a terrible cough that often brought up bloody phlegm. There were often fainting spells, anemia, weight loss, and an increasingly fragile demeanor. The thin, pale, weak, and listless victims often came to resemble a living corpse. Oddly, due to the romantic and beauty standards of the time, these symptoms made the victims, especially young women, strangely alluring. As the illness progressed, they became more beautiful - while their bodies, health, and strength were consumed by the incurable disease.

It was probably easy for early New Englanders to imagine this wasting away - the process of being consumed by the disease - as the result of a vampire preying on the very life of the victim. No doubt, to some, the resulting mysteriously heightened feminine beauty was evidence of a transformation from victim to vampire. A seemingly bizarre component of the disease contributed to the illusion - consumptives occasionally experienced surprising periods of manic energy. Many were known to have powerful sex drives. Some have suggested that these attributes proved that the individuals were clinging to life in a manner that could survive the grave.

At some point in New England's history, it came to be accepted that when someone died of consumption, that they could come back from the dead and drain the life from their surviving relatives. To stop this, family members would open their grave and attempt to kill them again. When relatives opened the coffins of the recently deceased consumptives, the corpses, formerly thin and frail, were often found to be bloated and engorged. Fingernails seemed to have grown into claws, and perhaps the most damning evidence was blood often found in the mouth. There were even some accounts of bodies jerking and gurgling as the remains were being mutilated.

Of course, all of this "evidence" of vampirism could be explained scientifically in these modern times. The decomposition of the body caused it to bloat, the flesh receded from the fingers, making the nails look as though they had grown, and a loss of tissue in the lungs from the disease caused blood to remain in the mouth. At that time, though, those who looked for it easily found "proof" that the dead person was a vampire.

But driving a wooden stake through the heart of the vampire was not practiced by New Englanders. That was a European tradition. Instead, the technique to destroy the monster was to remove its heart and burn it. Decapitation was also popular, as were other mutilations of the body. In each case, disturbing the body seemed to bring the trouble to an end - and it kept the dead from leaving the grave.

One of the earliest stories of a vampire in New England was recorded in Manchester, Vermont, and dates to the late eighteenth century. The account was discovered in the personal papers of Judge John S. Pettibone and was written down at some point between 1857 and 1872.

The story, by all accounts, was true.

The events began on March 8, 1789, when Captain Isaac Burton married a beautiful young woman named Rachel Harris. She was from a prominent family in the region, and the marriage was praised in the Manchester community. The captain seemed to have found the perfect partner, but unfortunately, the marriage did not last long. Shortly after the wedding, Rachel's health began to fail. Consumption was prevalent in the area, and Rachel succumbed to it, dying slowly and painfully. Less than one year after she married Isaac Burton, she died on February 1, 1790.

Captain Burton was distraught over the death of his young wife, and he mourned her for many months. After nearly a year had passed, he decided to marry again. He took a new bride, Hulda Powell, daughter of a wealthy landowner, on January 4, 1791. Hulda was described as a lovely, fit, and healthy young woman - but she didn't stay that way for long.

A few months into the marriage, Hulda began to display symptoms of the same wasting disease that had taken Rachel. Her vitality faded away, she became unnaturally pale, and she developed a harsh, bloody cough. Desperate to save his second wife from death, Burton spent huge sums of money on her treatment, bringing in physicians from large cities to investigate his wife's condition. Although they offered opinions and prescribed tonics, they were of little use, and soon Hulda was confined to her bed, just as Rachel had been. The stories say that she became delusional in her illness, claiming that she saw Rachel in her room, her mouth covered in blood and smelling of dirt. The stories frightened Burton and his in-laws, and they took turns staying with her at night, looking after her, and perhaps protecting her from her delusions. As time passed, Hulda continued to deteriorate.

One of the relatives who sat beside Hulda's bed was an elderly aunt that was well-versed in the folklore of the region. She listened to her niece's tales of late-night visitations from a ghastly-looking Rachel Harris and talk turned to vampires. She offered Isaac a rather chilling explanation for what was ailing his sickly wife. Bluntly, she told him that she believed his late wife was draining the life from Hulda's body. The only way to stop it was to remove the body of Rachel from her grave and burn it. After that, Hulda had a chance to recover but, even then, recovery was not certain. It was certain that if nothing were done at all, Hulda would surely die - and soon, the vampire would perhaps prey on other members of the family.

Frightened and at a loss, Burton approached an old friend and town selectman named Timothy Mead to request the exhumation of Rachel's body. Mead refused, telling his friend that vampires were only a superstition. Rachel had been a respectable young woman from a good family, and she didn't deserve to be connected to such nonsense. The matter was put aside, and Hulda grew weaker with each passing day. The old aunt's beliefs seemed to be supported by her decline, especially after Hulda began to complain of feeling a pressing weight on her chest at night, as though someone was sitting on it. In addition, she now had flecks of blood around the sides of her mouth, as if someone had been taking it from her body. Burton and several relatives remained by the young woman's bed each night, only to be startled from sleep by Hulda's cries and screams that Rachel was in the room with her.

Rumors began to spread around town and whispers about a "demon vampire" began to be heard from every corner. Of course, the progress of tuberculosis in the body will produce a variety of symptoms, from coughing up blood to respiratory problems that might feel as if the victim is being suffocated to pale skin and feverish dreams. All Hulda's ailments could be attributed to the disease, but to Captain Burton and many of the people in Manchester, the symptoms only meant one thing - a vampire was at work.

Burton approached Timothy Mead again, and this time, aware of the rising tide of rumor and fear in town, Mead arranged for an exhumation. On a February morning in 1793, Rachel's coffin was removed from the cemetery and taken to the shop of the local blacksmith. Despite their fear, a large number of people gathered to watch the events. Once opened, the casket revealed a bloated corpse that was scarcely recognizable as the young and beautiful Rachel Harris. Around her mouth were dark stains of blood, which were noticed immediately by the crowd. The body was so bloated, the onlookers said, because it was engorged with blood. It was incontrovertible evidence that Rachel was indeed a vampire.

Her heart, lungs, and liver were removed and were cast into the searing heat of the blacksmith's forge. According to the account, the stench that came from the burning organs was nearly overpowering, and several onlookers later declared that they heard the sigh of a woman as the black smoke curled up into the sky. Others claimed they saw what looked like a black serpent slither upward in the smoke and vanish as it began to disperse.

If Isaac Burton expected his wife to recover after the gruesome task at the blacksmith shop, he was extremely disappointed. Hulda was too weakened by her illness and did not survive. She died on September 6, 1793, and despite some initial fears that she might return from the grave as Rachel did, nothing was ever heard from her again.

The story of Rachel Harris Burton, the wife who returned from the grave to take a blood and wasting sort of revenge on her successor, spread wildly throughout New England. It reinforced old beliefs, not only about vampires but about the presence of evil in the land and about the necessity of living a good and proper life. All over the region, the tale became a staple of local folklore and would be revisited many times over the century to come.

Within three years of the exhumation of Rachel Burton, another vampire account reared its ugly head in New England. This tale involved Cumberland, Rhode Island, and the death of a young woman named Abigail Staples, who died near the end of 1793 at the age of only 23. It was believed that she died from consumption, but unfortunately, her deathbed was not the last time that her family would see her.

On February 8, 1796, Abigail's father, a prosperous merchant named Stephen Staples, approached the Cumberland town council with an unusual request - he wanted to dig up the body of his dead daughter. In what he described as an "experiment," he wished to exhume Abigail, who had died several months before, to see if this might save the life of his other daughter, Lavinia.

Abigail had been a moody, unhappy girl who, while never married, often dreamed of a husband and children. When her sister married a young man named Stephen Chace, it was believed that Abigail harbored deep resentment toward the marriage. Her own dreams of matrimony were cut short by consumption, and she died.

Shortly after her sister's death, Lavinia began to exhibit similar symptoms, and her health began to deteriorate. She was confined to her bed for a time, and, as she slept, she had visions of a dark figure crouched at the end of her bed. It jumped onto her chest, crushing her with its weight and stealing the breath from her body. Her family assumed that the dreams would pass with the sickness, but then one morning, her husband was very disturbed when she sat upright in bed and cried out a single word - "Abigail."

Stephen was troubled by her outburst and went to see his father-in-law. Staples listened to what the young man said. He knew the legends of vampires but had never put much faith in the stories. However, the incident occurred at an interesting time. Several people in the area were also suffering from tuberculosis, and, in keeping with the religious fervor of the times, several local ministers had proclaimed that the illness was God's punishment on his wayward people. The Devil was near at hand, they said, and would soon make his presence known. Staples was a man who took his faith seriously and so he decided to take his son-in-law's concerns to the authorities.

The members of the town council reacted with skepticism. While they were sympathetic toward the girl's grieving father and husband, they believed that vampires belonged in the realm of folklore and ignorant superstition. But they were also acutely aware of the sermons being given by ministers in the area and how they had stirred up notions of ever-present devils and demons. Sensing their uncertainty about how to proceed, Staples pressed the issue, saying that if the Devil was close at hand, then vampires might be among them, too. Stephen Chace then made his impassioned plea, suggesting that it would be for the good of the community to dispel the terror that gripped so many people. Abigail's corpse should be exhumed and inspected and, if nothing were amiss, the girl would be reburied with decency. Somewhat reluctantly, the council authorized the exhumation. They only had one stipulation - the "experiment" had to be kept as secret as possible, and no written record of it could be kept.

In keeping with the council's request, Staples, Chace, and three hired men went out to a small graveyard on the Staples' property. They arrived after nightfall, lanterns in hand, and unearthed Abigail's body. No record exists about what they found, but local legend recalls that whatever young Stephen Chace saw when the coffin was opened that night almost drove him mad. He wandered the countryside, muttering to himself until sunrise. Stephen Staples never again spoke of that night or what he had witnessed, but he was a changed man after that. For the rest of his life, he was troubled by horrible nightmares. Legend also claims that one of the workmen who unearthed the coffin committed suicide a short time later.

What became of Lavinia Chace is unknown. She simply vanished from history after that. She might have recovered, or she, too, might have perished from consumption. There is no marker to identify her grave to say when or how she died, and no mention is made of her in any subsequent account.

There is no record of any similar occurrences in the region, and it is unclear if any similar deaths took place in the wake of Abigail's demise. However, there is a curious headstone that was erected nearby for a man named Simon Whipple Aldrich. It can be found in the Union Cemetery Annex, and it bears a very odd inscription: "Although consumption's vampire grasp had seized thy mortal frame."

Simon Aldrich was the youngest son of Colonel Dexter Aldrich and his wife, Margery. He died on May 6, 1841, presumably of tuberculosis. However, the strange mention of the word vampire in the inscription has intrigued historians over the years. Why was it included on the headstone? It may, of course, be only a turn of phrase, but it may also be a reminder of the dark days of Abigail Staples - and perhaps proof of the indelible mark that she left on the community.

The graves of Simon Aldrich and his wife, Marietta. Simon's stone contains the epitaph, "Although consumption's vampire grasp had seized thy mortal frame."

Stutley Tillinghast was a prosperous apple farmer who lived Exeter, Rhode Island. He was liked and admired in the community and was active in the local church. He was a good provider, probably everyone in town agreed, and he was an excellent father. He and his wife, Honor, were parents to 14 children, and all of them, against the odds in those days, had survived into early adulthood.

Then one night, the farmer awoke after an unsettling and disturbing dream. The nightmare was especially vivid and had left him in a cold sweat. He dreamed that he was walking between the rows of his apple orchard. On one side, the trees were healthy; their limbs weighed down by an abundance of fruit. On the other side of the orchard, the trees had withered and died. The branches had dropped their leaves, and rotten apples lay scattered about on the ground. Somewhere, in the dark shadows of the dream orchard, he heard the voice of his daughter, Sarah, calling to him. As he turned to see where she was, a cold wind blew through the trees and chilled him to the bone. Branches creaked in the trees, and dry leaves swirled about his feet, scraping and rustling. The voice faded, and as it did, the stench of decay spread from the diseased side of the orchard, and he knew that half of his crop had been lost. Tillinghast awoke with a terrible feeling of dread. He was sure the dream was some sort of portent of things to come - but of what?

Fearing that the dream predicted something terrible about that year's apple harvest, the farmer was greatly relieved when it was successful as always. He thought about the nightmare for a short while longer, but then his fear began to fade as the family settled in for the winter.

A short time later, Sarah, the couple's oldest daughter, grew sick. Sarah had always been a moody young woman, preferring to stay in her room and read and wander alone to a nearby graveyard instead of spending time with the rest of the family. At first, no one noticed when she began to skip meals or stay in bed a little longer than usual. But as she became weaker and grew pale and sickly, her mother realized that she was terribly ill. At the end of 1799, she died. The cause was, of course, given as "consumption," and she was laid to rest in the family plot, a short distance from the Tillinghast house.

But it was soon believed that she had returned from the grave.

A few weeks after Sarah's death, the Tillinghast's youngest son, James, came down to breakfast one morning looking pale and shaken. He claimed that his chest hurt badly, "where Sarah touched him." His mother assured him that it had only been a bad dream, and yet she could hear an unhealthy rattle in his lungs. He was sent back to bed with high piled blankets to keep him warm. In the nights that followed, he continued to claim that Sarah came to visit him in the night and would often touch him. He grew sicker, and his parents assumed that the stories were the result of his fevers, no matter how real they seemed to the boy. He didn't have bad dreams for long, though. James followed his sister to the grave.

A short time later, another of the Tillinghast girls, Andris, became sick. Her sister, Ruth, also began wasting away. Both girls died, and their parents began to fear that God had turned against their family. Before the girls died, they began to complain repeatedly about their dead sister Sarah and claimed that she was coming to them in the night. She came as a ghostly figure, they said, entering the room through the window. Sarah would then come to the side of the bed and push down on each girl's chest, making it difficult for her to breathe.

In the days and weeks that followed, more of the Tillinghast children weakened and died. The fifth child, Hannah, was married and lived several miles away with her husband. She often visited her parents and helped Honor with the daily chores. On several nights, though, after leaving the Tillinghast farm, she was convinced that she was being followed. One night, she caught a glimpse of someone in the shadows and thought it was her sister, Sarah - but Sarah was dead. Oddly, she had dreams that night that Sarah was in her bedroom with her. A short time later, Hannah grew sick and began wasting away. She died in the spring of 1800.

By the time Hannah died, Stutley Tillinghast began to recall the strange dream that he had experienced about the apple orchard. In this vision, exactly half of the orchard had withered and died. He finally realized what the dream had been trying to tell him. In despair, he realized that seven of his children were going to die. He didn't try to ponder the supernatural meanings behind the dream, however. At this point, he was trying to puzzle out the meaning behind his children's complaints about nighttime visits from Sarah. Before each of them died, they claimed their sister came into their room at night. What could this mean?

Another death followed, and then the seventh Tillinghast child, Ezra, also began to complain of strange feelings of fatigue and of seeing Sarah in his room at night. He died soon after.

The Tillinghast family plot, where Sarah and other members of the family were buried. Sarah's father believed she had returned from the grave.

And then, Honor began to weaken - and dream of Sarah coming to her in the darkness.

After talking it over with some of his neighbors, Tillinghast began to believe that Sarah was responsible for the string of deaths in his family. Knowing the only way to save the rest of them was to take action, Stutley, along with two of his hired men, made his way to the cemetery where the body of Sarah had been buried. They took along shovels, ropes, and a flask of oil.

Throughout the night, the men unearthed the coffins of all of the Tillinghast children. All of them had been in the earth for more than six months when the caskets were opened, and they found the bodies to be rotting and decayed - except for one. Sarah's body, it was said, was in perfect condition. She was lying as if in repose. Her hair and nails had grown, her flesh was soft and supple, and her eyes were open, staring up into the sky. When the coffin lid was removed, and one of the workmen looked down on her face, he immediately fell to his knees and began to pray.

When Tillinghast saw his daughter, he was seized with horror, and he rushed to the wagon and returned with the can of oil. Taking a large knife from his belt, he bent down into the coffin and cut open Sarah's chest. Her heart and liver were sliced out, and Tillinghast doused them with oil and set them on fire. As they burned, a sharp stench filled the air, and the men watched as the smoke curled into the air above the burial ground. The organs turned to ash, and the men, still shaking, judged that the danger was past. They reburied all the coffins and left the cemetery as the sun began to rise.

Honor Tillinghast survived her illness, recovered her health, and later bore her husband two more children. All the remaining children outlived their parents. In Tillinghast's vision, half of his orchard was lost to an unexplainable scourge, just as half of his children had been. The eerie dream had come true.

The story of New England's last vampire, Mercy Brown, is a shadow that still lingers over Rhode Island today. Even though it came to a cruel and bloody end in 1892, the tale had its beginnings years before, in 1883, when consumption was claiming lives in the area around Exeter.

George Brown was a hard-working farmer who prospered in this part of southern Rhode Island, not far from Providence. He and his wife, Mary Eliza, had raised six children and lived a comfortable, but simple life. In late 1883, the first in a series of terrible events occurred on the Brown farm when Mary began to show the telltale signs of having contracted consumption. The sturdy, once healthy woman began to suffer from fainting spells and periods of weakness. Most of all, she was gripped with a harsh cough that kept her awake through the night. After these horrible fits of coughing, the handkerchief that she kept pressed to her mouth would be covered in blood. The disease began to ravage her body, and on December 8, she slipped into unconsciousness and did not awaken. She died at the age of only 36.

Seven months later, the Browns' oldest daughter, 20-year-old Mary Olive, also came down with the dreaded illness. She developed the now familiar symptoms of weight loss, weakness, and a wracking cough. Mary Olive grew paler and weaker with each passing day, and on June 6, 1884, she followed her mother to the grave.

Several years of peace followed the death of Mary Olive, and during this time, Edwin Brown, George and Mary's only son, got married and bought his own farm in nearby West Wickford. He hoped to make a life for himself and his new bride while he worked in a store to support his family and save money for the future. All was going well until 1891 when Edwin noticed the symptoms of the disease that had killed his sister and mother. He resigned from his job and, following advice from friends, moved west to Colorado Springs. The city had begun to develop a reputation for helping to ease the suffering of consumption patients, and Edwin hoped the nearby mineral waters and the drier climate might restore his health.

While Edwin and his wife were out west, things took a dark turn for the Brown family in Exeter. In January 1892, Edwin received word that his 19-year-old sister, Mercy, had also become sick and died. Her consumption was diagnosed as the "galloping" variety, and she quickly passed away and was entombed in the receiving vault at Chestnut Hill Cemetery in Exeter.

Meanwhile, Edwin realized that his health was not improving in Colorado. He and his wife decided that they should return home so that Edwin could spend the remainder of his days with family, friends, and loved ones. They made the journey back to Rhode Island and moved in with Edwin's in-laws.

By the time Edwin returned to Rhode Island, his father was in a dreadful and worried state. Friends were convinced that the family was being preyed on by a vampire and suggested that Brown should exhume the bodies of the other family members and see which one of them it was. While upset and worried, he refused to go along with such nonsense. It was superstitious fear, and he would not be a party to it.

But one of Brown's younger friends - his identity was never documented - took matters into his own hands. He decided to pay a visit to Dr. Harold Metcalf, who was not only the district medical examiner but was also the physician who had treated Mercy Brown during her illness and ask for his help. He told him that Edwin was also suffering from the same disease and that several friends and neighbors believed that the only way in which his life could be saved was to have the bodies of the mother and two daughters exhumed to ascertain if the heart of any of the bodies still contained blood. If any of them did, then that dead body was feeding off the living tissue and blood of Edwin. Metcalf considered this as absurd as George Brown did and sent the young man away.

At some point over the next week, Brown's friends finally convinced him of the possibility that one of the dead women was indeed a vampire. Perhaps, only because he had exhausted all his other options, Brown agreed to the exhumation - but only if Dr. Metcalf would also attend. The young man who had previously gone to see the doctor returned to his door once again. He told him that George Brown, though not believing in the superstition himself, wanted to pacify his friends by allowing the graves to be opened. Because of this, he asked Dr. Metcalf if he would attend and perform the autopsies. Dr. Metcalf again balked at the idea but eventually agreed to go along, realizing that he could not persuade them from what they believed was their duty.

By the time Metcalf arrived at the cemetery, the bodies of Mary Brown and her daughter, Mary Olive, had already been unearthed. Mary had been in the ground for almost nine years at this point, and she was in an advanced state of decay. Some of her muscles and flesh remained in a mummified state, but there were no signs of blood in her heart. The men then opened the coffin of Mary Olive, who had also died years before. According to a newspaper account, only a skeleton and a thick growth of hair remained. Dr. Metcalf stated with certainty that they were "just what might be expected from a similar examination of almost any person after the same length of time."

Mercy's body had not yet been buried. Since she had died in the winter, the ground was too hard for burial. Her body had rested for the past two months inside a small crypt on the cemetery grounds. The coffin was placed on a small cart inside the tomb. Once the casket was opened, Dr. Metcalf looked inside and began a quick autopsy of the

The grave of Mercy Brown - America's most famous vampire

corpse. He noted some signs of decay and the marks left by consumption on her lungs. This did not convince him that she was a vampire, so he finished his examination and announced his findings to the men who had gathered to see the gruesome tasks at hand. Metcalf told them that there was nothing amiss with the body, but they didn't see things the same way that he did. When he was unable to convince them, he left the cemetery.

To the other men - and perhaps even to Edwin, who was present for the exhumations - Mercy seemed relatively intact, or at least more so than she should be after being dead for two months. Besides, they were also sure that her body had moved. She had been laid to rest on her back, and somehow the corpse was now resting on its side. Could she have left the casket? Dr. Metcalf, they believed, was simply trying to protect his reputation as a man of science and wanted no part of vampires.

The men were suspicious that something was wrong with Mercy Brown, and what happened next convinced them entirely. One of the men opened her heart with his knife and was startled to see fresh blood come pouring out of the organ. It was quickly removed from her chest. They also cut out her liver because, even though it contained no fresh blood, it was in a remarkably preserved state. The organs were burned, and then the ashes were gathered with which to make a tonic that would hopefully cure Edwin of the disease.

Edwin consumed the macabre mixture, but it did him little good. On May 2, he joined his mother and sisters in death and was buried at Chestnut Hill. While his death was tragic, all was not lost. He became the last of the Brown family to die from consumption - or the ravages of a vampire, depending on what you believe.

The exhumations, autopsies, and burnings that were designed to save the living of New England from being consumed by the dead- ended with Mercy Brown. The germs that caused tuberculosis had been discovered in 1882, and the fact that the disease was contagious was established not long afterward. The discovery dismissed the superstitious belief that the illness was caused by vampires that fed on the living, but news of such discoveries was slow in arriving at places like rural New England. Even if the Brown family and their friends heard such accounts, the claim that consumption was caused by invisible organisms that were passed from one person to another would have seemed perhaps even more unlikely than the idea that people weakened and died after being preyed upon by a monster.

The accounts of the Mercy Brown exhumation had a brief life in the newspapers of the day, all of which seemed more focused on pointing out the superstitious ignorance of country-folk than in studying the effects the old folklore had on the lives and deaths of the people involved. Mercy was finally placed in her grave soon after the incident took place - but that was not the end of her story. Mercy Brown lived on, not only in Rhode Island legend but in other ways, as well.

Author H.P. Lovecraft wrote a horror story called *The Shunned House* in 1924, and it was first published in the October 1937 issue of

Weird Tales magazine. While not the primary focus of the story, the 1892 exhumation is mentioned when Lovecraft refers to the Exeter "rustics" and even names one of the characters in the story, Mercy. Lovecraft relished New England folklore and legends and incorporated many of them into his stories.

A more important appearance of Mercy Brown in literature occurred in 1897 when the story of her exhumation was used in an altered form for Bram Stoker's novel, *Dracula*. When Stoker died, his years of collected articles and book materials were sold. Among them was the material that he used to research his groundbreaking vampire novel. Among the material were clippings about Mercy Brown. He used the bare facts of the story to create the staking of Lucy Westerna by Dr. Van Helsing and his group of vampire hunters in the story - earning Mercy Brown a place in vampire literature history.

To this day, Mercy Brown has not been forgotten by the people of Rhode Island. She retains a place of honor as the last New England vampire, and she casts a long shadow that stretches back to a time when vampires and consumption were both a part of everyday life. Over the years, tuberculosis claimed many more victims than so-called "vampires" ever did, but the end result for both was the same.

Both were conquered by science.

The belief in vampires faded as superstitions about them became a thing of the past. Tuberculosis, though, was much harder to kill. It was many years after Mercy Brown before effective treatments and cures could be developed to treat the illness. Literally millions died before tuberculosis finally became - just like the vampires of New England - a thing of the past.

3. SPIRITS IN THE STONE

Grave headstones. Grave markers. Gravestones. Tombstones.

The past of monuments to the dead is as varied as its many names. Marking the grave of the deceased reflects our need for a hallowed site of remembrance - a place to which we return, alone or with others, to renew the ties with someone who is now "gone, but not forgotten." Many of us return to the grave of a loved one like a wife, husband, parent, or child, especially in the first months after a death. Bringing flowers, a token of life, can soften the pain of death. Some will talk to the dead in the belief that the spirit still lingers near the corpse.

A grave marker is meant to be a touchstone of good memories and a life well-lived - but it was not always that way. The first markers to designate burial sites were stones and boulders that were used to keep the dead from rising out of their graves. If heavy rocks were placed on the graves of the deceased, it was reasoned, they would not be able to climb out from underneath them.

But in time, a need arose to create a reminder of the person who had died. This was not always possible. Many early American settlers were buried in unmarked graves. Those who died in floods, storms, and blizzards were never found. Even under normal circumstances, or because of a shortage of natural stone, many families could not afford a tombstone. Many simple markers were made from wood, which did not last long in the weather. The dead were forgotten with the changing of the seasons.

The grieving demanded change. Humans have a great desire to know where their loved ones are buried, and they wanted something more permanent.

And they got it - no matter how terrifying it was.

Gravestones and monuments in New England were once used to instill fear in the living. They were carved with crude, frightening motifs like winged skulls, skeletons, and angels of death. Some stones had small openings at the top to represent the passage to the afterlife - a horrific place for the sinner. The stones were meant to frighten the living with the very idea of death, becoming more righteous after seeing the decay and horror that awaited them in the boneyard. It would not be until the middle nineteenth century that scenes and messages of eternal peace would replace those of damnation.

Eventually, making grave markers, monuments, and tombs became a craft, as well as an art form. In those days, many bricklayers and masons began to take side jobs as gravestone carvers, but soon demand became so great that companies formed to meet the needs of this new trade. Stonework companies started all over the country, especially in Vermont, where a huge supply of granite was readily available. Many stones and monuments that were carved and cut in Vermont were done by Scottish immigrants. The most delicate carving was done by the Italians, though. As children, many of them had trained in Milan, going to school at night to be carvers. Despite the thousands of statues and mausoleums that were created, only a few dozen carvers could handle the most intricate work.

The peak for the new funeral industry - and graveyard art and mausoleums - came during the Victorian era. During the period known as the "Victorian Celebration of Death," American cemeteries were packed with massive, ornate, and beautiful statues and tombs. This was a time when maudlin excess and ornamentation was greatly in fashion. Funerals were extremely important to the Victorians, as were fashionable graves and mausoleums. The skull and crossbones tombstones had all but vanished by this time, and now cemeteries had become very  survivor-friendly and, of course, heartbreakingly sad. Scantily dressed mourners carved from stone now guarded the doors of the tombs, and angels draped themselves over monuments in agonizing despair. The excessive ornamentation turned the graveyards into a showplace for the rich and the prestigious. Many of them became inundated with artwork and crowded with crypts as society figures attempted to outdo one another with how much of their wealth could be spent celebrating death.

Gaudy and maudlin artwork like furniture, carved flowers, and life-size (and larger) statues dominated the landscape. Realistic representations of the dead began to appear, as did novelty monuments that told entire life stories or would spin on a round dais to be seen easily from any direction.

There was nothing as elaborate in the Victorian cemetery as the mausoleum, however. Tombs for the dead had already been around for thousands of years. The pyramids are the largest and most famous, but even ancient man entombed their leaders and chieftains in subterranean and aboveground structures. Most of these were domed chambers created from circular mounds of earth, although some of the stone structures still exist today.

The word *mausoleum* comes from the name of Mausolus, who was the king of Halicarnassus, a great harbor city in Asia. When Mausolus died in 353 B.C., his grief-stricken wife, Artemisia, constructed a huge fortress to serve as his tomb. Inspiration for what would become the world's first mausoleum is believed to have come from the Nereid Temple, which boasted statues and friezes of battling warriors and female statues standing between Ionic columns. The tomb at Halicarnassus was similar to the temple, but much larger, standing a full five stories and having hundreds of statues decorating almost every bit of available space. It was said to be surrounded by a colonnade of 36 columns and a pyramid-like structure that climbed 24 steps to the summit. At the top was a four-horse chariot, cut from marble.

Nothing remains of the tomb today save for a few stones from the foundation. It was most likely damaged during earthquakes and by the Knights of St. John of Jerusalem, who plundered the structure in the late fifteenth and early sixteenth centuries. They took the stones to strengthen their own castles and destroyed the underground tomb chambers. During its heyday, though, the tomb attracted many sightseers, including Alexander the Great. The tomb is still considered one of the Seven Wonders of the Ancient World.

The Greeks adopted the tomb of Mausolus as the new standard and began building their own "mausoleums" and coining the word. The Romans emulated the Greeks and influenced the modern styles of the nineteenth century, thanks to the fact that many great archaeological finds were uncovered during this period.

The rise of the American mausoleum came with the founding of Mount Auburn, the first American garden cemetery, near Boston. The creation of this cemetery meant the end of the horrifying graveyards of the past and a new era for burial grounds. Although grave markers dominated the cemeteries, mausoleums experienced a Golden Age, starting in the mid-nineteenth century and ending around the time of the Great Depression. They became the most desired burial spots in any cemetery for bankers, industrialists, robber barons, beer barons, entrepreneurs, and anyone else with plenty of money to spend.

Committing their mortal remains to a mausoleum, they saw themselves as the pharaohs of Ancient Egypt, who if they were not remembered for their accomplishments, would be remembered for their tombs.

The best architects were hired, and extravagant amounts of money were spent. Most mausoleums of the era were made from granite, marble, and various types of stone, and often the imaginations of the designers ran wild. They created everything from gothic cathedrals to classic temples to even Egyptian pyramids. One can find just about everything imaginable decorating the tombs of the period, from nude women to macabre animals and the sphinx. They have been constructed in every architectural style imaginable and can only be classed as "uniquely funerary."

But for cemetery enthusiasts, gravestones have proven to be just as fascinating as the even the most eccentric tombs. The earliest American stones were copies of the old European ones with skulls, crossbones, and death's heads decorating their surfaces. Later, carvings on the stone began to represent the grief of the family and began to make a statement about the life of the person buried beneath it. A variety of different images were used to symbolize both death and life, like angels, who were the emissaries between this world and the next. In some cases, they appeared as mourners and on other graves, as an offer of comfort for those who are left behind. As time passed, even the plainest of illustrations began to take on a new significance - a sort of code that could be read by those who visited the cemetery and knew what the motifs and illustrations meant.

Broken columns, inverted torches, spilled flowerpots, and funeral urns were meant as simple images of lives that were ended too soon. Some graves were marked with the image of an hourglass with wings that represented the fleeting passage of time or with ferns and anchors that were meant to give hope to grieving loved ones. Much the same can be said of clasped hands, bibles, and pointing fingers. These symbols

direct the mourners to look toward heaven and know that the worries of the world are now past.

Flowers, like roses or lilies, were common symbols that represented love and purity or that life is like a blooming flower, never meant to be permanent. There are other monuments where depictions of discarded clothing, opened books, or forgotten tools have been etched or carved. Such items are meant to symbolize the fact that the dead have left behind the burdens of life.

The depiction of wheat or a sickle would show the reaping of the soul and the gathering of the harvest to the next world.

Suns, moons, planets, and stars have various meanings in the cemetery, from that of rising saints to that of glorified souls. They can also signify that heaven is the abode of the stars and the planets.

Trees - especially the famous "willow tree" motif - stood for human life and the fact that man, like a tree, must reach for the heavens. The willow itself often stood for mourning. Trees could also have other meanings, especially when the monuments were made to look like wood. Cemetery visitors can often find examples of chairs, centerpieces, and even entire monuments that are designed to look like the rough wood of a tree. These markers symbolize the fact that the tree has died, and its life has been taken away, just like the life of the person the stone honors.

Perhaps the most heartbreaking - and often spookiest - monuments mark the graves of children. These images include the images of disembodied hands from heaven reaching down to pluck flowers from the earth and small lambs, lost and alone. Cribs and beds

are sometimes seen, holding the images of sleeping children, or are often empty, symbolizing that these little ones are gone forever. Most disconcerting of all is the life-size images of the children themselves. They stare out at the cemetery visitor with lifeless eyes that can send a shiver down your spine.

Gravestones, markers, monuments, and statues have a wide range of meaning, from comfort to grief, but there is no question that, under the right circumstances, they can also be unnerving. It is no surprise that within the boundaries of the haunted cemetery, there are many strange tales of cemetery markers with a life of their own, so to speak.

There are stories of curses, the macabre, the haunted, even cemetery relics that move on their own. This is a chapter that might have you questioning - as you walk alone through a cemetery some evening - if you are ever truly alone in an American graveyard.

The Devil's Chair

This is an old classic of mine - a story that I have been talking about now for more than 25 years. It doesn't get mentioned nearly as often as it used to, but the story has always stuck with me.

I grew up in the Midwest, and years later, I would discover that some tales and stories were unique to our region and, as it turned out, most popular during certain periods. In this case, it was the 1980s and 1990s, and the tale was that of the "Devil's Chair," a generic name for the stone seats that could be found in cemeteries scattered across the Midwest. When I was growing up, many people accepted the stories of these "cursed" chairs as factual ones, offering second- and third-hand accounts as proof. I heard them over and over again and eventually decided that I needed to see if I could find whether the stories of "Devil's Chair" had any basis in truth.

The roots of the "Devil's Chair" could be found in the Appalachian Mountains of the mid-nineteenth century. According to legend, on certain nights, a chair would rise out of the ground in the local graveyard. Anyone who sat in the mysterious chair could make a pact with the Devil and receive his or her heart's desire for the next seven years. At the end of that time, the Devil would come and take their soul.

The legend changed over the years as it traveled from the Appalachians to the Midwest, and its mythology became simpler. The stories began to say that if you sat down in one of these chairs in your local graveyard, you were sure to die within a year. I'm not sure what the incentive was to try this out, but that was what the legend stated.

A typical mourning seat that can be found in cemeteries all over the Midwest. These chairs have nothing to do with curses or the Devil, but many have mistaken them for the chairs of the legend.

But few chairs that are found in Midwestern cemeteries have anything to do with the Devil. Most of these chairs are simply "mourning seats" that usually date back to the Victorian era and the "golden age" of cemetery décor. They were placed next to the grave of the recently deceased so that loved ones would have a comfortable place to sit while visiting the dead. The chairs were of simple design, and most that I have seen are made from stone, carved to resemble a tree trunk with branches for the arms and back. The tree motif was mentioned earlier in the chapter. These chairs were readily available in the monument catalogs of the period.

But those were not the only style of mourning seats - and that's where the trouble began.

Some graveyard chairs were larger, and some even described them as throne-like. It was this kind of chair that accidentally resurrected the legend of the "Devil's Chair." Over the past few decades, many of these cemetery seats have been destroyed, creating an addition to the legend that claims the chairs were broken apart by grieving parents or friends of an unlucky teenager who sat

As the legend traveled from Appalachia to the Midwest, these kinds of cemetery chairs - or "thrones," as the stories called them - were believed to be cursed.

in the chair and then was killed a short time later, usually in a car accident.

Quite a few of these chairs could be found in Midwestern cemeteries when I was growing up, and nearly all of them had a story of a strange death connected to it. Truth or fiction? It was hard to say because literally everyone swore the stories were true. However, only once did I ever meet a person who was actually present when a person sat in a chair and later died. Otherwise, they were always unsubstantiated or relied on the stories of a distant cousin or a "friend of a friend." The stories were popular for years and, at one time, were almost always the first anecdotes that were recalled when people started telling me about their local legends.

Were people dying after sitting in the chairs? That's hard to say, but they were undoubtedly causing a problem. In the middle 1990s, an

Illinois cemetery superintendent told me: "We used to get people coming here every night to see the thing. The cemetery is closed after dark, but that didn't stop them, they'd just climb the fence. Finally, we moved it to a storage shed,"

The chair had stirred up the local teenagers so much that there making nightly treks to the cemetery to get a look at it. The story attached to the chair claimed that a local boy - who had been recently killed in an auto accident - had dared to sit in the chair the previous Halloween. Now, everyone wanted to see it.

First, the caretakers moved the chair to make it more difficult to find, and then finally, with the family of the deceased's permission, they removed the chair from the grounds and placed it in storage. As far as I know, it's still gathering dust in a shed somewhere while its legend is slowly forgotten.

How did such stories get started? No one really knows. And I can't tell you if there is any truth behind the stories either. I never found out. But I can tell you one thing - after spending years tracking down these stories and trying to get to the bottom of how they all began, I have never taken a seat in any of these chairs.

You know, just in case.

Stones That Won't Stay Still

Large stone balls in cemeteries are almost always purely decorative. They don't seem to have any special meaning, but, depending on the size of them, they can be eye-catching.

And in some instances, downright weird.

In the Oak Hill Cemetery of Taylorville, Illinois, there stands a monument that seems to have a life of its own. It was constructed around 1910 and bears the family names of Richardson and Adams. It's not a unique monument - there are hundreds like it in cemeteries across the country - it's merely a large marble ball that has been placed on top of a pedestal at the center of a family plot. It is so nondescript that it's been a forgotten ornament in this cemetery for many years.

And then, people began to notice that it moved.

The stone ball, which weighs several hundred pounds, is set into a granite base and is not designed to rotate. Somehow, though, it managed to move and slowly begin to spin, exposing the rough bottom of the sphere, where workers had tried to seal the stone to the base. Caretakers were puzzled. It would take several men with pry bars and a block and tackle to move the granite ball, and yet somehow, it happened. Perplexed, the officials at the cemetery poured concrete into the stone base and set the sphere back into position. Two months later, it was discovered to have moved again, and the rough bottom patch was once again visible.

It still turns to this day - I've seen it myself. If you visit the cemetery and find the stone, you can see the rough bottom of the sphere. When you visit the next time, it will be somewhere else.

Why does it move? That remains a mystery, but it's not the only revolving stone in the country.

The "moving" stone in Oak Hill Cemetery. This photo shows the rough spot that is supposed to be on the bottom of the stone sliding around toward the top.

There is another in Marion, Ohio. Another large sphere rests over the gravesite of Charles Merchant and his family. The monument was built in 1887 and is a white stone column that is topped with a granite ball. It was also, like the stone in Taylorville, far from unique - except that it rotated on its own, of course.

When news spread, curiosity-seekers began traveling to the cemetery. One geologist theorized that the movement of the stone occurred because of unequal expansion caused by resting in the sun on one side and shade on the other. Others believed that the weather might be the culprit. If moisture on the stone froze at night and then thawed in the daylight hours, the ball might shift slightly in its base as the dampness lubricated it. This theory seemed to hold up in the winter months, but what about in the summer, when the stone was also reported to move? The rotation was first noticed in July and has continued to turn ever since.

And there is also that pesky problem of how - like the Taylorville stone - it moves at all if it's designed to stay in one place.

The mystery of the revolving stones remains unsolved.

A Roadside Attraction

The small southwest Missouri town of Nevada has many tales to tell, not the least of which is how it became the home of outlaw Frank James, older brother of more infamous Jesse James. But there is another story of Nevada that must be included here. It is the story of an unusual grave, the man buried in it, and the reason why he is unable to find rest.

On March 4, 1897, the body of a young man who had been apparently struck by lightning was found just outside of town. An article in the local newspaper stated, "Death Came Without Warning," and added that his "clothing was torn from his body." The man had been so badly scorched that he was unrecognizable at first, but eventually, his father identified him as Frederick Alonzo "Lon" Dorsa. He had apparently been carrying an umbrella to shelter from the rain, which was struck by lightning.

Lon left behind a widow, Neva, and two young children, Beatrice and Fred. The couple had only been married for two years. Her grief over his shocking death led her to commission a very peculiar grave for her husband - one that would lead to her being ridiculed for years and would also turn the small town into a tourist attraction.

Lon's funeral - in which he was displayed in a "neat casket," the newspaper said - was well-attended, and there was a large procession to the cemetery and burial with full military honors.

But Lon's first burial was only temporary.

Neva had arranged an elaborate resting place for her husband, but it wasn't ready in the short time between his death and the funeral. She had ordered a large, above-ground enclosure for his grave from

Frederick Alonzo "Lon" Dorsa's grave in Nevada, Missouri. Although in poor condition today, the sliding Bible on top of the grave is still there, although it no longer moves.

the Brophy Monument Company in Nevada. The stone had to be shipped in by railroad car, and when it arrived, it was too heavy to move, so a local stonecutter had to spend the next month chipping away at it until it was light enough to be pulled by away by horses. One news story claimed that the stone was "12 feet long, 4 feet wide, and 5 feet night. Its weight at completion was 11,000 pounds."

Before Lon was exhumed and placed inside, Neva made one addition to the enclosure - she had a hidden glass window installed so that she could look at her husband's face. A piece of stone, carved to look like a Bible, could be moved aside to let her peer into the tomb. Or as the newspaper described it - "It can be lifted easily by the widow's hand, and when Mrs. Dorsa's grief becomes unusually poignant, she goes to the cemetery and gazes for hours at a time upon the face of her dead husband."

The *Nevada Daily Mail* went into great detail about the changing of Lon's grave. It noted that his casket had been submerged in water while in the ground but noted, "The remains looked perfectly natural, and there were no evidences of decomposition having sat in. No odor whatever. A little mold had gathered about the roots of his hair, and on the neck, otherwise the body looked as fresh as when buried."

After Lon was placed in his new enclosure, Neva managed her grief by visiting his grave often. Her home was only a short distance away. During the three years after her husband's death, Neva was employed as a dressmaker, and she cared for her two children.

In 1905, though, stories about the details of Lon's specially designed, above-ground crypt began making the rounds outside of the immediate area. It's unknown where the story was reported first, but the *Topeka Daily Capital* - located about 150 miles from Nevada - published a story. The strange tale later spread to St. Louis, Chicago, Pittsburgh, and beyond.

In 1906, it made the front page of the *Staunton Spectator and Vindicator*, a paper published in Virginia - half a continent away from southwest Missouri. The story noted, "The strangest tomb in America, if not in the world, is that which rest the remains of Lon Dorsa in Deepwood Cemetery, Nevada, Mo. It is so constructed that the widow can look upon her deceased husband at will, by the turning of a key in a lock which holds a stone Bible just above the remains."

The story began to take on many weird elements, depending on who was doing the telling of it. One article claimed that scientists had told Neva that since Lon's remains were in an airtight tomb, they would be well-preserved. But decomposition had already started, causing the body to turn "almost black, but the general outline of the features remains unchanged."

I doubt that Neva Dorsa ever spoke to a scientist in her entire life.

Local lore suggests that the town turned against Neva after the crypt began making news and drawing curious visitors to their town. It was said that she was closely watched when she arrived at the cemetery in her buggy to visit the grave. Children called her names, and "if she saw them, she'd go after them with a whip, shrieking like a madwoman."

Rumors also state that the publicity, along with Lon's deterioration, drove Neva to insanity. Some say she was locked away in the state asylum that was then located in Nevada - a believable tale since Deepwood Cemetery has no record of Neva being buried there.

Stories of her being driven insane, though, are simply not true. Neva eventually remarried and moved to California. She died in Los Angeles in 1945.

Before she left town, she had the stone Bible on Lon's grave sealed with cement. The window over his face was permanently closed.

Unfortunately, though, Lon was not allowed to rest in peace. In July 1986, vandals broke into his tomb, and they stole his head. It was recovered the following year and put back where it was supposed to be. Talbot Wright, the Deepwood Cemetery board president at the time, told the local newspaper that Lon's hair, skin, and clothing were "well-preserved" until the vandals tore loose the stone Bible and broke the glass. The reclaimed skull was photographed, and it showed that it had no hair or skin on it. Both had quickly decomposed after the head was stolen. The skull was reburied in an undisclosed location to thwart any new grave robbers, and the tomb was resealed to prevent any further damage.

Lon has been resting quietly ever since.

The Uncooperative Gravestone

There is an unusual tombstone that can be found in Bardstown, Kentucky, that seems to be influenced by the presence of the man who was buried beneath it.

His name was John Rowan and was once considered one of America's most prominent men. He was a Kentucky state judge, served seven terms in the state legislature, and was elected to the U.S. Senate. In 1836, Rowan and two other men founded the Louisville Medical Institute, the forerunner of the University of Louisville medical school. The next year, Rowan was chosen as the school's first president, serving in that capacity until 1842 He also served as the first president of the Kentucky Historical Society from 1838 until his death.

Need another prominent place for him in Kentucky history? His cousin, Stephen Foster, was the famous songwriter of the nineteenth century, and he wrote the state song, "My Old Kentucky Home," about Rowan's mansion, Federal Hill.

But tragedy plagued Rowan's life. When he was a boy, he was so sickly that his family never expected him to live to be an adult. In hopes that fresh country air might invigorate the ailing child, his father, William, moved the family west to Kentucky. John was enrolled in a school run by Dr. James Priestly, and he began to thrive, physically as well as intellectually. He became a brilliant scholar, studied law in Lexington, and was in demand as an attorney by 1795.

A few years earlier, John had met and married Ann Lytle. His new father-in-law deeded him a huge section of land, and the construction of Federal Hill began a short time later. In the early years of the nineteenth century, the Rowans hosted many dignitaries, including Henry Clay, James K. Polk, James Monroe, and many others.

The fine home became John Rowan's greatest achievement, but it also became the scene of his greatest heartbreak. In 1801, Rowan was forced into a duel with an acquaintance, Dr. James Chambers. Their disagreement began during a card game. After what I'm sure were more than a few glasses of local bourbon, the men began arguing over which of them was more conversant in Latin. The argument became so heated that when Rowan made a disparaging remark about Chambers' wife, the other man challenged him to a duel, a custom of the time. Rowan immediately regretted his words and made a public apology, but Chambers insisted that the duel take place. The two men met on the field of honor, but only one of them fired true. John Rowan was the one who walked away that day. He regretted the incident for the rest of his life.

In 1833, tragedy struck Federal Hill when four members of the Rowan family and 26 of their slaves died during a cholera epidemic. Rowan's oldest son, also John, had just been appointed as the Secretary of State for President Andrew Jackson. He had paid a visit to Federal

Hill to see his family on his way to Washington. He never made it to the capital. While home, he contracted cholera and died.

A decade later, in July 1843, John Rowan died. Before his death, he had made his wishes clear - he did not want any sort of monument or stone placed on his grave. His parents had been buried without grave markers, he said, and he would be disrespecting their memories if he was given an honor that had not received.

As far as he was concerned, Federal Hill was the only monument that he needed to leave behind.

When he died, his family and friends ignored his wishes. Rowan had been a great man, and a suitable monument was needed to mark his burial place. He was interred in Bardstown Cemetery, and a tall obelisk was placed at the site.

John Rowan's troublesome tombstone in the cemetery in Bardstown, Kentucky

And, of course, the trouble began a short time later.

Within days of the monument being placed over Rowan's grave, it mysteriously toppled over. Members of the family - a little disturbed by the controversial decision to go against John's wishes and mark the grave - quickly summoned a stonemason to repair it and put it back into place.

When the workmen arrived at the cemetery, they were puzzled by the fact that the stone had fallen. One suggested that perhaps the ground had settled or that tree roots - which would have had to grow *very* quickly - had knocked the stone over. They weren't convinced by rational explanations, and rumors spread around town about the monument.

The stories became even more heated a month later when the workmen were called to the cemetery again. Rowan's stone had again fallen over - and again, there was no explanation for it. A few of the men refused to return to the gravesite.

The stone was repaired and placed upright again. But a short time later, it again fell over. This time, it had become loose from its base and had fallen directly onto Rowan's resting place. Locals were convinced that John was unhappy and knocking over the grave marker that he hadn't wanted.

Each time it was repaired, the stone fell again. Eventually, all the stonemasons refused to return to the cemetery, and, after the stone continued to fall over, its repair was left to the cemetery workers. For quite some time, it was left lying on its side because workers feared that Rowan was displeased by their efforts.

It was eventually cemented back into place, but rumor has it that it's still known to tip over on occasion. Workers quietly put it back in place again.

It appears that John Rowan meant what he said when he died - Federal Hill was the only monument that he wanted to stand in his memory.

The "Miracle Child" of Chicago

Located in the Chicago suburb of Worth is Holy Sepulchre Cemetery and tucked away on the grounds of this ordinary graveyard is a grave that is anything but ordinary. In fact, it has been said that it can heal the sick and the dying. It is a sacred place, many believe, because it holds the remains of a young woman named Mary Alice Quinn.

Over the years since Mary's death, hundreds of people have allegedly experienced miraculous cures near her gravestone. Others tell of paranormal visitations and experiences, making her innocuous-looking tombstone the subject of visits by religious pilgrims and supernatural enthusiasts alike.

Mary was born on December 28, 1920, the first child of Daniel and Alice Quinn. Mary appeared to be a healthy child until she was around five months old. It was then that her parents noticed that her lips sometimes turned blue, and her fingers became enlarged. She was taken to specialists, and the family learned that her heart was twice the size that it supposed to be. In those days, there was nothing that could be done for her. Doctors predicted that she wouldn't live past the age of two. There was no hope that she would outgrow the problem, they said. Alice Quinn simply said that she and her husband "never gave up hope and just trusted to prayer."

And Mary continued to live.

Before she turned three, she knew all her prayers by heart and joined her parents

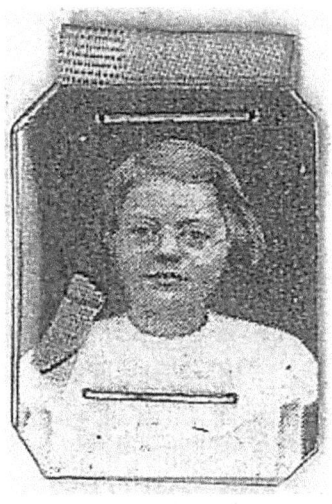

Mary Alice Quinn

in their nightly prayers for her health. The little girl became devout, praying fervently, and visiting the church to make a novena. Sometimes, she was so weak that she had to lie down in the pew until she could gather the strength to walk home. Her friends asked her why she went to church so often because it wasn't making her any better. Mary replied, "If God wanted to make me well, he would make me that way."

Mary rarely played outside. She preferred to stay inside with her mother and was determined to learn new things every day. Then when she was seven years old, she reported a visitation from the Virgin Mary. It happened again when she was 12.

In late May 1930, Mary was confirmed and made her first Holy Communion. She was too sick at the time to be given her Confirmation name, so her mother went in her place. When she told one of the nuns that Mary had chosen the name "Mary Alice Madeline Sophia Wanda Quinn," both women laughed and decided that "Madeline" would be enough.

In September 1930, Mary took a big step and began attending the St. Laurence Elementary School. Her grades would not have been important since she had already lived much longer than her doctors had expected, but she studied hard and continued her religious devotion. She was often praised by the sisters for saying the rosary in class. Mary kept a small envelope that she filled with slips of paper on which were written the number of times that she planned to say the rosary each day. If she failed, she forced herself to do without dessert or endured some other small punishment of her own choosing.

One morning when Mary was in fifth grade, Alice was summoned to the school. According to Father Touhey, he had been giving Mary communions when something appeared to him that he could not explain. He told Alice that her daughter would be a greater saint than Saint Theresa. The priest left on vacation soon after the event - but died while he was on his trip.

Mary finished at St. Laurence in 1935, but her health didn't allow her to continue to high school. Her body was finally failing her, but Mary refused to remain in bed. She wanted all the time she had left to be spent boldly serving God.

On November 1, 1935, Mary and her mother received communion together, and while they were having breakfast, Mary told Alice that she wasn't feeling well. She was in and out of bed the following day, but on Sunday, November 3, she got dressed but was too weak to attend Mass. She rallied a little during the day, but that evening, when saying the rosary, she couldn't get up from her knees. Her eyes were bothering her, and she said she was having trouble reading.

The next day, Mary asked for a priest. Alice asked her if she was sick, and Mary replied, "You are always better when you have the priest." Father Corley came to the house and gave her communion and offered his prayers, but the end was near. Alice called Mary's doctor, but he told her there was nothing else that could be done. Even though death was close, Mary's spirit never wavered. She remained happy and tried to cheer her parents, who were already stricken with grief. Around 7:30 that evening, Mary stood in the dining room and uttered her final words.

"I am going up, up up!" she cried.

She went back to bed and sank slowly into oblivion. She continued to breathe through the night and into the next day. Monday was cloudy and dark with rain until the afternoon when the sun broke through the clouds. Buoyed by the sunshine, Alice went to Mary's bedside and found her bathed by the light from the window.

The young woman took her last breath at 2:20 p.m. on November 5, 1935.

Mary's wake was held at Drumm's Undertaking Parlor across the street from St. Laurence Church. While her casket was open, dozens of people claimed to see a veil that appeared above her body. Her mother called it a "veil of grace."

Mary was buried on November 8, a plot donated by a kind family named Reilly. At first, her burial site was kept secret. It was feared that the graveyard might be overrun by curiosity-seekers who had heard her story and wanted to find her resting place. As word spread of the strange events that began to occur, though, her name was eventually carved into the stone.

But what strange events?

While she lay dying, Mary had told her parents that she wanted to come back and help people after her death. The faithful believe that she has, and in fact, the miracles began before she had been buried. Two nuns from St. Cyril's Elementary School prayed for a favor, asking for Mary's intercession, and they received it almost immediately.

On the first anniversary of Mary's death, her spirit appeared to her sister, Patricia. About five months later, she appeared to a Mrs. Queen who lived at 1721 West 63rd Street. A short time later, she appeared to the same woman a second time, placed her hands-on Mrs. Queen's stomach, and healed her of an ailment that her doctors had told her was incurable. She continued to appear to others in the Chicago area throughout the 1930s and 1940s, and Mary Alice Quinn sightings became almost commonplace.

A woman named Walsh, who lived at 7526 Langley Avenue, had been given a lock of Mary's hair, which she kept in a gold case. On January 31, 1938, while she was holding the relic and praying, she claimed to see the Lord's face in the hair. Her husband had recently suffered a paralyzing stroke, and her prayers - along with Mary's help - had healed him.

A woman named Sullivan, who lived on Dorchester Avenue - who was not a Catholic - was cured of stomach cancer with Mary's help.

The gravesite of Mary Alice Quinn is now a place of pilgrimage for many who come hoping for healings and miracles.

Another woman, a Mrs. Kerns, reportedly had a birthmark on her face for more than 70 years. Each time she washed her face, it would bleed. She asked Mary Alice for help, and the birthmark went away. That same woman's sister had been committed to an insane asylum, but after prayers to Mary Alice, the sister was sent home and restored to health.

Mary Alice's brother, Gorman, became ill with the measles on his later sister's birthday a few years after her passing. To make things worse, the illness enflamed his appendix, and doctors feared it would rupture. His fever climbed to 105 degrees. Doctors feared he would die at any moment. At one point, they gave him less than 24 hours to live. Alice and Daniel prayed for their daughter to intercede on his behalf, and he recovered without an operation. "He was entirely cured," Alice said, "to the doctor's amazement."

In the years that followed, her parents received thousands of letters from people all over the country who had heard about Mary and offered prayers that she would intercede on their behalf. There were scores of incredible, impossible healings that credited Mary for the cures.

The legend of the "Miracle Child of Chicago" was born.

Today, Mary's healing powers have taken on another manifestation - one that is connected to her grave at Holy Sepulchre. Thousands of people have come to the site over the years, most of them bringing prayer cards, tokens, rosaries, coins, candles, and photos to leave as offerings and to ask that Mary help them. Many say they have been healed of their afflictions after visiting the grave, and others have been healed by extension, finding relief from a small bit of dirt that was gathered at her grave.

Eerily, many also report the phantom scent of roses around the gravesite, even though there are no roses nearby. The smell is said to be especially strong in the winter months when the scent of fresh roses would be impossible to mistake. The smell is powerful, overwhelming - and unexplainable.

To the faithful, this is proof that Mary's presence is still nearby, helping as many people as she possibly can from beyond the grave.

The Face on the Tombstone

A grave marker in Washta, Iowa, has a sinister story to tell. The tombstone dates to the early twentieth century, and its tale concerns an elderly couple named Henrich and Olga Schultz and their mysterious farmhand, Will Florence.

According to the legend, the older couple operated a small farm outside of town and were well-liked in the community. Schultz had hired Will Florence during the haying season, even though many of his friends and neighbors were suspicious of the stranger. They had already turned him down when he asked for work and prodded Schultz to do the same. The kindly older man hated to see anyone down on their luck, so he hired Florence, providing him with food and board and a small salary.

Florence was a sullen and quiet man. He offered no information about himself, other than to say that he had moved to Texas to recover from some medical problems. He claimed that he had worked outdoors in the past, but Schultz found him to be clumsy and inexperienced with farm work. But Schultz continued to show him kindness and patiently instructed him with his chores.

But Florence repaid that kindness with murder.

One afternoon, Shultz received word that the bank in town was in fear of failure. These were uncertain days, and banks were closing all over the country. Fearful about his savings, Schultz went into Washta and withdrew most of his money from his account. He felt that it would be much safer at home until the bank crisis had passed. On his way out of town, Schultz waved a friendly greeting to one of his neighbors.

That was the last time any of them saw him alive.

Three days later, a friend decided to check on the Schultzs because no one recalled seeing them for several days. He stopped by the house and opened the front door to find Heinrich and Olga lying in the kitchen in a huge pool of blood. Both were dead, and their heads had been split open by an ax. The house had been wrecked, the money withdrawn from the bank was gone, and Will Florence was missing.

The authorities were quickly notified, and Florence was tracked down a few days later in Nebraska. He was arrested and returned to Washta for questioning. Convinced of his guilt, the local prosecutor convened a grand jury and pushed for an indictment. Sadly, there was just not enough evidence to hold him for the crime, and the officials were forced to let him go. He quickly left town and was never seen again.

A short time later, a strange story began making the rounds in Washta. Something unusual was happening with the tombstone of Heinrich and Olga Schultz. There was some kind of marking on it that had mysterious appeared - a marking that looked like a face. As more and more people began traveling to the cemetery to look at the stone, rumors spread that the marking looked like the face of Will Florence. No one could agree, though, if the resemblance were genuine, or simply the power of suggestion.

A marble dealer was brought to the cemetery to examine the stone and try to explain what was happening to it. He reported that the features were developing because of the "atmospheric influences of the rust and veins in the marble." He predicted that the face would grow plainer, and it did. He believed that the strange event was caused by entirely natural means, but locals didn't think so. More and more, they were starting to believe that the tombstone was trying to name the killer of the Schultzs.

Finally, after much urging, two police detectives agreed to visit the cemetery and examine the stone. They soon returned with other officers. Even the most skeptical of them agreed that the face in the marble did resemble Will Florence. But what could they do about it?

They certainly couldn't arrest the man again based on a ghostly image on a tombstone, but they could at least reopen the case for another look. When they did, they discovered new evidence that had been overlooked the first time. The new evidence solidly implicated Will Florence, and a warrant was put out for his arrest.

But they never found him.

Florence simply vanished into history. All we could do is hope that the killer got what he deserved. I think he did - and I think it happened just around the time that a spooky-looking face was appearing on the tombstone of Heinrich and Olga Schultz.

The Blood-Stained Mausoleum

Located in the southeastern Tennessee city of Cleveland is Saint Luke's Episcopal Church, a historic chapel built in the 1870s. At the rear of the church is a marble mausoleum that, over the years, has attracted curiosity-seekers from all over the region. The tomb is the burial place for the Craigmiles family, four members of which have become legendary for their tragic deaths.

Some say that this is the reason that the white stone of the tomb is streaked with a crimson stain - a stain that is the color of blood.

John Henderson Craigmiles came to Cleveland from Georgia around 1850. He and his brother, Pleasant, operated a successful mercantile business, but John soon grew restless with small-town life and traveled west to the California gold fields. He soon discovered that prospecting held little appeal for him, but out west, he did make a realize something that would both change his life and create his fortune - that to get to the gold fields, men needed a way to get to California. He would soon make his fortune in the shipping business.

Traveling overland to California in those days was a lengthy, costly, and dangerous endeavor. It was much easier to travel by sea.

John purchased a small fleet of six ships and began a shipping line between California and Panama. Not only could he trade back and forth between Central America and the West Coast, but he could also carry passengers from the eastern United States who booked passage to Panama and then on to California.

The shipping business prospered for some time, then disaster struck. Mutinous crews hijacked five of John's ships at sea and made off with the vessels and cargo. Claims from his creditors soon wiped out his fortune, but Craigmiles refused to give up. He borrowed $600 from his brother, Green, and set out to rebuild his business with the one ship that he had left. By 1857, he returned to Tennessee, once again a very wealthy man.

Soon after his return, John began courting a young woman named Adelia Thompson, the daughter of a local doctor, Gideon Blackburn Thompson, and on December 18, 1860, they were married.

A few months after the wedding, the Civil War began. The Secretary of State for the Confederacy, Judah P. Benjamin, recognized John's head for business and appointed him the chief commissary agent for the South. He held this position throughout the war and reportedly used it to great advantage. Buying cattle and speculating in cotton, he sold goods to the Confederacy at a profit and made a fortune from the war. He was also wise enough to know that paper money was of little value and only traded in gold. After the defeat of the Confederacy - when the paper money printed in Richmond turned out to be worthless - John was not ruined as many other southern businessmen were.

In August 1864, Adelia gave birth to the couple's first daughter, Nina. John soon became absolutely devoted to the little girl, and thanks to John, Adelia, her grandparents, and her uncles, she became wonderfully spoiled. Perhaps no one loved the little girl more than her grandfather, Dr. Thompson. He took long walks with her in downtown Cleveland, where she was popular with the shopkeepers, and often took her on medical calls in his buggy. They would spend entire afternoons enjoying the fresh air and traveling about town.

It was during one of these outings that tragedy struck. On October 18, 1871, Nina and her grandfather were off on a short jaunt in the buggy. How it happened remains a mystery, but somehow, Dr.

The "bloodstained" Craigmiles mausoleum in Cleveland, Tennessee

Thompson steered the carriage in front of an oncoming train. He was thrown clear, but Nina was instantly killed.

The whole town grieved for the little girl. John, Adelia, and the entire family were crushed by the loss and could barely function during the funeral services. When it was over, John began making plans to build a church in his daughter's memory. The Episcopal congregation in town had no permanent meeting place, and John felt that a new church in Nina's honor would be fitting. The ground was broken the following August, and Saint Luke's was completed on October 18, 1874, the third anniversary of Nina's death.

Almost as soon as the brick and stone church was completed, the family began construction on a mausoleum for Nina's body. It was built at the rear of the church and was constructed from expensive marble with walls that were four feet thick. The marble spire of the tomb rose more than 37-feet from the ground. Inside the tomb, six shelves were built into the walls, and in the center was a marble sarcophagus, into which Nina's body was placed.

As time passed, other members of the family followed Nina to the grave. The first to die was an infant son who was born to John and Adelia but only lived a few hours. He was never named, but his body was placed next to his sister.

John Craigmiles died in January 1899 from blood poisoning. He was walking downtown and slipped and fell on the icy street, and an infection developed and turned into blood poisoning. He died a short time later.

Adelia, who remarried Charles Cross many years after John's death, was also tragically killed in September 1928. She was crossing Cleveland Street when she was struck and killed by an automobile. She was laid to rest with the other members of her family in the mausoleum.

The stories say that the bloody stains first began to appear on the Craigmiles mausoleum after Nina was interred there. With the death of each family member, the stains grew darker and more noticeable. Some of the locals began to believe that the marks were blood, coming from the stone itself, in response to the tragedies suffered by the family. Attempts were made to remove the unsightly blemishes from the walls, but they refused to be washed or scrubbed away.

To this day, the "bloody" marks remain as a sad reminder to the tragedies of the family whose bodies lie within.

The "Flaming Tomb of Josie Arlington"

Located on the outskirts of New Orleans is Metairie Cemetery, the most beautiful and fashionable burial ground in the city. It's on the site of a former county club and racetrack that was a favorite of the wealthy elite. The club refused to allow Charles Howard to become a member because he was "new money" and, worse, a Yankee, so he vowed that he would one day buy the club and turn it into a graveyard. When money was tight after the Civil War, the people who supported the club fell on hard times, and it was eventually put up for auction.

Charles Howard kept his promise.

He incorporated the racetrack into the driveways of the graveyard, added more roads, dug ponds, planted flowers and trees, and turned it into am opulent park-like cemetery that appealed to the same families that had once turned their nose up at the money Howard made as the head of the Louisiana State Lottery.

The cemetery has since become the final resting place to 11 Louisiana governors, 9 New Orleans mayors, dozens of Confederate officers, and an area called Millionaire's Row, thanks to the price of the real estate in that part of the cemetery. Attorney Ray Brandt paid over $1 million for an eight-crypt mausoleum for his family there and shrugged it off. "I guess it's the last house I'll buy," he said.

Among the notables buried in the cemetery are General Pierre Gustav Beauregard, General Richard Taylor, General Fred N. Ogden, and General John Bell Hood. At one time, Jefferson Davis was also buried at Metairie, but his body was moved.

There are musicians buried there like jazz trumpeter Al Hirt and Louis Prima, who gained fame with songs like "Jump, Jive, and Wail. There are also important names in the New Orleans food world like Ruth Fertel, who put the name "Ruth" on Ruth Chris Steak House in 1927, and Al Copeland, the Popeye's Chicken King. Owen Brennan also rests there. He was the patriarch of New Orleans restaurants, and there are now 10 Brennan's restaurants operated by his heirs in the city. Brennan was a larger than life character who started his first restaurant after the owner of Arnaud's made the snarky comment that an Irishman wouldn't be able to run anything better than a hamburger joint. Brennan proved him wrong.

Jim Garrison, the district attorney who helped create the conspiracy theories about the death of JFK, is also buried here. So, is Stan Rice, the artist-poet husband of author Anne Rice, who will also be interred here eventually.

But, for many years, the most-visited tomb in the cemetery did not belong to any Confederate military leader, wealthy politician, musician, or chef - but it did belong to royalty. It was the tomb of Josie Arlington, once the Queen of New Orleans' Storyville.

Her tomb drew so much attention and such large crowds to the graveyard that police officers were often forced to remain all night around her tomb to maintain order.

Why? That's not a simple story to tell.

During the heyday of Storyville, Josie was one of the most colorful and infamous madams in New Orleans. She operated a well-known sporting house that catered to rich and discerning gentlemen who were looking for company. It was the finest bordello in the district, with the most beautiful women, the best liquor, the most delicious food, and the hottest music, and anything else that money could buy.

Storyville was the brainchild of a city alderman named Sidney Story, who suggested that the vice in New Orleans could be better controlled if it was segregated to a central district where prostitution - and all the vices that went with it - would be legal. By the time of the proposal in 1897, bordellos, saloons, and drug dens could be found all over the city. Story suggested moving them to a 38-block section of the city - and taxing them, of course. The licenses and fees required to run the bawdy houses and taverns would raise a tremendous sum for the city. The proposal passed a vote from the City Council, and the new vice district was dubbed "Storyville," much to the embarrassment of the alderman.

Josie Arlington

Courtesy of the Louisiana and Special Collections Department, Earl K. Long Library, University of New Orleans, Louisiana.

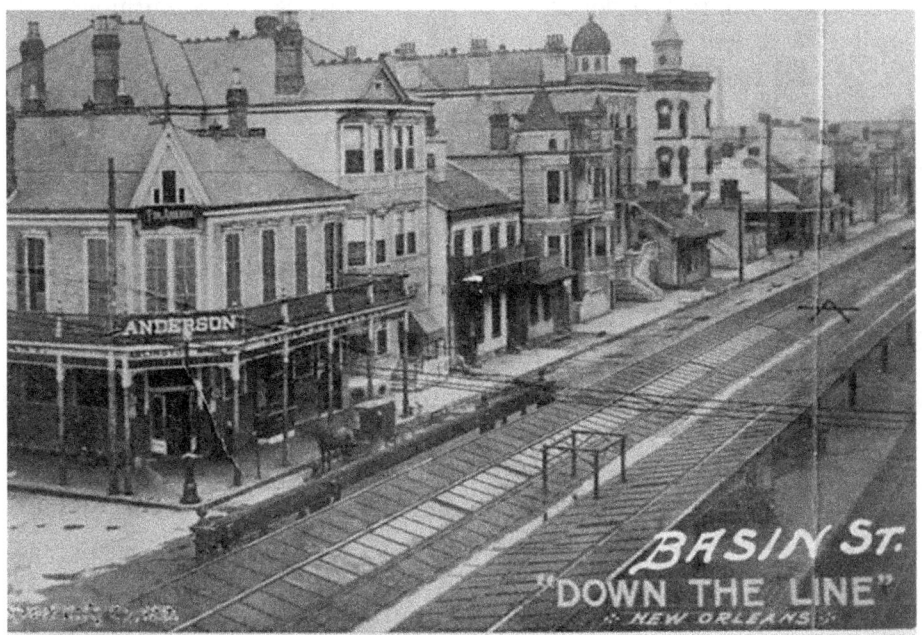

Storyville during its heyday in the late 1800s and early 1900s

Within a few years, Storyville became the most celebrated red-light district in the United States, and tourists came from all over to both see and experience it. The gateway to Storyville was the property of Thomas C. Anderson, saloon-keeper, political boss of the Fourth Ward, member of the legislature for two terms, owner of at least one of the most prosperous sporting houses in the district, and the unofficial "mayor" of Storyville. Anderson owned a restaurant and cabaret on Rampart Street he called the Annex. It was the district's unofficial town hall.

Storyville boomed during Anderson's years as leader. The area along North Basin Street was the site of the new district's swankiest brothels. The imposing three- and four-story mansions were bordellos where business was conducted with considerable elegance and ceremony. Rudeness and lewd behavior on the part of the customers was frowned upon, and drunken gentlemen were tossed out. When a man entered the parlor, he was expected to buy a drink - incidentally, at great profit to the house - but the girls were not brought out for inspection unless he requested it. All the sporting houses were more or less expensively furnished and equipped, with as much satin and velvet as the madams and their financial backers could afford. Many of them had one or more rooms with mirrored walls and ceilings, which were available at special rates; ballrooms with hardwood floors for dancing; and curtained stages for erotic performances that were given whenever sufficient money was offered.

Storyville became an important venue for jazz music. At first, the establishments of the district were reluctant to hire bands - if customers were busy dancing, after all, they wouldn't be buying drinks or women. But eventually, the new music became too popular to ignore. Hot ensembles were soon playing regularly at Storyville clubs like Nancy Hank's Saloon and the Big 25. Tom Anderson's Annex began by hiring a string trio - piano, guitar, and violin - but eventually became a spot for larger bands, too. The brothels also wanted the new jazz sound. It was often in the form of a single piano "professor" playing in the parlor while clients chose their partners for the night, but it was something.

According to some reports, Countess Willie Piazza was the first madam to bring music into her sporting house, hiring a legendary pianist known as John the Baptist to play on her famous white grand. Other pianists like Tony Jackson, Clarence Williams, and Jerry Roll Morton eventually found their own regular gigs in the district.

Storyville may not be the birthplace of jazz, as has sometimes been claimed, but the various venues in the district did provide many early jazz artists with employment and helped to bring their music to a wider - and usually non-black - audience. Of course, this was what earned jazz its early reputation as "whorehouse music," but the musicians that played it didn't much care so long as they had an audience, and they were getting paid.

The groundbreaking musicians soon reached another audience, namely the reporters who were writing stories about the brothels of Storyville, thus connecting jazz and vice for their readers. Whether the connection was deserved or not, Storyville began the careers of many musicians who went on to great fame. It also provided a home to perhaps 200 or more other musicians who worked the mansions of the district but of whom little record remains today. They are only recalled as whispered legends from a time when music rolled out of brothel windows and echoed down the street.

Unlike jazz, though, Storyville didn't last. It was doomed by America's entrance into World War I in 1917. In August, Secretary of War Newton D. Baker issued an order forbidding open prostitution within five miles of an Army camp. A similar rule was made for naval bases, and later that same month, Bascom Johnson, representing the War and Navy Departments, visited New Orleans, inspected Storyville, and informed Mayor Martin Behrman that it had to be shuttered. Mayor Behrman protested all the way to Washington, but it was no use. If the city didn't close Storyville, the military would do it for them. A short time later, the district was closed for good.

There is almost nothing left of Storyville today. Once located along Basin Street between Canal Street and St. Louis Cemetery No. 1, most of the district was leveled as part of a slum clearance project in 1940. It was turned into the Iberville public housing project, but then that was torn down in 2013 to make room for a new federal housing project. There are only three buildings from Storyville standing today and the only one you can visit - Frank Early's My Place Saloon, where you just might hear some of the music that was heard from the windows of the Storyville sporting houses.

Three buildings left - but only one ghostly story. It's the story of Josie Arlington and her infamous tomb.

Josie Arlington wasn't her real name, of course. She had been born Mary Duebler in New Orleans around. In 1881, she fell in love with a gambler and pimp named Philip Lobrano, and she was his mistress for nine years. During that time, she worked in various brothels in the city, using the name Josie Alton.

Around 1888, Josie began using the name Lobrano and opened a place of her own on Customhouse Street. It soon became known as one of the toughest houses in New Orleans, but Josie still made enough money to support several members of her family and Lobrano, who lived in the house with her. Lobrano hated her relatives, and during a terrible fight in which Josie and all her girls were involved, Lobrano shot and killed Josie's brother, Peter Duebler. Lobrano was tried twice for murder and was acquitted at the second trial.

After the shooting, Josie ended things with Lobrano and changed her name to Arlington. She dismissed all the cheap girls who worked for her, remodeled her house, and hired cultured women who she felt better appealed to the tastes of gentlemen of refinement. She re-opened her renovated bordello, which she called the Arlington, in Storyville and it became known as one of the grandest and gaudiest in the district.

Josie ran the place for ten years and amassed a considerable fortune. She had everything she could ever want - almost. The only thing that Josie still craved was social acceptance, which was something she could never have. She was shunned by the families of the city and even publicly ignored by the men she knew so well. Her money and charm meant nothing to the society circles of New Orleans.

But Josie Arlington would have her revenge. What she couldn't have in life, she would have in death.

She purchased a plot of land in Metairie Cemetery, the city's most fashionable burial ground, and built costly red marble tomb, topped by two pillars. On the steps was placed a bronze statue that ascended the staircase with a bouquet of roses in the crook of her arm. The tomb was an amazing piece of funerary art, designed by an eminent architect, and although it cost Josie a small fortune, it was worth every penny to her because of the scandal it created. Tongues wagged all over the city, and the gossip only increased after Josie died in 1914.

A few months after her death, the city installed a traffic light on the road alongside the cemetery. At night, the glow of the light struck the marble tomb in such a way that it gave the perfect illusion of a red light shining at the door of the brothel-keeper's tomb. The monument was soon dubbed "Josie Arlington's Flaming Tomb."

Word quickly spread, and people came in droves to witness the bizarre sight. The cemetery was overrun with people every evening, which shocked the cemetery caretakers and the families of those buried on the grounds.

Scandal followed Josie even after her death.

And that wasn't the end of the story. Soon, an alarming number of sightseers began to report another weird event. Many swore they had seen the statue on the front steps move. Two of the cemetery gravediggers even swore they had witnessed the statue leave her post and move around the grounds. They claimed to follow her one night, only to see her suddenly disappear. Records say that on two occasions, the statue was found in other parts of the cemetery. Most blamed vandals, but, of course, the legends said otherwise.

Josie Arlington's "Flaming Tomb"

People who lived near the cemetery claimed that the statue of the "Maiden on the steps," as she was called, would sometimes become angry and begin pounding on the door of the crypt. This spectral pounding would create a din that could be heard for blocks. Anyone who asked about the noises would be told that it was the Maiden "trying to get in." The story was that Josie had lived by a certain rule regarding her bordello in Storyville. The rule was that no virgins would ever be allowed to enter her establishment. The stories say that she placed the statue of the Maiden on the steps of the tomb to symbolize this lifelong code of honor.

Others say that the statue is Josie herself. As a young girl, she stayed out too late, the stories say, and her father locked her out of the house. Even though she pounded on the door and pleaded with him, he would never allow her to enter again. After that, she went away and began a career that eventually made her one of the richest women in New Orleans.

Still, others say that while the statue may be Josie Arlington, they say it symbolizes Josie as an outsider to the society circles that she always wanted to be inside of. They say that no matter how hard she "knocked," the doors would never open for her.

The tradition of the flaming tomb has been kept alive for many years, but unfortunately, it has a rational explanation. It was caused by the nearby traffic light when it swayed in the wind.

But what about the statue of the maiden?

No one has ever been able to explain the eyewitness accounts of the tomb's statue, moving around the cemetery and knocking on the door of the mausoleum. That part of the story remains a mystery, which is likely just how Josie would have wanted it.

It's true that she was never accepted in life, but Josie Arlington is certainly still on the minds of many in New Orleans long after her death.

Inez Clarke – The Girl in the Box

Graceland Cemetery is located on the north side of Chicago. It's an old cemetery - created after the Old City Graveyard in what became Lincoln Park was relocated - and a historic one. It's filled with famous people, Chicago notables, mayors, politicians, businessmen, robber barons - and some say, ghosts.

It's in Graceland Cemetery that a visitor will find the ominous statue that famed sculptor Lorado Taft called "Eternal Silence." The brooding and menacing monument guards the final resting place of late hotel owner and businessman Dexter Graves. The figure was black when it was first created, but over the years, the black has weathered away, except within the deepest folds of the figure's hood. That shadowy face has given birth to many legends, including that anyone who stares into the statue's eyes will get a glimpse of his or her own death to come.

In addition, legend has it that the statue is impossible to photograph, and no camera will work in its presence. But, as you can see, that isn't true, so that sort of calls into doubt all the other stories that surround this malevolent-looking character, too.

But without a doubt, the most famous spirited sculpture at Graceland Cemetery is that of Inez Clarke. In 1880, this little girl died at the age of six, allegedly killed during a lightning storm while on a family picnic. Her grieving parents commissioned a life-sized statue of Inez to be placed on her grave. The sculpture was enclosed in a glass box to protect it from the Chicago weather. Thanks to this, it's in almost perfect condition today.

The famous "Inez Clarke" statue that rests in Chicago's Graceland Cemetery

Even in death, the little girl charms cemetery visitors. She is perched on a small stool, wearing her favorite dress, and carrying a tiny parasol. Her face wears a small smile. It is not uncommon to come to the cemetery and find gifts of flowers and toys on her grave. It's one of the most popular places in the cemetery and, if these stories are true, it's one of the most haunted.

And I must stress here - *if* the stories are true.

You see, no one by the name of Inez Clarke is buried here.

Affixed to the front of the case that holds the statue of the little girl is a plaque that reads "Inez" and "Daughter of J.N. & M.C. Clarke. Born Sept. 20, 1873, Died Aug. 1, 1880." There's also a note that her parents - John and Mary Clarke - are buried just to the north of the site. That seems legitimate, but it turns out that, according to cemetery records, there is no one named Inez Clarke buried in Graceland.

The records say that a man named Amos Briggs is buried under the statue, next to an infant named Delbert Briggs. According to the 1880 census, there was no one living in Chicago at that time named Inez Clarke. The Graceland Cemetery files also contain an affidavit filed in 1910 by Mary C. Clarke, stating that her daughter from her marriage to John N. Clarke was still alive, and neither she nor her husband had any other children.

So, what was the statue doing there? It was suggested in 2007 that the statue was placed there by the sculptor, Andrew Gagel, as a sample of his work so that he could drum up new business. This was originally an unoccupied section of the cemetery, so it would not have been that strange.

But that turned out not to be accurate either.

Author John Binder began digging into the history of Inez Clark and the statue and made some interesting discoveries in 2011.

No one named Inez Clarke died in Illinois prior to 1916. However, there was an Inez Briggs who died in Chicago of diphtheria on August 1, 1880 - the same death date listed on the monument for Inez Clarke. It's also the same date that "Amos Briggs" died; the man believed to be buried under the statue. On the death certificate for Inez Briggs, the word "Graceland" is handwritten, indicating that she was buried there. Binder believed that name "Inez" was mistaken for "Amos" on the cemetery record because of bad handwriting - try writing the names in cursive, and you'll see what he means. The cemetery card was transcribed in 1929. Graceland has no record of anyone named Inez Briggs buried there, so there's no Inez Briggs buried in the cemetery. But if you try and find an Illinois death record for Amos Briggs before 1916, you won't find that name either. This adds credence to the theory that the name was erroneously written when the record was transcribed.

In the 1880 census, Inez Briggs is shown living with her grandparents, David R. Rothrock and Jane McClure Rothrock, in Chicago. They are buried at Graceland next to Delbert Briggs and "Amos" Briggs.

The relationships here get a little confusing. The Rothrocks were married in 1872. In 1880, a fourth person was living in the Rothrocks and Inez Briggs - Philander McClure, the son of Mrs. Rothrock from a previous marriage.

In the 1860 census, Jane McClure and her previous husband, Amos, lived in Michigan. Amos died during the Civil War. They had a son, Philander, and a five-year-old daughter named Mary.

David Rothrock divorced his first wife, Sarah, in 1872. He claimed she deserted him, but Sarah claimed that David had run off with Jane McClure, who kept a house of prostitution in Lansing, Michigan. David and Jane eventually moved to Chicago.

In 1872, Mary McClure - Jane's daughter - married Wilber Briggs in Cook County, Illinois. This was about one year before their daughter, Inez, was born. Their marriage did not last, though, and in 1880, Mary married John C. Clarke. The 1882 city directory lists the residences for both David Rothrock and John Clarke as the same. This continues at three different addresses over several more years. The families lived together and were eventually buried together. Mary C. Clarke - who was once Mary McClure and Mary Briggs - was the daughter of Inez Briggs - also known as Inez Clarke.

But what about the 1910 affidavit filed by Mary, denying the existence of her children? The reason for this will likely never be known, but we can say almost for certain that she did have a daughter named Inez and that she is buried under that beautiful statue in Graceland Cemetery.

But does she rest in peace?

In 2007, accusations were made that Inez Clarke - who was not found in the cemetery records - was a fictional character. If that was true, then this meant the stories that had been told for years about her ghost haunting her gravesite were fictional, too.

Strange sounds - like laughter and disembodied weeping - had been reported near her grave for many years, and some even claimed that the statue of the little girl moved under its own power. It was said that the statue of Inez would sometimes vanish from inside of the glass box. Many years ago, a night watchman for the Pinkerton agency stated that he was making his rounds one night discovered that the box that held Inez's statue was empty. He left the cemetery that night, never to return. Other guards have also reported it missing, only to find it back in place when they pass by again, or the following morning.

The stories were called into question when researchers exposed the "truth" about Inez Clarke, but when further research revealed that Inez Briggs had once been a real-life little girl, they suddenly didn't seem so wild after all.

Does the spirit of little Inez still manifest around her grave? The stories of the haunting certainly haven't stopped. Recent accounts maintain that visitors to Graceland still sometimes see a child playing among the gravestones in the part of the cemetery where he grave can be found. She disappears whenever she is approached, though.

Inez only seems interested in entertaining herself.

The Black Angel of Oakland Cemetery

In Oakland Cemetery, on the north side of Iowa City, Iowa, stands a foreboding, mysterious statue. Locals tell tales of the mysterious powers and the curse that is linked to the strange monument.

For those who have grown up in the area, a nighttime visit to the "Black Angel" is almost a rite of passage, a necessary part of growing up and facing your darkest fears. Most can recite dark tales about the statue's frightening past, but they dismiss the story is nothing more than a local urban legend.

But the Black Angel is not just a legend. It has a very real history and one that might convince you there is reason to be afraid.

Teresa Feldevert commissioned the bronze statue in 1911 as a monument for both her husband, Nicholas and her teenaged son, Eddie. Many consider it to be one of the greatest works of art in the region,

The infamous Black Angel of Oakland Cemetery in Iowa City

having been created by Daniel Chester French, the same sculptor responsible for the gigantic statue of Abraham Lincoln at the memorial in Washington.

No one knows how the stories of death and curses got started, but perhaps they have something to do with the appearance of the statue itself. The eyes of the figure are truly eerie with swirled irises that seem to bulge from the blankness of the rest of the eye. They seem to stare at the visitor from beneath strangely drooping eyelids - an effect that can be very unnerving. The sheer size of the statue does little to convince the visitor of the angel's celestial goodwill either. Some claim that looking directly into the mysterious eyes of the Angel at midnight will result in a fatal curse upon the gazer.

Unlike most angelic graveyard art, the Black Angel is staring at the ground, and her wings point downwards. The imposing figure seems to be making no effort towards entering Heaven. Instead, she remains here on Earth, standing as a reminder of pain and death, and inflicting those very things upon those who disrespect her.

And then there's the color. The statue was made from bronze, so why does it look so ominous? Stories associated with the statue always address its mysterious change in color. Over time, the mournful winged angel has transformed from its brilliant bronze tint to its dark and foreboding black hue. All attempts to restore the statue to its original gleaming incarnation have failed, and the Angel continues to get darker and more eerie looking with each passing year.

There are a few legends that attempt to explain this drastic change. One story says that the matriarch of the family beneath the angel, Teresa Feldevert, was a witch in life. Her evil was so great that even in death, it managed to taint the monument directly above her. Another legend states that when Teresa's husband buried her, he swore never to dishonor her memory by sleeping with another woman. As time went on and he managed to move past his grief, he found another sweetheart and slept with her. This breaking of his graveside promise resulted in the Black Angel's discoloration.

Of course, neither of those stories are true. Teresa was the one who commissioned the statue when her husband died - not the other way around - and there's no evidence to suggest that she was a witch.

Regardless of why the Angel turned back or even why it's cursed - there are a slew of stories about the dangers that the statue poses for the living. Many legends involve kissing in front of the statue at midnight. It is said that if a girl is kissed directly in front of the Angel, the statue will return its original golden color - but only if that girl is a virgin. But another legend says that any girl kissed in front of the monument will die within six months.

One girl who should never be kissed is the Black Angel herself. It's said that any man foolish enough to attempt this feat will die instantly. Even touching the Black Angel reportedly results in the offender coming down with a mysterious and incurable illness. Anyone who attempts to vandalize the statue will also be struck down. One story says that a group of men once urinated on the statue and got in a fatal car accident on their way home from the cemetery that very night.

Are any of these stories true? I couldn't say. It's doubtful but consider the idea that almost every wild legend usually has some kernel of truth at the heart of it. What's the truth to be found when it comes to the Black Angel of Oakland Cemetery? I don't know, but I don't plan on waiting around the cemetery until midnight to find out!

The Curse of "Black Aggie"

When General Felix Agnus, the publisher of the *Baltimore American* newspaper, died in 1925, he was buried in Pikesville, Maryland's Druid Ridge Cemetery, right outside of Baltimore. On his grave was placed a rather strange statue. It was a large, black mourning figure that was dubbed "Grief."

In the daylight hours, the figure was regarded as a beautiful but eerie addition to the graveyard art of the cemetery. The sculptor was one of the premier artisans in Maryland at the turn-of-the-century, and the statue was highly regarded - at least until darkness fell and the legends began.

Augustus St. Gaudens was a premier American sculptor of the late nineteenth century. Before his death in 1907, he created some of the most honored works in America, including the figure of Diana that once topped Madison Square Garden and monuments to American heroes and statesmen like Lincoln and Sherman. One of his most personal pieces of work was a memorial for Marian Adams, the wife of Henry Adams. Marian, called "Clover" by her friends, had fallen into a dark depression after the death of her father in 1885. In December of that year, she committed suicide by drinking potassium.

Henry Adams plunged into despair and in search of comfort, traveled to Japan in June 1886 with his friend, artist John La Farge. When he returned from his trip, he decided to replace the simple headstone that he had ordered for his beloved "Clover" in Washington's Rock Creek Cemetery with a more elaborate memorial. He turned to St. Gaudens and asked him to create something with an "eastern" feel to it, perhaps combining the images of the Buddha with the work of Michelangelo.

The endeavor took over four years, frustrating Adams, but created what some called "one of the most powerful and expressive pieces in the history of American art, before or since." It was placed in the cemetery in 1891, and Adams was delighted with both the design and the setting. The statue was never officially named - most just called it the "Adams Memorial" - but later it gained the popular name of "Grief." The stories for this nickname vary. Some say that the statue was eventually named by St. Gaudens himself, and others say the name was coined by Mark Twain, who viewed the memorial in 1906.

The monument created a stir and provided grist for the rumor mill. People talked about the death of Marian Adams and her husband's strange reaction to it. He had discovered her body collapsed in front of the fireplace in their Lafayette Square home in Washington. He never discussed the circumstances of her suicide, and when Adams wrote his autobiography, Marian was never mentioned. As time passed, he spent less and less time in their former home, and neighbors began to claim that it was haunted. At dusk, they reported the sounds of a woman weeping inside of the dark mansion, and even after it was sold later, residents claimed to experience a persistent cold spot in front of the fireplace. They could never explain this, especially when the fireplace was piled high with burning logs. Another story claimed that the apparition of Marian could sometimes be seen sitting in a wooden rocking chair in her old bedroom. It was said that she often appeared in front of several witnesses at one time, and a terrible feeling of loneliness would overwhelm each of them. In moments, the ghost would simply fade away. Stories are still told about the house today.

Adams never even publicly acknowledged the enigmatic monument. He didn't name it and never used its nickname. Thanks to his silence and the fame of his esteemed political family - he was the grandson of President John Quincy Adams - there was a great curiosity about the monument. Adams made things worse by refusing to have Marian's name inscribed on it and then having a wall of trees and shrubs planted around it to make it harder to find. Of course, curiosity-seekers were up for the challenge, making it even more of a must-see site. Public interest was fueled by word of mouth, guidebooks, and magazine articles.

It was almost inevitable that the design of the statue would be stolen.

Within a few months of the statue being placed on Marian's grave, Adams reported that someone had apparently made a plaster casting of the piece. He wrote to Edward Robinson that "Even now, the head of the figure bears evident traces of some surreptitious casting, which the workmen did not even take the pains to wash off."

He was right. Within months of the cast, sculptor Edward L.A. Pausch began mass-producing an unauthorized copy of "Grief," and they began to be sold through monument catalogs across the country. Even today, copies of the statue can be found in hundreds of cemeteries, but there is only one copy that has gained even more notoriety than the original.

General Felix Agnus purchased the Pausch copy of the sculpture in 1905, perhaps after having admired the original work at the Adams grave.

Agnus was born in France in 1839. At the age of only 13, he traveled around the world and, at 20, fought in the army of Napoleon III against Austria and later served with General Garibaldi's forces in Italy. In 1860, he came to New York and went to work as a silver chaser and sculptor at Tiffany's. When the Civil War broke out, he enlisted as a private in the Union Army and began a war record so incredible that he was promoted to the rank of Brigadier General by age 26. He saw action in dozens of battles, including Big Bethel, Richmond, the Siege of Port Hudson, and the Battle of Gaines' Mills. He was wounded 12 times by both bullet and saber. His friend, writer H.L. Mencken, later said that Agnus "had so much lead in him that he rattled when he walked."

After a severe shoulder injury at Gaines' Mills, then Lieutenant Agnus was sent to Baltimore for treatment. There, he met Charles Carroll Fulton, the publisher of the *Baltimore American*, and his daughter, Annie, who nursed Agnus back to health. Fulton had met the young officer at the Pratt Street Pier when the medical steamer docked and had taken him to his home for care and rest. When the war was over, Agnus returned to Baltimore and asked Annie to marry him. She quickly accepted. After that, Agnus continued his remarkable career,

Black Aggie as she looked in 1966. As the stories claimed, no grass would grow in front of the monument.

Courtesy of Pat Bailey

working briefly in the Internal Revenue Service, then as Consul to Londonderry, Ireland, for the United States Senate. He later left this position to take over for his father-in-law at the newspaper. He remained the publisher of the newspaper until his death.

In 1905, Agnus began construction of a family monument in Druid Ridge Cemetery. It was during this time that he purchased the copy of "Grief" and then had a monument and pedestal created that would closely match the setting of the Adams Memorial in Washington. The first burial in the family plot was that of the General's mother, who had been brought over from France.

A year later, the widow of the artist Augustus St. Gaudens sent a letter to Henry Adams to inform him of the poor reproduction of "Grief" that was in Druid Ridge Cemetery. There was nothing legally that could be done about the theft of the design, but St. Gauden's widow traveled to Baltimore to see it for herself. She discovered a nearly identical statue, seated on a similar stone, but with the name "Agnus" inscribed on the base. She found the whole thing tasteless and publicly declared that General Agnus "must be a good deal of a barbarian to copy a work of art in such a way."

I'm assuming that she had no idea just how many copies had been made of the statue. If she found out, that might have been too much for her to handle.

Agnus quickly responded to her and claimed to be the innocent victim of unscrupulous art dealers. The artist's widow then requested that he give up the sculpture and file suit against the art dealers. Agnus did sue - and was awarded $4,500 - but he refused to give up the copy of the statue.

His wife, Annie, died in 1922, and Agnus himself died three years later at the age of 86. He was laid to rest next to his wife at the feet of the statue. A short time later, "Aggie," as she would come to be known, became a legend.

While the Agnus Monument seemed innocent enough in the daylight, those who encountered the statue in the darkness, added to her nickname and dubbed her "Black Aggie." They saw her as a symbol of terror, and her legend grew. Stories sometimes appeared in the newspaper about the statue, but the legend really spread through word of mouth. As time went on, the stories got wilder and more menacing.

Black Aggie's eyes would glow red at the stroke of midnight. The spirits of the dead rose from their graves and gathered around her on certain nights and that anyone who dared to return her gaze was struck blind. Pregnant women who passed through her shadow - where, incidentally grass didn't grow - suffered miscarriages.

A local college fraternity decided to include Black Aggie in their initiation rites. Candidates for membership were ordered to spend the night in the cold embrace of Black Aggie - sitting on her lap until daybreak. According to one story, "she once came to life and crushed a hapless freshman in her powerful grasp."

Some ventured into Druid Ridge at night to test their courage by visiting Black Aggie. One night, at the stroke of midnight, the cemetery watchman heard a scream in the darkness. When he reached the Agnus grave, he found a young man lying dead at the foot of the statue. He had died of fright - or so the story goes.

One morning in 1962, a watchman discovered that one of the statue's arms had been cut off during the night. The missing arm was later found in the trunk of a sheet metal worker's car, along with a saw. He told the judge that Black Aggie had cut off her own arm in a fit of grief and had given it to him. The judge wasn't buying it, and the man went to jail.

But there were a lot of people who did believe the man's strange story. After the incident, huge groups of people began gathering in the cemetery at night until the police finally had to send them home. The public attention brought Black Aggie new followers, and her reputation grew.

Years ago, a man that I always refer to simply as "Frank" told me about his first-hand encounter with Aggie. Frank grew up in New Jersey bout heard the stories about Black Aggie and took a trip from Atlantic City to Baltimore with two friends to see her for himself. The trip was also meant to be a reunion with three Baltimore girls they'd met earlier in the summer. The group decided to do some sightseeing and, of course, one of the top attractions on Frank's list was getting a look at Black Aggie. The girls directed them to the cemetery and told them some of the local stories.

Frank and his pals walked over for a closer look. The girls said that people often left coins in Aggie's hands for good luck. As Frank was digging in his pocket for a dime, but friend, Freddy, thought it would be funny to snuff out a cigarette in Aggie's hand instead.

Frank told me later: "We told him not to, but Freddy just laughed. He didn't believe in any of that stuff. But about ten years later, Freddy was found in a dump in South Carolina. He'd been shot in the back of the head, Mafia-style. They never found out who did it."

Frank paused for a moment and appeared thoughtful. "It's been many years now, but I will never forget the feeling that I had standing in front of Aggie that night - as if she knew the future and could see what lay ahead for us."

The lurid tales of Black Aggie brought scores of people to trample the Agnus gravesite. The suburb of Pikesville, where the cemetery was located, was relatively isolated in those days, so it was easy to get in and out of the cemetery without trouble. The site was visited - and often vandalized - by thousands of people over several decades. In addition to the statue's arm being stolen, hundreds of names and messages were scrawled on the statue, the granite base, and the wall behind Aggie.

Cemetery officials did all they could to discourage visitors. They even planted thorny shrubs around the site. There is no indication as to why the cemetery was not better patrolled at night, but perhaps they just couldn't afford it. For every trespasser arrested, dozens of others managed to reach the statue - and left their mark behind.

Eventually, the number of nighttime visitors and the destruction they caused became too much for the cemetery to handle. By the 1960s, it had gotten so bad that the descendants of Felix Agnus elected to donate Black Aggie to the Maryland Institute of Art Museum. For some reason, though, the donation fell through, and the statue remained at the Agnus plot until 1967. On March 18, the Agnus family donated Aggie to the Smithsonian Institution for display.

For many years, this donation would prove to be a mystery for those of us who attempted to track down the whereabouts of Black Aggie. According to the Smithsonian, they didn't have her. Despite some people who claimed that Aggie was displayed in the National Gallery for a brief period, officials at the Smithsonian stated they had never displayed her at all. There was some suggestion that perhaps the Smithsonian learned of Aggie's mysterious past and decided not to put her on display - just in case.

"Maybe, just maybe," wrote a columnist for the *Baltimore Sun*, "they're not taking any chances."

The solution to the mystery would not be that strange. At some point, the staff at the Smithsonian gave Aggie away, which explains why she does not appear in their records. They had no interest in displaying her and instead, gave her to the National Museum of American Art, where she was then put into storage. For years, she remained in a dusty storeroom, shrouded in cobwebs.

Then, in 1996, a young Baltimore area writer named Shara Terjung did a story on Black Aggie for a small local newspaper. After having been fascinated with the legends, she became determined to track down the present location of the statue. Finally, shortly after Halloween, she got a call from a contact at the General Service

Administration who was able to discover where the elusive Aggie had ended up. The statue can still be seen today at the Federal Courts building in Washington, in the rear courtyard of the Dolly Madison house. She remains there now, seated on a stone pedestal gazing forlornly at those who cross her path.

Black Aggie may be gone from Druid Ridge Cemetery, but she's certainly not forgotten. "We still have people coming to Druid Ridge, asking for Black Aggie all the time," said one of the cemetery spokesmen in an interview. "I don't think there's a week that goes by when we don't get a call about it."

The Agnus gravesite is well cared for today and shows little sign of the disturbance of the past. Grass grows now in the place where for many years, it did not. The only lingering evidence of Black Aggie is a chipped area on the granite pedestal and a faint shadow where she once rested.

Well, that's the lingering evidence that can be seen.

Is there more? Who knows? Whether Aggie's old resting place is haunted or not, the mysterious statue has left an indelible mark on Druid Ridge Cemetery and in the annals of the supernatural in America, as well.

4. GHOSTS FROM AMERICAN GRAVEYARDS

Fear about the uncertainty of the afterlife is deeply rooted in human nature, but as we all know, fear fascinates all of us. There is probably no greater fear than death. Throughout history, the mystery of death has captivated writers, artists, scientists, philosophers, and theologians. Symbols and stories about death permeate our great works of art, our architecture, our literature, and our folklore. Our interest in death, along with what may lie beyond, is reflected in our popular culture, with books and films that present spooky and transcendent themes of the afterlife, ghosts, and creatures that return from the dead. Many of these themes are ancient, hearkening back to times when people not only believed in miracles but also felt a deep connection to nature and a sense of being surrounded by unseen entities.

Combine these things, and it's easy to understand how stories of haunted cemeteries first came about. Our fear of death - mixed with our fear of ghosts and monsters - created a natural inclination to see a graveyard as a place where few would want to venture, especially after dark.

But are graveyard tales merely folklore and legend? Are they just stories, nervous fictions created to patch up holes in an incomplete narrative to explain why we "whistle past the boneyard at night?" Perhaps. People do it in every town across America, even today. They create stories to explain things like why a woman in white is seen along a certain stretch of highway, or why a certain tombstone leans just a little too far to the left. We might never claim to be writers, but every one of us is filled with stories.

But can we say that are *all* just stories? What happens when the solid clues start to add up to be something tangible? Is it okay then to feel afraid?

Yes.

We can call these stories rumors and folklore all we want, but when the evidence is right there, staring us in the face, it's time to consider what we honestly believe in.

Don't misunderstand - some graveyard stories are harder to believe than others, but, as we have already established, almost every legend has a kernel of truth at its heart.

Are you willing to gamble on which part of the legend is true?

Ephraim Gray's Empty Grave

Ephraim Gray was a reclusive older man who lived in Malden, Massachusetts, in the mid-nineteenth century. Gray was a mystery to the people who lived in town. He seemed to have no employment or visible means of support, and yet he was never without money to spend. He lived in an old, dark house near the center of town, and his only companion was his butler, a faithful, tight-lipped man who conducted all of Gray's business for him. Gray had never been married and, in fact, had never been seen in the company of any woman.

Gray kept to himself. He was only ever seen peering out the windows of his large house or glimpsed puttering around the backyard, hidden by a fence and a wild row of shrubs. Aside from that, he rarely left the mansion - but people knew he was there.

They often commented on the strong chemical smell that came from the property. Rumor had it that the noxious odors were so powerful that people literally became sick after inhaling them. They asked each other what Gray could be doing in that rambling old house, but no one knew. He remained a mystery until - and after - his death.

One morning in 1850, Gray's butler walked into the Malden police station to inform the authorities that his master had died. When he had tried to awaken him that morning, he discovered that Gray had died peacefully in his sleep.

Whispers about what Gray's will may contain spread rapidly. Since he had no family, his entire estate had been left to his butler. The only condition was that the man had to make sure that nothing happened to Gray's body before he could be buried. He did not want any harm to come to his corpse - no autopsy or attempt at preservation. Gray's will stated that, as a chemist, he had been working on a formula that he believed would guarantee eternal life. If he should die before it was completed, though, the formula would be used to maintain his corpse in perfect condition for centuries. The patent for the mixture was also given to his servant. He would become extraordinarily rich, the will said, with the formula for the embalming chemicals alone. Knowing this, the butler was determined to make sure that Gray's last wishes were carried out.

The formula that Gray had created for "eternal life" - or at least to mummify his corpse - will always remain a mystery because his butler never had time to market it. He died soon after his master did, and the formula, along with Gray's eccentric claims, were eventually forgotten.

Twenty years later, though, a medical student at Harvard University heard a strange and intriguing story from a friend who had grown up in Malden. He only recalled portions of the story but told his friend about a strange inventor and his mysterious formula for preservation. A group of students was gathered one night - and I'll imagine there was alcohol involved - and decided to pay a visit to Ephraim Gray's tomb in the cemetery in Malden.

They easily found it in the darkness, forced the door open, and went inside. By the light of a lantern, they opened the casket and looked in on Gray's corpse. To their surprise, he looked very much alive, as if he were only sleeping. There were no signs of decay on the body, even after two decades.

The students closed the tomb and returned to Cambridge. They decided to keep their excursion a secret but were determined to discover Gray's secret formula. Unfortunately, though, all their discreet inquiries led nowhere. The young doctor from Malden found that the formula had been lost after Gray's death. His butler had died before the secret could be revealed.

But there is one final twist to the story.

In the early 1900s, the Malden Cemetery had to be relocated to make way for a new road construction project. The work went according to plan - until they reached the tomb of Ephraim Gray.

When his casket was opened, it was found that his body was missing.

An investigation that lasted for several weeks followed, but the case remains unsolved a century later. The authorities could find no evidence that the crypt had been opened or the body removed without leaving any trace behind. The seal that the medical students had used years earlier remains unbroken. So, what happened to the well-preserved corpse of Ephraim Gray?

Had the medical students, intrigued by the possibilities of the strange preservation formula, returned to steal the body? Or could, as it appeared, Gray have simply revived after 20 years in "hibernation" and walked out of his own tomb?

The questions remain unanswered today, but logically speaking, it would have been impossible for Gray to have awakened and walked out of his tomb after all those years - right?

Maybe, or maybe not.

Poe and the Haunted Catacombs

I love Baltimore, Maryland - I always have. It's a place of history, hauntings, crab cakes, Fell's Point, Bertha's Mussels, and the last place that Edgar Allan Poe ever walked the earth - in physical form, anyway.

Poe - one of America's most celebrated horror and mystery authors and poets - continues to intrigue us, even more than a century and a half after his death. There has never been another writer like him and much about his life - and his death - remains a mystery, which is probably just how he would have wanted it.

Even the cemetery where Poe was buried - twice, by the way - is mysterious. It is one of the strangest on the East Coast, largely because many people are unaware that a portion of it exists. It is called the Old Western Burial Ground, and, besides Poe, it holds the remains of Francis Scott Key's son, the grandfather of President James Buchanan, five former mayors of Baltimore, and 15 generals from the Revolutionary War and the War of 1812.

Edgar Allan Poe

When the Westminster Presbyterian Church - now Westminster Hall - was built over a portion of the cemetery nearly a century after it was started, many of the graves and tombs disappeared. They didn't vanish, though. They were simply relocated underground - into the catacombs that exist under the building. It's an eerie place and one that is filled with a history of ghosts.

But the ghosts are not the strangest elements of this historic burial ground. There are many mysteries here.

Legends say that the ghost of Edgar Allan Poe has been seen lurking near his grave in this cemetery. First, we'd have to ask - which grave? He actually has two. His original grave is in the back of the

Poe's original burial site at Westminster Burial Ground

cemetery, where he was interred under a stone that had a carving of a raven on it. Years later, when cemetery officials realized that Poe's grave was a big draw for the graveyard, he was moved to a new resting place - with a much larger stone - just inside of the front gates.

Poe died in Baltimore at the age of only 40. He no longer lived in the city, and what he may have been doing there remains just one of the mysteries surrounding his death. He was supposed to be on his way to New York to meet his former mother-in-law, Maria Clemm, with whom he had remained close after the death of his first wife from tuberculosis years before. Poe planned to accompany her to Richmond, Virginia, where he planned to re-marry. He never made it to New York.

On October 3, Poe was found lying in the gutter and was taken to Washington Medical College, where he died on Sunday, October 7, 1849, at 5:00 in the morning. Poe was never coherent long enough to explain how he came to be in his dire condition, or, oddly, why he was wearing clothes that were not his own. Poe is said to have repeatedly called out the name "Reynolds" on the night before his death, though it is unclear to whom he was referring.

All medical records, including his death certificate, have been lost. Newspapers at the time reported Poe's death as "congestion of the brain" or "cerebral inflammation," which were common euphemisms for deaths from disreputable causes such as alcoholism. Speculative causes of his death range from heart disease, epilepsy, syphilis, rabies, mistaken identity, and outright murder.

Perhaps fittingly, we'll never know for sure.

Is it his unexplained death, or the disturbance of his resting place, that has caused his spirit to linger behind at the cemetery?

Or could it be that something else is keeping him here?

In the 1930s, a macabre tradition began each year on January 19, the birthdate of Edgar Allan Poe. A man who unofficially became known as the "Poe Toaster" began making nocturnal appearances at the author's grave.

The shadowy figure, dressed in black with a wide-brimmed hat, white scarf, and silver-tipped cane, would pour himself a glass of cognac and raise a toast to Poe's memory, then vanish into the night, leaving three roses in a distinctive arrangement and the unfinished bottle of cognac. Poe fans gathered every year in hopes of getting a glimpse of the Toaster, who never sought publicity and was rarely seen or photographed. Each time he came, he visited Poe's original stone and left roses that were believed to represent Poe, his wife, Virginia, and his mother-in-law, Maria Clemm.

On several occasions, the Toaster left a note along with the roses and cognac. Some notes were simple expressions of devotion, such as "Edgar, I haven't forgotten you." In 1993, a cryptic message stated, "The torch will be passed." In 1999, a note announced that the original Toaster had died the previous year and had passed the tradition to "a son." Subsequent eyewitnesses noted that the post-1998 Toaster appeared to be a younger individual.

The identity of the man was an intriguing mystery for years. Many people, including Jeff Jerome, the curator of the nearby Edgar Allan Poe house, did his best to protect the identity of the Toaster. He was quoted as saying that if he had his way, the man's identity would never be known.

For some time, rumors persisted that Jerome was the mysterious man in black, so in 1983, he invited 70 people to gather at the graveyard at midnight on January 19. They had a celebration in honor of the author's birthday with a glass of amontillado - the Spanish sherry featured in one of Poe's horror tales - and readings from the author's works. At about an hour past midnight, the celebrants were startled to see a man run through the cemetery in a black frock coat. He was fair-haired and carrying a walking stick and quickly disappeared around

The infrared photo taken of the "Poe Toaster" in 1990

the cemetery's east wall. The roses and cognac were found on Poe's grave, as usual.

Not to solve the mystery, but merely to enhance it, Jerome allowed a photographer to try and capture the elusive man on film. The photographer was backed by *LIFE* Magazine and was equipped with infrared night-vision photo equipment. A radio signal triggered the camera so that the photographer could remain out of sight. The picture appeared in the July 1990 issue of *LIFE* and showed the back of a heavyset man kneeling at Poe's grave. His face, shadowed by the black hat, was unrecognizable. The Toaster was never photographed again.

The tradition continued for a few more years after the 1998 announcement, but it was never the same again. Subsequent notes predicted a win for the Baltimore Ravens in the Super Bowl and, in 2004, was critical of France's opposition to the war in Iraq. Jeff Jerome suggested that the later notes reflected an unwillingness of the "son" to take the tradition as seriously as had the father. A final note– left sometime between 2005 and 2008– was so dismaying, Jerome said, that he decided to fib and announced that no note had been left. He declined to reveal its contents, other than that it was a hint, in hindsight, that an end to the tradition was imminent.

Meanwhile, a group of onlookers unsuccessfully attempted to intercept the Poe Toaster in 2006, breaking a long-standing tradition in Baltimore to never interfere with the Toaster's entry, tribute ritual, or departure. It was the only time that it ever happened.

Then, in 2007, a man came forward who claimed to be the Toaster. The man, a 92-year-old named Sam Porpora, claimed that he had started the Poe Toaster tradition. A former historian for Baltimore's Westminster Church, Porpora claimed that he invented the Toaster in the 1960s as a "publicity stunt," to reinvigorate the church and its congregation, and had falsely told a reporter at the time that it had begun in 1949. However, Porpora's claims turned out to be more fanciful than many of Poe's stories. Reports of the annual visits dated from well before the 1960s. For example, a 1950 article in the *Baltimore Evening* Sun mentions "an anonymous citizen who creeps in annually to place an empty bottle (of excellent label)" against the gravestone." After the many errors were pointed out in his stories - which changed every time he told them - Popora admitted that he'd made it up.

In 2009, the Poe Toaster returned to mark the bicentennial of Poe's birth, but he didn't leave a note behind. It became the last "official" visit of the Poe Toaster to the author's grave. It was believed that the bicentennial of his birth was a fitting time to bring the tradition to an end.

Since then, however, the Maryland Historical Society and Poe Baltimore have decided to hold auditions for a new "Toaster." He first started appearing a year later and, keeping with the old tradition, his identity has been kept secret. Although this watered-down version of the Toaster isn't nearly as compelling as the men who carried on the tradition on their own, at least it keeps the mystery of Edgar Allan Poe alive for new generations to ponder.

Poe's death - and the mystery Toaster - maybe be the most famous mysteries associated with the Western Burial Ground, but they

The spooky catacombs beneath Westminster Hall

are not the only ones. The catacomb beneath the church holds secrets of its own. While restored and kept in good condition today, visitors to this place will still experience an eerie shudder as they walk about this gothic chamber of horrors. Graves and crypts hold the bodies of those long since deceased and yet stories of the not so distant past tell of unexplained exhumations and a strange fascination that drew a number of people to commit suicide here in the years between 1890 and 1920.

I have been lucky enough to visit the catacomb several times over the years, and it's a fascinating and spooky spot. While I had no supernatural encounters while roaming the catacombs and tunnels, others have not been so lucky. There are a number of stories told of visitors who have felt icy spots that have no explanation have felt the soft caress of unseen hands and have heard the startling whispers from voices that simply don't exist.

Guided tours of the subterranean cemetery are available, but organized searches for ghosts in the catacombs have been few. I was a part of several of them myself. One outing, in August 1976, brought ten ghost hunters to the graveyard in search of the ghost of a little girl who has been reported here for decades.

Robert Thompson, the leader of the group and at that time, behind a drive to restore the cemetery, stated that while the ghost hunters didn't spot the small spirit, the investigation did not come up empty.

"We didn't see anything," he recalled in an interview, "but we sure heard things.... like footsteps. It scared the heck out of me is what it did".

Legends of Memory Hill

Located in the town of Milledgeville, Georgia is Memory Hill Cemetery, a small, 20-acre piece of land that was set aside as a graveyard back in 1803. This historic site holds the remains of many historic Georgians, including the famed southern author Flannery O'Connor.

And, if the stories are true, it holds a few ghosts, too.

One unusual resident of the cemetery is William Fish, who once lived in the town of Hardwick, just outside of Milledgeville. In 1872, Fish's wife and daughter contracted typhoid, and both died slow and agonizing deaths. In despair, Fish constructed a brick mausoleum for their bodies. For the next several months, he continued to mourn, unable to overcome his depression. Not long after the mausoleum was finally completed, he placed his old rocking chair inside of it, closed the iron door, sat down in the chair, and shot himself with a revolver. His body was placed next to his wife and daughter, but his rest was not a peaceful one.

Legends of the cemetery say that if a visitor knocks on the iron door of the small crypt, sometimes an answering knock will be heard in reply. It's merely William Fish, they say, letting you know that he is still watching over his wife and daughter.

But the most famous grave in Memory Hill belongs to a "witch."

Her name was Dixie Haygood when she was born in Milledgeville in 1861, but she would become famous under her stage name, Annie Abbott. The stories say that Dixie possessed amazing

Part of Dixie's act was using psychic power to make it so that three strong men would be unable to lift her off the ground. There were a lot of things that passed for entertainment in those days...

supernatural powers - although others claim that she was simply a skilled stage magician who took her secrets to the grave.

After seeing Lulu Hurst perform as the "Georgia Wonder" in 1884, Dixie developed a version of an act that was known as the "human magnet." It involved her displacing objects that were held securely by one or more strong men. Dixie became a huge success, mostly because she was a small, slender woman, which made her performances seem miraculous. During this era of the Spiritualist movement, she often claimed to be a gifted psychic medium. It was, she said, the spirits who created the bizarre effects.

It was said that she could cause a piano to move about a room and chairs to rise into the air. While in a trance, she could find lost objects for members of the audiences who came to see her, and she had an ability that could prevent five men from lifting her small body off the floor. On one occasion, Dixie was said to have lifted a table holding several men and was able to command the chairs around it to leave the room. Her audience watched in amazement as one by one, the chairs slid off the stage. Some of the spectators even checked to make sure there was nothing physically propelling them. Dixie would often simply place her hands on the back of a chair and, without holding onto it, make it rise from the floor. A dozen men were unable to break her hold on the object without twisting or jerking it away from her.

In 1886, her husband, a deputy marshal named Charles Haygood, was shot and killed on duty, leaving her as the sole earner for their three children. They never went hungry.

Dixie was an inventive self-promoter and numerous media outlets reporting on the physical tricks that made her act possible, her popularity was undiminished.

In 1888, Dixie had married again, this time a man named T.D. Embry, but that marriage also ended in tragedy. While in Cincinnati on tour, Embry told Dixie that he was afraid that she would lose her money, so he volunteered his services as treasurer of the family. Dixie allowed him to have $600 - all she had at the time - and she never saw him again. Embry had someone write letters to her, saying that he was dead, but while Dixie was visiting some relatives in Kentucky, she learned that he was alive and well in Mississippi. The couple was soon divorced.

But Dixie had no intention of sitting at home, worrying about her lost husband. In the 1890s, Dixie was invited to perform in London, and her successful six-week run there led to a two-year European tour. During this period, she performed for numerous world leaders, including Kaiser Wilhelm II of the German Empire, Emperor Franz Josef I of Austria-Hungary, and Tsar Alexander III of the Russian Empire, Queen Victoria, governors of Georgia, and presidents of the United States.

Dixie returned home with fame, jewels, and extravagant gifts from aboard - which made her a target for thieves. She was robbed on several occasions, including in one incident in New York when a thief made off with a satchel that contained nearly $30,000 in jewels.

Worse, in 1897, Dixie was robbed by a man who worked in a local freight yard and had an accomplice - Dixie's 14-year-old son, Fred. Both were locked up for stealing diamonds, watches, and other jewelry from a trunk in her bedroom. When Fred was returned home, Dixie threw her arms around him and wept, exclaiming, "Oh, Fred, how could you do your mother so?" Then she fainted and fell to the floor.

For a while in 1906, Dixie's friends and family thought she died in the massive earthquake that struck San Francisco. She hadn't, but she had gotten married again. This time, she married a man who was soon arrested for bigamy, charged with marrying Dixie while his wife, Lulu F. Day, was locked up in an insane asylum.

Lulu and Dixie met each other and compared notes. They were friendly at first, but then Dixie took out warrants on Lulu for allegedly stealing photos and trinkets from her. Lulu then sued Dixie for $10,000 in damages for slander. Neither case went anywhere.

At some point, Dixie came back home to Georgia and settled in a house in Macon. In 1912, it was reported in the newspaper that Dixie said she "thinks her power, which she terms magnetism, is dwindling and does not know whether she could perform the feats of strength now that she was capable of several years ago."

That same year, she took her son Fred to court and accused him of threatening her with a pistol. She also claimed he was not her biological son and that she adopted him shortly after the death of her real son.

Was Dixie losing her mind - or was something else going on?

Days after all the charges against him were dropped, Fred filed a writ of lunacy for his mother, and she was booked into the county jail. In court that summer, he told jurymen that she "would go into the back yard in the wee hours of the morning and there, in utter darkness, remain for hours at a time playing with toads."

While Dixie was behind bars, Fred sold her land and received only a few hundred dollars after her creditors and lawyers were paid. There was no mention of jewelry or anything else. Was it all gone? Did Fred steal it? Or had Dixie lost it herself, perhaps as she slowly going insane?

We may never know. Legends in Milledgeville claim that Dixie was once an inmate of the State Central Hospital for the Mentally Insane, but there are no records to say this was true. What we do know is that she was released from jail after 13 days, and she died three years later. In a brief obituary, it was mentioned that Dixie was a "mysterious actress who appeared before virtually all the royal houses of the world."

Her fame had vanished with her money.

Dixie was buried in an unmarked grave beneath a cedar tree in Memory Hill Cemetery, but her story wasn't over yet.

Some stories claim that before her death, Dixie put curses on some of the families she knew when she was growing up - families who never took her seriously, some say. One of those was the Yates family, whose burial plot is located near the tree under which Dixie was buried - and where her spirit is believed to linger.

For the past century or so, a sinkhole has appeared in the Yates' plot every year just before Christmas. The hole has been so bad that the gravestone of Mr. Yates and one of his daughters sometimes sinks out of sight. Many blame this odd phenomenon on the winter rains, and in the past, city crews have filled the hole with cement, gravel, and stones. No matter what they do, though, the hole always comes back.

Could it be the curse of the "witch," Dixie Haygood? Or is it merely a case of a story that has been created to explain something that no one can understand?

You can decide that answer for yourself.

The Graveyard Light

There is no question that the state of Georgia is a very haunted place. Ghost stories here abound, both in the small towns and in the large cities. One haven for ghost lore is a line of islands that stretch along the southeastern shoreline of the state. These islands are rich in legend, lore, history, and hauntings, but none of them can claim as many ghost stories as St. Simon's Island.

The stories on the island had been passed on for generations. There is the story of "Mary the Wanderer," a grieving woman who roams the deserted roadways in a search for her drowned lover. There are the ghosts of the Africans who were brought to America as slaves but chose to take their own lives rather than give up their freedom. Still wearing their chains, they walked off into Dunbar Creek, and some say their chanting can still be heard along the water today. There is the St. Simons Lighthouse, where the ghost of a former lightkeeper still walks up and down the staircase. There is also the former owner of Kelvyn Grove Plantation, who wanders the grounds, looking for the man who killed him.

Christ Church Cemetery on St. Simon's Island, Georgia

But none of these hauntings are as famous as the mysterious light that appears in Christ Church Cemetery. Nearly everyone who lives on the island can tell you a version of the woman whose fear of the dark prompted her husband to place a lighted candle on her grave every night after her death.

A candle that continues to return many decades later.

Emma had always been afraid of the dark. When she was a child, her father initially took her fear lightly. He assured her that there was no reason to be afraid, but even a few moments in darkness would have his little girl screaming in terror. At the child's insistence, a servant placed a lighted candle by her bedside every night. Emma's father indulged this for years, always believing she would overcome her fear when she was older. But she didn't. Finally, his patience at an end, he ordered her to bed one night without the candle.

Emma's nanny reluctantly put the candle away. At bedtime, she put out the lamp and closed the door, and then hurried from the house so that she would not have to hear Emma's screams. The child wailed and cried for hours, but her father forbade his wife, or any other member of the household, to go and comfort her. At last, he could stand it no more and went to Emma himself. He was determined to harshly stop her crying, but when he found the girl in hysterical tears, he embraced her instead. Emma collapsed into his arms, and his anger vanished. He left a candle burning next to her bed and quietly left the room. From that time on, a candle remained at Emma's bedside.

Even when Emma was nearly an adult, her fear of the dark remains. She became very anxious about how many candles were in the house, frightened the family might run out. She began hoarding the discard stubs of wax, hiding them in a drawer until her mother found them one day and started to throw them out. Emma became so upset that her mother then allowed her to keep them in a box in the corner of the pantry.

Except for her horrific fear of the dark, Emma was a normal, happy, and attractive young woman. She had many friends and was invited to all the social occasions on the island. Although her friends sometimes teased her about being afraid of the dark, they all accepted it as a rather romantic notion, especially with a lone candle burning in her window at night as if signaling some illicit lover.

One evening at a party, Emma met a young man named Phillip. He had recently moved to Brunswick, Georgia, from the Carolinas to work in a cotton brokerage firm. He and Emma fell in love, and not long after, they were married at Christ Church. Phillip soon learned to live with Emma's intense fear of the dark and never complained about the candle that was left burning beside their bed each night. They soon moved from Brunswick to Frederica on St. Simons Island. Phillip went to work managing his father-in-law's plantation and his shipping company, and the couple had an incredibly happy life together.

Time passed, and one day Emma was making candles when she accidentally spilled hot wax on her arm. She was severely burned, and for some reason, the wound did not heal properly. It became infected, and despite attentive care from the local doctor, blood poisoning set in. In less than a week, Emma died.

Phillip was heartbroken. Despite the kindness and caring of Emma's family, he barely survived the funeral. That afternoon, he returned home, and he sat in a chair on the porch and watched as the sun slipped from the sky. Twilight shadows were creeping across the lawn when Phillip went into the house and took a candle from a box that Emma had made. He walked down the road to the cemetery at Christ Church and went to his wife's grave. He pushed the candle into the soft dirt and lit the wick. The light flared up, and Phillip managed to smile. "You'll always have a light," he whispered.

Every night, for as long as Phillip lived, he made a solitary journey to the graveyard, and he placed a candle on Emma's grave. When the weather was rainy or windy, he placed it inside of a glass lamp, but he never failed to leave a light for her. His friends and neighbors sadly remarked on his faithfulness, and they always explained the significance of the candle to strangers who asked about it.

When Phillip finally joined his beloved wife in death, he was laid beside her in Christ Church Cemetery. For several nights after he died, people passing by the graveyard still saw the familiar light on Emma's grave. They were startled at first but then realized that perhaps friends of neighbors were simply carrying on the tradition of placing a candle there.

But as talk of the light spread across the island, it was realized that no one was responsible for the new light. No one was taking a candle to Phillip and Emma's grave.

The source of the light was - and remains today - a mystery.

Since Phillip's death, hundreds of people on St. Simons Island have seen a glowing light that looks just like a candle flame appearing near an old grave in Christ Church Cemetery. A brick wall was later built around the graveyard, hiding the interior from the road. However, those who walk into the graveyard at night and stand beneath the Spanish moss that hangs from the ancient oaks will sometimes still see a strange, flickering light among the tombstones.

Phillip has kept his promise.

The Grave of Carl Pruitt

In 1938, the stories go, rumors of a "killer ghost" began to spread in Eastern Kentucky. Although no one ever saw this malevolent apparition, the specter was believed to have caused five unexplained deaths in Pulaski County.

In June 1938, a man named Carl Pruitt came home from work one night and found his wife in bed with another man. After her lover escaped, Pruitt strangled his wife with a small piece of chain. Then, in a fit of madness, he committed suicide. The Pruitts were buried in the same cemetery but on opposite sides of the grounds.

A few weeks after the funerals, visitors to the cemetery noticed a weird pattern that was forming on Carl's tombstone. It looked like the links of a chain. Most assumed that it was just an unusual discoloration of the stone until it formed the shape of a cross. At that point, it stopped growing. A few of the more superstitious locals suggested that the tombstone be removed from the graveyard, but officials scoffed at the idea.

A month later, a group of boys were riding their bicycles past the cemetery one afternoon. One of them, a boy named James Collins, decided to throw a few stones at Pruitt's "cursed" gravestone, probably just to prove that he wasn't afraid of spooky stories. One of the rocks chipped the gravestone. As the boys started home, Collins' bicycle suddenly began to pick up speed until he could no longer control it. It veered off the road and collided with a tree. Then, in some unexplained way, the sprocket chain tore loose, flipped upward, and wrapped itself around the boy's neck, instantly killing him. Rumors quickly spread about this remarkable occurrence, especially after an examination of Pruitt's tombstone didn't reveal the damage the other boys claimed they had seen.

It wasn't long before people were talking about a vengeful ghost.

James Collins' mother was especially heartbroken over her son's death. Less than a month after his accident, she went out to the cemetery and destroyed the Pruitt gravestone, shattering it into dozens of pieces. The following day, she was hanging the family wash on the line. Ironically, the clothesline was made from a small linked chain rather than the usual rope or wire. Somehow, she slipped and fell, and her neck became entangled in the chain. She fought to get free, but it was no use. She strangled to death. She had told several friends about her destruction of the tombstone, but it was found to be just as it had been, undamaged, in the cemetery.

A short time later, a local farmer and three members of his family were driving a wagon past the cemetery. For some reason, the farmer announced that he had no fear of ghosts and fired several shots at the Pruitt stone with his revolver. Chunks flew from the marker, and immediately, the horses pulling the wagon began to run. As the wagon careened down a hill, all the occupants but one jumped to safety. The farmer held on, trying desperately to stop the horses. Just as the wagon veered around a curve in the road, the farmer was thrown from his seat, and he tumbled forward. His neck snagged on one of the trace chains, and the motion of the horses snapped his neck. Once again, the stories claimed, Carl Pruitt's stone showed no signs of the damage that had been done to it.

Locals were now convinced of the fact that the grave marker was cursed. Things got so bad that complaints to the local congressman convinced him to send two police officers to the cemetery to investigate the stories. When they arrived at the graveyard, one of two men laughed about the stories and complained about wasting their time. Regardless, they took some snapshots of the stone and left to go and talk to the witnesses who had called the congressman.

As they were driving away, the skeptical officer looked in the rearview mirror and saw a bright light coming from Pruitt's tombstone. At first, he assumed it was a reflection of the sun off the stone, but then it seemed to move closer to the car. He hit the gas and drove off, but the light continued to follow them. He drove faster and faster, but the light stayed behind them. Even after his partner begged him to slow down, he refused. He couldn't explain his terror. He only knew that he had to outrun the strange light.

The car veered into a sharp curve, and he tried to slow down, but it was too late. They missed the turn, narrowly shot between two posts, and plunged down a hill. The car rolled over several times. The officer in the passenger seat was thrown clear of the wreck, only slightly hurt, but the driver was dead. His death had occurred just as the car had left the road. As it had passed between the two posts, a chain that had been hanging between them had broken the car's windshield and wrapped around the driver's neck. The force was so great that it had severed his head.

After this accident, locals avoided the cemetery completely. Only one man, Arthur Lewis, dared to go there. He was determined to prove that the stories of a "cursed" tombstone were superstitious nonsense. One evening, after telling his wife what he intended to do, he went to the graveyard with a hammer and chisel and began to destroy the grave marker methodically. A neighbor later reported hearing the hammering coming from the cemetery - followed by a bloodcurdling scream.

Several men grabbed flashlights and went to investigate. When they arrived, they found Lewis dead with the long chain that had been used to close the cemetery gate wrapped about his neck. Apparently, something had frightened him, and he had started running, forgetting about the chain across the entrance gate. Oddly, even though at least a dozen people had heard Lewis hammering on the tombstone, there were marks or broken places on it.

The death of Arthur Lewis was the last straw for the neighborhood. The cemetery was closed. Bodies of their relatives were exhumed and buried in other graveyards until only Carl Pruitt and his wife were left. As older folks died and younger folks moved away, the old burial plot was eventually forgotten. The site became overgrown and tangled with weeds. In 1958, it was destroyed once and for all by a strip-mining operation. The five strange deaths - all linked by chains - were never explained.

But the curse of Carl Pruitt was finally ended - or so the story goes.

I first heard this story in the late 1990s and was apparently the first person to post it on the internet around that same time. I assumed it was an old story, but I have no idea where I heard it first. I wish that I did. It's a detailed and fantastical story about a vengeful ghost, which is something that we don't often hear. The power of a ghost story lies in the fact that the mere existence of a ghost is enough to scare us. It introduces us to evidence that the unknown may exist. But the fear of a normal ghost story is compounded many times over when the possibility of a murderous spirit - like Carl Pruitt's ghost - is introduced. None of us want to consider the idea that harm might be inflicted on us from beyond the grave.

Perhaps that's one of the reasons I liked this story so much when I first heard. It was also incredibly detailed - documenting the time and place where it occurred and even offering the names of two of the spirit's victims. As it later turned out, though, the names and the details were what revealed this story to be a little too good to be true.

When I began researching this book, I knew I wanted to include the legend of Carl Pruitt as a vengeful graveyard ghost. I had the basics of the story, but I have many more resources at my disposal for research than I had in 1999 or so. Knowing that everything that happened in the story occurred between 1938 and 1958, I assumed it would be easy. It seemed certain that a murder-suicide would have made the newspapers of the day, not to mention the deaths of several residents, including a young boy and a police officer. Sadly, a rather extensive search the newspapers - as well as census and death records - failed to turn the names of James Collins, Arthur Lewis, or even Carl Pruitt.

The only possible match was Enos Prewitt, who shot himself with a pistol at the age of 43 on November 7, 1910. But not only was the date wrong, so were the circumstances of his death - and, of course, the "curse" surrounding his tombstone was never reported. There was also a farmer named Arthur Lewis who died in 1914 in Whitley, Kentucky - only a couple of counties away from Pulaski - but there is no record of anything supernatural being linked to his death. Could those men have inspired the ghost story of Carl Pruitt's grave? Sure, but it seems unlikely.

What is more likely is that the story never happened at all. I took it at face value more than two decades ago, and since then, it's been borrowed and repeated across many websites. It's too bad because I wanted to believe it. A story with so many names, dates, and witnesses should have been evidence of proof of the supernatural. Instead, it seems to be the opposite.

But, who knows, maybe it's not. I included it in this book for a reason. As mentioned already, almost every ghost story gets started for a reason - that often-elusive kernel of truth. Is there any truth to the story of Carl Pruitt? Perhaps, and perhaps we just haven't found it yet.

On the other hand, maybe some ghost stories aren't supposed to be anything other than a tiny whisper of the unexplained. And maybe that's because ghosts themselves are simply a tiny whisper of the explained that, as the truth in this story, continue over and over to slip through our hands.

The Girl by the Grave

The small community of Mansdale, Mississippi, is about 15 miles north of the larger town of Jackson. Among the historic buildings in Mansdale is the Episcopal Chapel of the Cross. Its churchyard lies next to it on a small knoll, mostly hidden from the road by a grove of trees.

The cemetery is the final resting place of a tragic figure in Mississippi history named Henry Vick. It would be to his grave here that his lover, Helen Johnstone, grieved for him in the weeks and months after his death in May 1859.

The legends say that she grieves here for him still.

The short-lived affair of Henry and Helen began during the holiday season of 1855. Helen and her mother, Margaret, were spending Christmas with Helen's sister, Mrs. William Britton, at "Ingleside," the home that John Johnstone had built as a wedding gift for his oldest daughter. The house had been Johnstone's first construction project, which was to have been followed by a manor house called "Annandale," an estate designed for himself and his wife. The plans for the house had been delayed by Margaret's insistence that they first build a chapel, but sadly, Johnstone died before the chapel could be completed. Margaret proceeded with the plans, however, and personally supervised the building of the church. By the time it was consecrated in 1852, her husband's body had already been moved to the small churchyard behind it. Three years later, Margaret began the construction of her husband's "Annandale" and work had just begun before the holiday season.

One night, just before Christmas, the family was seated to dinner at the Britton home when a knock came on the front door. The servant who answered it returned to the dining room to inform William that a young man named Henry Vick wished to speak with him. Vick, spattered with mud, was there to ask for help in getting his carriage repaired. While servants tended to the carriage, Vick became a guest at "Ingleside." He stayed for several days, and while he was there, he and Helen fell deeply in love.

And it wasn't only Helen who was charmed by the young man. Margaret was impressed and with him and made it known that she approved of the match. Over the next three years, Henry visited with the Johnstones and the Brittons often. Since Helen was only 16 when they met, Margaret requested that they wait before getting married. A date for the ceremony was eventually set for May 21, 1859, and it would take place at the Chapel of the Cross. The reception would be held at "Annandale," which had finally been completed.

A week before the wedding, Henry boarded a steamer in Vicksburg. He was traveling to New Orleans to buy a new suit for the wedding. Soon after he arrived in New Orleans, he stopped in a billiard room where he had a chance meeting with James Stith, a former friend that had caused him many problems in the past. A passing insult from Stith caused the two men to get into a heated argument and an altercation. Henry, in the heat of the moment, challenged the other man to a duel. Stith quickly accepted.

Hours later, when his passions had cooled, Henry regretted his hasty actions and sent a friend to try and cancel the duel. Stith refused to accept his apology, however, and the duel was scheduled to take place in Alabama within days. They traveled to Mobile with their seconds and met early in the morning at a place called Holly's Garden. This was to be one of the last duels ever fought in the city - they had, much earlier, been designated as illegal - and the weapons were Kentucky rifles, fired from 30 paces. Henry was wounded fatally in the head. He fell over, dead before he hit the ground.

Stith and his friend escaped from Mobile, but Vick's second, A.G. Dickinson, was delayed by an undertaker who had to take charge of his friend's body. Before he could leave Mobile, the authorities issued a warrant for his arrest. He took refuge in the home of a friend who was a local physician and managed to avoid the search for a few days. Finally, though, guilt-ridden over his part in Vick's death, Dickinson sent a message to the Mobile chief of police, Harry Maury, and confessed to his role in the duel. He asked that he be permitted to take his friend's body back to Vicksburg. Maury was so impressed by the man's honesty that he sent his own carriage to take Vick's body to the riverfront docks.

The grave of He nry Vick, where Helen Johnstone mourned for her lost love.

Henry's body was taken to New Orleans and loaded onto a packet boat going upriver. Ironically, the caterer, cooks, and helpers who were on their way to "Annandale" for Helen and Henry's wedding dinner were on the same boat.

Their supplies were loaded right alongside Henry's coffin.

Helen and her family buried Henry in the same graveyard where her father's body was laid to rest. Day after day, Helen sat on an iron bench near the grave and wept for her beloved Henry. When darkness fell, some members of the family would gently lead her home, but she would return early the next morning to resume her vigil. She was said to have made her family promise that the plot next to Henry would always remain empty - she wanted to be buried there when she died.

Months passed, and Margaret, fearing that Helen would never recover, took her to Europe so that she would have time for her broken heart to heal. They remained away for many months, and by the time they returned, Helen had recovered from her depression. She later married Reverend George Harris, but never forgot about Henry Vick. She and her husband later moved to the northern part of the state, and Helen died in 1916.

She never was buried in the empty plot next to Henry.

Today, the space next to Henry's grave at the Chapel of the Cross remained unused, but Helen has returned after all. The legends say that her ghost still appears there, weeping for her lost love. Many visitors to the secluded cemetery have told of seeing a young woman kneeling in grief beside Henry's gravestone. When they try to approach her, she looks up and then vanishes before their eyes.

From A Steamboat to A Grave

Norman T. Staples still walks in the Bladon Springs Cemetery in Bladon Springs, Alabama, even though he died more than a century ago. The steamboat captain and ship designer died by his own hand in 1913 and now watches over the graves of his wife, several of his children, and the one that holds his own mortal remains. During his life, he was a restless man, and he remains so after his death.

Norman Staples was born in 1869 and was raised along the banks of the Tombigbee River in Alabama. From his early days, he was fascinated with steamboats, and when he was old enough to do so, he chose the river as his life's work. He found employment on a riverboat and soon became a skilled navigator on the Tombigbee. Soon, he was offered his first command and became an accomplished pilot. His family was impressed with his career, but it was his sister, Mary, who did the most to help him succeed. She had married a wealthy man named Fred Blees, and she convinced him to finance her brother so that he could build his own boat. Fred agreed, with the only stipulation being that the boat would be named in Mary's honor. Norman didn't need much convincing.

Mary's confidence in her brother paid off, and soon the *Mary S. Blees* became one of the most profitable vessels on the river. Staples was able to repay his brother-in-law's generous loan in less than two years, so they worked together to commission another ship, the *Mary E. Staples*, which was named after Norman's mother. The new boat was soon traveling up and down the river, too, carrying passengers and cargo and making a large amount of money for the owners.

A few years earlier, Norman had married Dora Dahlberg, but, unfortunately, his family life was not as successful as his professional one. Norman was an inattentive husband and was rarely home. When he was, he was usually occupied with some piece of business. Despite this, Norman and Dora had two children - a daughter named Mable Claire and a son named James, who died soon after he was born. More daughters followed - Beatrice, Bertha, Melanie, and Mary Faye - and another stillborn son. The deaths of his sons caused Norman to concentrate even harder on his business, and he and his wife drifted apart. He loved his wife and daughters, but his drive for success overshadowed everything else.

Norman was working hard to create the plans for what would be his greatest ship yet - a huge and impressive steamer that he planned to call the *James T. Staples* in honor of his father.

In 1907, as he was still trying to complete the new ship, tragedy struck his family. Over that winter, all the children suffered from influenza and high fevers. Bertha and Mable did not survive, and the Staples marriage barely did. Their grief did not bring them together. It drove them further apart. A heartbroken Dora turned her attention to her surviving daughters, and Norman became even more deeply involved in his work.

Every penny he had went into the construction of the boat, and it was finally finished in 1908 - just in time for the heyday of the steamboat to come to an end. The competition had never been greater because as fewer boats were needed, small, independent companies were being put out of business by a large company called Birmingham and Gulf Navigation. They were determined to own and operate all the remaining boats on the river and soon began undercutting Norman and the few others that had survived. This forced Norman also to lower his rates, putting him even deeper into debt. At this same time, a new railroad spur was constructed that ran right next to the river. Many companies that had once shipped by riverboat had turned to the railroad, chipping away even more at Staples' failing business.

Somehow, he managed to keep the company operating until December 1912. Shortly after Christmas, though, his creditors called in his loans, and he was forced to declare bankruptcy.

On January 2, 1913, Captain Norman Staples committed suicide, unable to cope with the loss of his lifelong dream. His wife and two daughters wept bitterly as his body was lowered into the grave. Staples had been able to bear the deaths of his children, but the loss of his steamship company had simply been too much for him to stand.

Meanwhile, the creditors who had taken away Norman's dream vessel, the *James T. Staples*, were having problems of their own trying to operate the ship. No one wanted to work the boat without Captain Staples, who had been considered a good and fair man and a friend to everyone on the river. It took weeks to assemble a crew, but they didn't last long. Two of the ship's firemen claimed to see Norman himself lurking around the boiler room. He had walked through the boiler room as if he still belonged there and then had vanished. Frightened, the firemen quit their jobs, and after hearing the story, many of the other workers left too.

With great difficulty, the new owners got another crew together. This time, it was made up of men who had never worked with Norman and knew nothing about the sighting of his ghost on the boat. A few hours before the vessel was scheduled to depart, when the passengers and their luggage were being loaded on board, the crew members noticed something very strange taking place. It was the rats. They were common on any boat - but not acting like this. Before the boat could leave the docks, the rats suddenly began escaping from the hold and scurrying off the ship. A few of the superstitious crewmen declared that rats leaving a ship was a bad omen - as if something terrible was going to happen - and they abandoned their posts.

The ships' departure was delayed by several hours while new crewmen were found. The passengers were assured that everything was operating normally, and soon, the boat left Mobile and headed upriver.

It was an uneventful trip until they reached Powe's Landing, a port about 100 miles from Mobile. The crew was unloading freight, and the passengers were taking their noon meal. All was calm, and then, suddenly, one of the boilers in the ship's bow exploded with a tremendous roar. The steaming hot water shattered the decking and gushed over the crew and passengers, killing many of them instantly. The front of the ship burst apart, and the river became a frothing, writhing scene of horror. Dozens were killed, including the captain and first mate, both scalded beyond recognition.

The *James T. Staples* burst into flame, and as the ropes securing it to the dock burned, the vessel drifted out into the middle of the river. It sluggishly drifted along the Tombigbee until it came to a point on the river just below the Bladon Springs Cemetery, where Norman Staples was buried. Then, with a great shudder, the steamboat rolled over and sank to the bottom of the river. There were 26 people killed in the explosion, and another 21 were seriously injured.

An investigation of the accident followed, and the ship was hauled up from the river bottom for inspection. The conclusion was reached that the boilers had malfunctioned, but no one was able to explain why. They had been inspected in December and had been in perfect working order.

The mystery caused many to remember the sightings of Norman's ghost that had taken place in the boiler room of the ship. They had been dismissed as wild imagination, but now people were not so sure. Had Norman reached out from the beyond the grave as a revenge against the people who had forced him out of business?

After the ship was gone, sightings of Norman's ghost began to be reported in the Bladon Springs Cemetery. Over the years, visitors to the graveyard have reported the apparition of a man matching his description near his gravesite. They say that he sits there, holding his head in his hands as if he has some great regret.

What keeps his spirit here? Does he wish that he had spent more time with the family that is now buried beside him? Does he regret ending his life too soon?

Or could his regret be about something much worse?

Some say that Captain Norman Staples will never rest. Eternal peace will always elude him because of what happened in 1913 that caused the deaths of those on board the ship that he'd built with his own hands - and sabotaged from the other side.

Father Padilla's Bones

The deserts of New Mexico are filled with ghostly tales. Many of them concern the colonial days of the Spanish Missions and the men who came to bring God to the native population - whether they wanted it or not.

One such ghost story involves the bones of one of those early priests, Father Juan F. Padilla. He was murdered in 1756, although accounts vary as to the method of his violent death. One story says that Indians near Gran Quivira killed him, while another claims that he was stabbed to death by a jealous husband who believed that the priest was his wife's lover.

Regardless of how he died, though, Father Padilla was wrapped in a shroud and buried beneath the altar of one of the region's mission churches at Isleta Pueblo. This was a fairly common practice at the time, and Father Padilla was not the first priest to be buried under the altar, nor would it be the last.

His burial would, however, be the strangest.

Father Padilla's body rested for nearly 20 years beneath the earth, and then, in 1775, his remains rose inexplicably out of the hard-packed earthen floor. It was a startling event to all who witnessed it - and a seemingly impossible one. What was even stranger was the macabre condition of the priest's body. All the accounts claim that it had not decayed at all and went on to say that his flesh was soft and pliable and had a pleasant, earthy smell. Although it was undoubtedly a supernatural event, the accounts say, no one in the church - even the little children - were frightened by the sight of the appearing corpse.

The parishioners were baffled about the meaning of this bizarre event, but some speculated that perhaps Father Padilla no longer wanted to be buried in the earth. They fashioned a coffin for him from the hollowed-out trunk of a cottonwood tree and placed the body inside. He was buried again and this time, remained beneath the altar for the next 44 years.

Then, in 1819, he rose from the earth again.

An account of the 1819 resurrection was discovered by Father

The church at Isleta Pueblo, where Father Padilla's body rose from the earth beneath the altar

Angelico Chavez, a historian, and restorer of the early missions, and he published an article about it in 1947. This time, the priests of the church, along with many of the parishioners, investigated the coffin and the ground beneath the altar. The cottonwood tree coffin had also been unearthed. When it was opened, they found that Father Padilla had mummified over the last half-century. Both the coffin and the body were examined, but no rational explanation could be found for why they had again risen from the ground. An overnight wake was held, and Father Padilla was buried again.

This time, he stayed beneath the church floor for 76 years. Time had passed, the church had been expanded, and a wooden floor had been installed in the sanctuary of the building - which meant that Father Padilla's next appearance was the most dramatic one yet.

On Christmas Eve 1895, a special ceremony was held at the church, incorporating some of the dances still practiced by the Native Americans in the community. Almost as soon as the performance was completed, a series of heavy thuds and knocks sounded throughout the church. No one could figure out where it was coming from, but then a few people noticed that the church altar was rocking back and forth. Candles, along with a plate and chalice used in Holy Communion, were jumping into the air with each of the knocks - the noises were coming from underneath it.

The services were halted, and several men pried up the floorboards. Beneath the floor, they discovered that the coffin of Father Padilla had unearthed itself again and was banging against the underside of the altar.

In the presence of the Bishop of Santa Fe - the Most Reverend Placido Luis Chapelle - the casket was opened once more. The mummified body was examined by Dr. W.R. Tipton. The parishioners gathered around the coffin and peered inside. Once again, no one could explain how - or why - the strange event had occurred again. After discussion and suggestions, Father Padilla was buried for the fourth time.

Over time, many have tried to explain why the body of Father Padilla refused to remain in its grave. Some suggested that perhaps the coffin had become buoyant in the shifting desert sands, in much the same way that it might in water, and this forced it upward over time. But this does not explain the first, non-decayed postmortem appearance of the priest - nor does it explain why none of the other bodies buried under the church's altar never rose out of the ground as Father Padilla's did.

Others have suggested that perhaps Father Padilla hadn't been ready to die when he did. In whatever manner he had been killed, his life had ended suddenly and prematurely, leaving work to be accomplished on earth. He may have been trying to call attention to that - a classic reason for a ghost to linger behind.

Did he receive the attention he wanted? Perhaps, because his appearance in 1895 was the last time that his coffin emerged from beneath the church. Since then, Father Padilla has apparently rested in peace.

Ghosts by the Book

The Sweetwater County Library in Green River, Wyoming, doesn't look like it should be haunted. The modern brick and glass building was constructed in 1980 and doesn't have a history that might suggest it could be infested with ghosts - until you consider what was once located on this property.

The library was built on top of the city's oldest cemetery.

The graveyard had been started in the 1860s, but the occupants had rested there peacefully - many in unmarked graves - until 1926. The town had decided to expand and used the land where the cemetery was located. The bodies were exhumed and moved to the site of the community's current graveyard, but as often happens, quite a few of them were accidentally left behind.

After World War II, the land was used to build housing for veterans, and it soon became obvious that not all the remains had been moved two decades before. Bones were being found almost daily as foundations were dug, and construction was started. Each time a new set of remains was discovered, they were moved to the new cemetery, but many workers began to wonder just how many might have been missed. There's still no answer to that.

In 1978, when the county purchased the land for the new library building, another grim discovery was made soon after the groundbreaking when workers found 12 more bodies on the property. And they weren't alone.

Architect Neal Stowe from Salt Lake City watched a heavy tractor moving back and forth, loosening the soil. He later recalled, "I walked right through the middle of the site, where something that looked like a deteriorated coconut was sitting on top of some freshly churned dirt. I picked the thing up, turned it around, and recognized it as part of a skull. Little tufts of brown hair were still clinging to it."

Stowe stopped work at the site and summoned city officials to try to determine the size of the old burial ground finally. Unfortunately,

The Sweetwater County Library in Green River, Wyoming was built over an old cemetery, leading to rumors and stories of ghosts

there were no records or physical clues as to how many bodies might have been left behind. Workers from the crew started probing the area with hand shovels and discovered pieces of rotted wooden caskets, as well as bits and pieces of human bones. The bones were collected, and these remains were also moved to the new cemetery.

Stowe soon had other problems on his hands. Local historians asked the city to consider other burials that had also taken place in the same area. After scraps of silk with Asian designs on them were found in the excavations, rumors spread that there had once been a Chinese graveyard for railroad workers at the site.

Others insisted that, after an epidemic in the region in the nineteenth century, there had also been unmarked burials of smallpox victims nearby. This story led to accusations that the library construction was endangering the community by unearthing infected remains. But the rumor proved to be unfounded. While there had been a smallpox epidemic among railroad workers in the 1860s, the victims had been buried elsewhere, and their graves were not disturbed.

What was disturbing, though, was what started occurring at the new library after it opened. Staff members began experiencing strange noises, lights turning on and off, disembodied footsteps, and more.

Worse, human remains continued to be discovered.

In the spring of 1983, landscaping work was done outside the front doors, and one of the contractors uncovered what he thought was some old wood. When he looked closer, though, he realized it was bones. Since not all the remains could be removed without tearing up the sidewalks, only portions of the skeletons were reburied in the local cemetery. The rest of the bones remained behind.

In 1985, it was discovered that one section of the library had started to settle, and some structural work became necessary. When the construction crews began drilling into the foundation, they found a small coffin with the body of a child inside. Oddly, they claimed the body was almost perfectly preserved, although the "flesh was like gelatin."

Meanwhile, the library staff was still hearing and seeing things they couldn't explain. Even though staff members and maintenance workers had been talking about the odd happenings for a few years, Library director Helen Higby didn't hear about anything unusual until the summer of 1986. The first thing she noticed involved a security gate that people had to pass through when leaving the library. If a book had not been checked out properly, an alert would sound. The gate was made from wrought iron and was just over waist height.

She recalled the incident: "One night, two of my staff were the only ones left in the building, and at ten minutes to nine, they were getting ready to close up. Each one was at least 15 feet from this bypass, but all of a sudden, it slammed as hard as it could, swung open again, and then oscillated back and forth for several seconds until it came to a stop. That was the first that I'd heard about any unexplained phenomena, and the two women were so upset that they didn't want to talk about it. But afterward, I started hearing about other weird things that had happened."

Many of the staff members spoke of events involving electrical disturbances, like lights turning on and off by themselves. One maintenance worker turned off the lights one evening in the multi-purpose room and then returned a few minutes later to find them on again. He was the only person in the building at the time.

Another maintenance worker spoke of trying to operate a vacuum cleaner one evening. He was vacuuming between the stacks of books and accidentally went too far and pulled the plug from the wall. He switched the machine off and went to plug it back in again at a more accessible outlet. After he plugged it back in, he walked back over to the machine. Before he could switch it on, though, the vacuum turned itself back on again. He immediately turned it off, unplugged it, rolled up the cord, and went home for the evening.

Nearly all the staff members reported feeling as though they were being watched in the library, especially in the multi-purpose room. A worker was vacuuming in there one day and noticed that the curtains were open on the adjoining stage. A community event was scheduled to occur soon, and the stage had already been set up for it. As she was running the vacuum, she happened to look up again and now saw that the curtains were closed. An electronic switch operated the curtains, and the cleaning woman guessed that the staff members at the circulation desk were playing tricks on her. She playfully called to them - only to learn after confronting them that the only switch for the curtains was in the multi-purpose room itself.

Strange sounds often occur. One Friday night, a group of staff members were closing and, according to Judy McPhie, "We heard a noise like someone hammering on a door, trying to get out. It seemed to come from the back part of the building - but we couldn't find anyone."

A maintenance worker once heard the voices of a man and woman arguing violently in the multi-purpose room. He could only catch an occasional word, but it was obvious that they were having a very heated discussion. Curious, because he had just passed through that room while taking out some trash and there had been no one in it, he opened the door and looked inside. Immediately, the muffled voices come to an abrupt stop. He looked around, but there was no one in the room and no place that anyone could have gone. He later discovered that he was not the only person to hear the voices. One former assistant was so terrified that she refused to talk about them - and quit working at the library altogether.

Since most of the strange events seemed to occur in the evening, director Helen Higby arranged schedules so that no one ever had to work alone after dark. That seemed to help. Even though activity was still reported, it didn't seem as frightening when others were present.

But it seemed that those who worked alone could still count on the restless spirits for a scare. One night, not long after the new rules went into effect, the library's business manager came in to do some work on a holiday when the building was closed. Since she knew she'd be by herself, she brought her dog with her. After working in her office for an hour or so, she saw the dog suddenly get up and walk over to the open door that opened into a dark hallway. He stood there for a moment, then cocked his head as if he could hear or see someone in the hall. After a few moments, he laid back down again. He repeated this several times over the next hour - always seeming to look at someone that his owner could not see - and finally, the business manager became so unnerved that she decided to go home.

A Gateway to Hell

Far removed from the horrible story of The Exorcist *or the bizarre black masses recently discovered in Los Angeles and tucked away on a rough county road between Topeka and Lawrence is the tiny town of Stull. Not unlike the town of Sleepy Hollow, described by Washington Irving in his famous tale, Stull is one of those towns' motorists can miss by blinking. Stull and Sleepy Hollow have another thing in common. Both are haunted by legends of diabolical, supernatural happenings.*

- *"Legend of Devil Haunts Tiny Town" by Jain Penner*

I hesitated to include this story in the book. If I had written this 15 or so years ago, then this cemetery would have undoubtedly made the list as one of the most legendary haunted places found in the vast and open landscape of Kansas. But we all know a lot more now than we did 15 years ago, don't we?

In truth, this story probably has no place in a book that is purported to include true accounts of haunted graveyards, but as I've already said, I feel the need to include some stories that are simply too good to be true because they illustrate the need we have to create order out of the madness by giving it a face, a name, and an explanation.

In this case, that explanation is the Devil.

At some point, probably in the 1970s, Stull Cemetery in Kansas was given a reputation that went beyond a mere haunting. It entered the world of the diabolical as one of the few places on earth where the Devil would appear to mingle with his followers. It was, the stories claimed, a literal gateway to Hell.

The cemetery, which included an abandoned chapel for many years, is in the small, nearly forgotten community of Stull. There is little left of the town today - a few houses, a church, and about 20 residents. The number of people buried in the graveyard far outnumbers the living. Somehow, though, this village became the source of dozens of tales of ghosts, witchcraft, and supernatural happenings, all linked to the claim that it allegedly one of "seven gateways to Hell" that exists on the earth.

Legends claim that such stories about Stull date back more than a century and yet, strangely - or not - none of them appeared in print until 1974. That November, an article by Jain Penner appeared in the University of Kansas student newspaper, the *Daily Kansan,* called "Legend of Devil Haunts Tiny Town." It reported the strange occurrences occurring in Stull's graveyard. According to the article, the cemetery was "haunted by legends of diabolical, supernatural happenings," and it was one of two places in the world where the Devil himself appeared in person two times each year. These stories, the writer asserted, had been told repeatedly since the mid-nineteenth century.

Most students, the article continued, had learned of Stull's sinister reputation from their grandparents and other old folks, who recounted their first-hand experiences with the unknown. University

An older photograph of Stull Cemetery, which still shows the old church that was once located on the property.

Courtesy of Rene' Kruse

students who dared to venture out to the graveyard had their own unearthly encounters. One student said that his arm had been grabbed by something unseen, while others told of an unexplained memory loss after visiting the place. Others had run into figures in black robes who were conducting some sort of ritual, implying that devil worshippers and witches were frequenting the ground.

Students were stunned by the article, but most of them accepted it for what it was - a Halloween season prank, taking advantage of some local urban legends to cook up a scary story.

But not everyone thought it was funny. Interest in the story led to mentions of it in regional newspapers, and soon teenagers and curiosity-seekers began flocking to Stull. Locals were just now hearing these stories for the first time and were adamant that they weren't true. Some were amused by the attention, others annoyed, and the rest were downright angry. The pastor of the new church in Stull called out the stories for what they were - the invention of students at the university.

Unfortunately, many people missed the debunking of the tall tales - they took them seriously. According to the original article, the Devil was supposed to make an appearance at Stull Cemetery on the night of the spring equinox in 1978. Word of mouth spread the story further than a student newspaper ever could, and on the night of March 20, more than 150 people showed up in the cemetery to await the appearance of the Devil.

In addition, it was said that the spirits of those who were buried in the cemetery and had died violent deaths would rise from the grave on that same night. But the only spirits in the cemetery that night were in bottles. No ghosts and no Devil - but this didn't keep the legend from growing.

Throughout the next two decades, the stories got wilder and even hard to believe - and yet so many people believed them. Second- and third-hand stories from frightened teenagers were told in tabloid newspapers and paperback books, and when the internet arrived, stories of Stull Cemetery were easy to find.

One popular story involved two young men who visited Stull Cemetery one night and were scared when a strong wind began blowing out of nowhere. They ran back to their car - only to find that the vehicle had been moved to the other side of the highway and was now facing in the opposite direction.

Another man claimed to experience this same anomalous wind, but inside of the abandoned church in the graveyard. He claimed that the sinister air current knocked him to the floor and would not allow him to move for several minutes. Incidentally, it is inside of the same church where witnesses claimed that no rain would fall - even though the crumbling building had no roof.

Even the history of the town of Stull became fair game for writers. According to new versions of the story, the Devil had started to appear in Stull as long ago as the 1850s. They also insisted that the name of the town was originally "Skull" - it wasn't - but the witchcraft-practicing settlers became so repentant about their black magic ways that they changed the name to Stull.

The real story of Stull, Kansas, wasn't nearly as dramatic.

It first appeared on territorial maps as Deer Creek in 1857. The first settlers in the area, most of whom had come west from Pennsylvania, spoke German. A handful of the families organized a church that met in the homes of the members until 1867 when they built the stone Evangelical Emmanuel Church. Sermons at the church were preached in German until 1908. It was used until 1922 when the "new" church was built nearby. It is now Stull United Methodist Church.

In 1867, a cemetery was chartered for the town next to the church. I'm sure that no one then had any idea of the reputation it would gain in the years to come.

In the late 1890s, a telephone switchboard was installed in the home of resident J.E. Louk, and in April 1899, the town's first post office was established in the same building. The first postmaster was Sylvester Stull, and the town's name was changed from Deer Creek to Stull in his honor. Even though the post office closed in 1903, the name stuck.

Then, one Halloween night, the Devil came to Stull and took Sylvester away with him to Hell, and he was never seen again.

Actually, that's not true at all - but it easily could have been included in one of the "true" stories written about Stull Cemetery in the 1980s and 1990s.

What is true is that Stull had a school until 1962. It was used for church services by the Lutheran and United Brethren congregations on Sundays, and the rest of the week, it hosted debates, voting for general elections, baseball games, horseshoe tournaments, and cooking, baking, and quilting competitions. When the school closed, students were bussed to a nearby town to continue their education.

In the early 1900s, there were never more than 50 people living in town. Most of the population came from surrounding farms. Residents recalled that life in the community was "quiet and easy, sometimes even boring." A big city like Topeka seemed far away, and it was - sometimes four hours in the car. Boys from Stull played baseball on the town diamond and were part of a league with members from other nearby communities.

Several businesses were established in the town, but most didn't last long, except for the Louk & Kraft grocery store that lasted until 1955. In the 1920s, there was talk of establishing an interurban railroad line between Kansas City and Emporia that would run through Stull. Believing that the city was going to grow, plans were made for establishing a Farmer's State Bank, and a charter was even secured. But then the Depression came along, and plans were scrapped for the bank and the railroad.

Stull was mostly forgotten after that - by everyone by the Devil, I suppose.

Stull Cemetery nonsense seemed to get stirred up again every year around Halloween. A 1980 article in the *Kansas City Times* - which I'm sure was meant to be tongue in cheek - just made things worse. In this article, the writer claimed that the Devil chose two places to appear on earth every Halloween night, and one of them was the "tumbleweed hamlet" of Stull, Kansas. The other, where he appeared at the same moment, was on a "desolate plain in India." When he appeared, he gathered all the spirits of those who had died a violent death throughout the previous year so he could dance with them at midnight.

The article also offered yet another version of Stull town history. It claimed that the village had been cursed in the 1850s, when "a stable hand allegedly stabbed the mayor to death in the cemetery's old stone barn. Years later, the barn was converted into a church, which in turn was gutted by fire. A decaying wooden crucifix that still hands from one wall is thought sometimes to turn upside-down when passersby step into the building at midnight..."

The article neglected to mention that neither the Deer Creek Community not Stull have ever had an official mayor.

That article was, of course, not the end of the new additions to Stull mythology. It was claimed that the Devil came to Stull because he wanted to visit a witch that was buried in the graveyard, that a tree in the cemetery was once used as a gallows for condemned witches, and that the bones of a "child of Satan" are buried there. He was, it was said, born of the Devil and a local witch and was so deformed that he only lived for a few days. He was buried in Stull Cemetery, and his ghost still walks the grounds.

One of the tales even borrowed from a real-life tragedy that occurred in Stull in the early 1900s - the death of a young boy named Oliver Bahnmaier, who wandered out into a field that his father was burning and was killed. His death created the myth that if you stepped on Oliver's tombstone in Stull Cemetery, you would wake up to find yourself in Hell.

Rumors claim that the rock band The Cure canceled a show they had booked in Kansas because their travel would take them too close to Stull Cemetery. Needless to say, this isn't true.

And neither is the claim from pop singer Ariana Grande that she tried unsuccessfully to visit Stull Cemetery but was driven away after being attacked by demons.

Probably the dumbest story about Stull allegedly appeared in *Time* magazine - it didn't - and occurred in either 1993 or 1995, depending on the version of the story. It claimed that Pope John Paul II when visiting the United States, ordered the Vatican plane to fly around eastern Kansas - instead of over it - while on his way to a public appearance in Colorado. Supposedly, the Pope did not want to fly over "unholy ground."

I don't need to assure you this never happened either, do I?

In 1988, the crowds waiting for the Devil to appear grew to more than 500 people. Rowdy partiers knocked over tombstones, vandalized the empty church, and left trash, bottles, and beer cans all over the cemetery.

They found the police waiting for them on Halloween 1989. The crowd at the graveyard had gotten so large that Douglas County Sheriff's deputies were stationed outside to send people away. Anyone who ventured inside of the cemetery was given tickets for trespassing.

But the stories didn't stop, and neither did the curiosity-seekers and ghost hunters. They came back to Stull again and again, finding nothing but wild tales and urban legends.

Eventually, locals became irritated enough with the vandals and trespassers wreaking havoc in the cemetery where their loved ones and ancestors were buried that they installed a new fence around it. Sheriff's deputies began making regular patrols, and the break-ins slowed down - until October anyway.

By now, Stull Cemetery had reached even greater fame on the internet, and the stories had become even wilder, if that's possible. There was no question of how they had gotten started. This was not a case of horrific legends with kernels of truth - this was pure fiction, made up by a college newspaper as part of a Halloween prank. It wasn't done with bad intentions, and I don't think anyone could have realized the trouble that a single scary story could bring.

The stories about Stull showed no signs of slowing down in the 1990s. In 1996, what remained of the roof of the old church on the cemetery grounds blew off in a storm, and it was finally torn down a few years later.

Despite the dubious origins of Stull's scary tales, the legend of the cemetery is alive and well today. Even though the crowds don't gather at the old graveyard the way they used to, I wasn't going to offer a chilling story here to keep the mythology alive.

As I said, some stories get started for a good reason.

This story of Stull Cemetery? There wasn't one.

Billy Cook's Unmarked Grave

The Route 66 town of Joplin, Missouri, certainly has its ghosts.

The old Freeman Hospital, which began operating on land donated by John W. Freeman in 1922, was said to be haunted long before it became abandoned. Phantom footsteps were said to roam the hallways, and workers refused to stay alone on the unoccupied fourth floor. There were cries, moans, and whispers that simply should not have been there. Many who died at Freeman Hospital over the years have apparently never left.

Prosperity School, which served the children of miners in the Prosperity Township on the outskirts of Joplin from 1907 to 1962, is believed to harbor the spirits of former students still, or perhaps staff members, or perhaps the victim of a murder that may have happened there in the 1950s. After being left vacant for more than 30 years, it has since been restored and is now used as a bed and breakfast. Guests who have stayed there have reported voices, footsteps, lights that turn on and off, the tapping of high-heeled shoes, and the dark figure of a man who is often spotted walking between the kitchen and the front door.

And while such places are undoubtedly unsettling, there is nowhere in the Joplin area that is regarded with the kind of dread that so many people afford to Peace Church Cemetery, an old, ramshackle, 1850s-era burial ground outside of town.

Over the years, reports have circulated about strange sounds, voices, and eerie lights that have been heard and seen in the cemetery. There are also reports of a ghostly figure that has been spotted lurking in the trees, peering out at passersby, and then vanishing when approached. It would be safe to assume that one of the restless souls buried here does not rest in peace.

And when those who visit this place learn just who is buried in this cemetery, in a forsaken, unmarked grave - they find a likely suspect for the ghost.

Few mass murderers have ever gone on a worse killing spree than the one 21-year-old Billy Cook started on December 30, 1950. On that day, Cook, posing as a hitchhiker, forced a motorist at gunpoint to get into the trunk of his own car and then drove away. Over the next two weeks, Cook went on a senseless rampage. He kidnapped nearly a dozen people, including a deputy sheriff, and murdered six of them in cold blood, including three children. He also attempted other killings and terrorized the southwestern border states.

Cook was born in 1929 and grew up near Joplin. His early life was hard, and he had to make do with what he could between seven brothers and sisters. His father was an uneducated mine worker, and after the death of Cook's mother, he raised the children in an abandoned mine shaft. One night, after drinking in a local tavern, he hopped a freight train and left the children to survive alone. Authorities found them huddled in the old mine, living like animals. Welfare workers were able to find foster homes for all the children, except for Billy. His attitude caused people to stay away from him, and he had a sinister-

 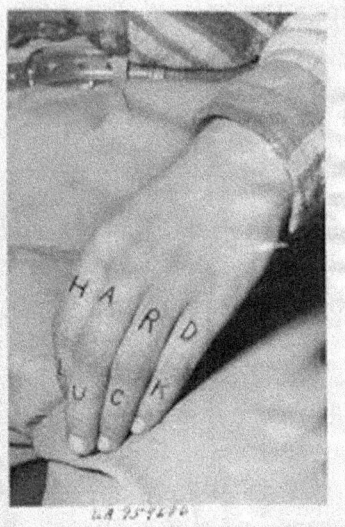

Billy Cook - even after he was arrested, he didn't want photos taken of his drooping eye. His tattoo artist probably should've told him that he had four knuckles on his *other* hand, too. That way, he didn't have to spell "hard luck" with only one hand.

looking affliction of the right eye that would not allow the lid to close all the way. He was finally taken in by a woman who did it purely for the money paid to her by the government, and she and the boy never got along.

As he got older, Billy stayed out at night, getting in trouble, and he ended up spending most of his formative years in reform school. He told a judge that he would prefer it to foster care, and he got his wish. He was simply born bad, most believed, and when he was young, he had the words "Hard Luck" tattooed across the knuckles of his hand. After being released, Cook immediately robbed a cab driver of $11 and stole a car. He was quickly arrested and sent back to reform school for five years. He became one of the most dangerous inmates in the institution and was sent to the Missouri Penitentiary to finish his sentence. While there, he beat another inmate so badly with a baseball bat that the man almost died.

He had made the mistake of laughing at Billy's drooping eyelid.

In 1950, Cook was released and returned to Joplin to look for his father. The reunion was short-lived, and Billy left town and started hitching rides through the southwest, ending up in Blythe, California. The only job that he ever held was there, washing dishes in a diner, but he soon grew bored and began to roam again, this time heading for Texas. Somewhere along the way, he picked up a snub-nosed .32-caliber pistol, and he kept it tucked away in his pocket.

Cook had little use for anyone and, frankly, hated people - all people - and he decided to put those feelings into action when he kidnapped his first victim, a motorist, near Lubbock, Texas. Cook locked him in the trunk of his own car, but the driver managed to use a jack handle to open the trunk from the inside. He held it down until Cook turned off the highway and onto a secondary road. Convinced that the young man planned to kill him, he jumped out when the car slowed down and escaped by running across the flatland.

Cook drove the lonely stretch of highway between Claremore and Tulsa, Oklahoma, before the stolen car ran out of gas. He left the vehicle on the side of the road and started walking. A few minutes later, he saw a 1949 Chevrolet coming toward him. Cook waved frantically as if he had encountered car problems, trying to get the car to slow down.

The driver, Carl Mosser, came to a stop. Mosser, his wife Thelma, and their three small children were on vacation from Decatur, Illinois, headed to New Mexico, when they picked up Cook alongside the road. Many wonder today why they would have picked up a hitchhiker with small children in the car, but those were different times, and Americans had not yet been bombarded with the gruesome images of death and murder that were to come in the media and entertainment. They had nothing to fear, they believed, and simply wanted to help a young man who was down on his luck.

Cook repaid the family's kindness by pulling a gun and forcing Mosser to drive into Oklahoma and then to Texas. Carl, frantically worried for his family, hoped that his twin brother, Chris, who lived in Albuquerque and was expecting the family for a visit, would start to worry and alert the authorities.

Cook forced him to drive to Wichita Falls, Texas, and Mosser desperately kept thinking of ways to try and get rid of the maniac. He thought he saw a chance in Wichita Falls when the car started to run low on gas. He urged Cook into a filling station for some fuel and food. Mosser pulled into the station and told the elderly attendant to fill the tank. When he asked, at Cook's orders, that some lunch meat be brought to the car, the attendant told him that he would have to get that himself. Mosser went inside, followed by Cook, and it was then that Mosser grabbed Cook and tried to pin him from behind. Frightened, the old attendant pulled an old revolver and waved it nervously at the two struggling men. He ordered Mosser to let loose of Cook and Carl tried to explain what was happening. Too scared to help, the older man ordered them out of the station. The two continued to fight until Cook broke away and pushed Mosser through a plate glass window.

The older man, now terrified, locked himself inside as Cook ordered Mosser back to the car. As the automobile drove off, the older man now jumped into his truck and gave chase. Cook saw him coming and fired several shots at him. With that, the attendant's bravery vanished, and he stopped the truck.

Cook was now seething with anger, and he forced Mosser to drive to Carlsbad, New Mexico, and then on to El Paso, Texas. From there, the terrifying journey continued to Houston and then to Winthrop, Arkansas. Cook then had Mosser turn the car toward his old stomping grounds in Joplin.

Finally - after more than 72 hours since the family had been kidnapped - Thelma Mosser became hysterical and started to cry. The children also began to wail, and Cook gagged all of them except for Carl. After Cook spotted a police officer that seemed to be paying too much attention to the Mosser car, Cook grew tired of his game and turned his pistol on the family. He shot and killed all of them and, for good measure, shot the family dog, too. He dumped their bodies in a place he knew well - an abandoned mine shaft near Joplin.

Eventually, the Mossers' car was found abandoned near Tulsa, Oklahoma. It looked like a slaughter pen, with the upholstery ripped by bullets and blood splashed everywhere. The victims' bodies were soon discovered but Cook left something behind in the car: the receipt for the handgun that he had bought. With the killer's identity known, a massive manhunt was launched.

Cook headed for California, where he was almost captured by a deputy sheriff. Cook turned the tables on him and took the deputy as a hostage. Billy forced the deputy to drive him around while he bragged about executing the Mosser family. After more than 40 miles, Cook ordered the lawman to stop and made him lie down in a ditch with his hands tied behind his back. He told the man that he was going to put a bullet in his head and then, for some reason, climbed into the car and drove away. The officer waited for the bullet, but it never came. He would never know why he was spared.

A short time later, Cook flagged down another motorist, Robert Dewey, and wounded him. The two men struggled, and the car left the road and careened out into the desert. Cook ended the fight with a bullet to Dewey's head, and he threw the body into a ditch.

By this time, an alarm had been raised all over the southwest, and so Cook decided to head into Mexico. He kidnapped two men and brought them along to Santa Rosalia, several miles across the border. Amazingly, though, Cook was recognized by the local police chief, Francisco Morales. He simply walked up to Cook, snatched the gun from the man's belt, and placed him under arrest. Cook was then rushed to the border and turned over to FBI agents.

Despite the slaying of the Mosser family, the Justice Department turned Cook over to the California courts, and he was tried for the murder of Robert Dewey. Cook displayed as much regret about this murder as he had the others --- in other words, none at all - and he was sentenced to death. On December 12, 1952, he died in the gas chamber at San Quentin.

And then things took a curious turn. Glen Boydstrun, an undertaker in Comanche, Oklahoma, had been around long enough to remember the crowds that had turned out to see the bullet-riddled bodies of some of the slain gangsters of the public enemies-era, like Pretty Boy Floyd. So, Boydstrun decided to try his luck at putting Cook's body on display in Comanche, even though the town had nothing to do with Cook or his crimes.

Peace Church Cemetery near Joplin, Missouri. Billy Cook is buried out here - somewhere.

Boydstrun contacted Cook's father, Will Cook, in Joplin and made a deal with him. He would pay for a proper burial for Cook's son if the man allowed Boydstrun to claim the body at San Quentin. The undertaker immediately drove to California, and three days after his execution, Cook's corpse, outfitted in a suit and tie, was placed on public display in Comanche. Boydstrun was disappointed with the first day's turnout, so he added loudspeakers and, like a sideshow barker, urged people to see the "last American desperado." Thousands came on the second day, including busloads of schoolchildren. In all, as many as 12,000 curiosity-seekers turned out, before Cook's siblings hired a lawyer, got the body away from Boydstrun, and returned it to Joplin.

Cook was buried in the dark of night at Peace Church Cemetery. According to a 1952 *Joplin Globe* article, a brief service was held with flashlights and lanterns with about 15 people in attendance. Just as the grave service ended, a reporter wrote, "the cry of a small child could be heard in the chill of the night air." As news spread, the public objected to the now infamous killer being buried in the cemetery, so the family quietly had his grave moved just outside of the grounds.

Over time, Billy Cook has proven to be a dark inspiration to several films, books, and even a song. He was cited as the inspiration for the film, *The Hitch-Hiker*, which was directed by actress Ida Lupino. In the film, two men on a fishing trip pick up a hitchhiker who turns out to be a psychopath who has committed multiple murders on the road. Lupino interviewed two men who were held hostage by Cook, as well as Cook's father so that she could integrate parts of Cook's life story into the film. When the film was released in 1953, it was marketed with the line, "When was the last time you invited death into your car?"

There is also the legend that Billy Cook was the inspiration for the Doors' classic song "Riders on the Storm." It's been said that some of Jim Morrison's lyrics were inspired by Cook's exploits: "There's a killer on the road; his brain is squirming like a toad; Take a long holiday; Let you children play; If you give this man a ride, sweet memory will die; Killer on the road..."

And that's not the only kind of mayhem that Cook has inspired. It is common to go to the cemetery and find items like flowers, notes, and candles left in various spots that people believe Cook's unmarked grave lies.

It has also been rumored that local teenagers have congregated at times to try and contact the spirit of Billy Cook. In 1987, three 17-year-old boys from nearby Carl Junction were discovered to have been killing animals and then murdered a 19-year-old acquaintance by beating him to death with a baseball bat. At trial, their defense claimed they had been engaging in satanic rituals and had been influenced to commit the murder by the spirit of Billy Cook. The jury wasn't buying it, and they were convicted of murder.

Despite what the jury believed, though, many people believe that Billy Cook does not rest quietly at the edge of this old graveyard. Throughout the years, stories have circulated about the shadowy figure that has been seen lurking about on the grounds and wandering among the nearby trees. Whoever this man is, he seems lost and confused, and some have remarked that he appears to be angry about something.

If this lingering spirit is that of Billy Cook, then his anger becomes clear. In life, Cook hated everyone and everything, and, likely, his hatred at simply being born hasn't gone away, even in death.

Legends of Stepp Cemetery

For many years, one of the spookiest legends in Indiana involved a small abandoned cemetery that was located off Old State Highway 37 in the Morgan-Monroe State Forest.

Called Stepp Cemetery, it can be found in a lonely place at the end of a narrow, dirt trail that winds through the woods. It's the kind of place that would have been forgotten many years ago if not for the ghostly tales that are still told about it. Only a few dozen grave markers remain within the burial grounds, and all of them are old and crumbling. No one has been buried here for many years, and yet the visitors continue to come.

They are hoping to experience the unknown.

And they hoped to find it waiting for them in what was called the "Warlock's Chair." Along the southern edge of the graveyard, near a row of tombstones, the chair was a worn tree stump that vaguely looked like a seat.

It was in the chair where the woman waited.

Depending on which version of the Stepp Cemetery legend you might hear, a nearby grave held the remains of the woman's child, or a road worker killed too soon, or a teenager who met a tragic end. But each story had one constant - the woman who watched over their grave during the darkest hours of the night. Scores of people had seen her there over the years, always watching, always waiting, always seated on the old tree stump.

Most of the ghost stories of Stepp Cemetery seem to have their root in the 1950s, but the cemetery itself is much older than that. Historians believe that the oldest burial - that of Isaac Heartstock, a veteran of the War of 1812, dates to 1851.

It was simply a rural cemetery until the early twentieth century when the first hint of anything unsavory was connected to the burial ground. It was around 1909 that stories about the Crabbites began making the rounds. This mostly undocumented, fringe Christian sect is believed to have used the cemetery for some of their ritualistic sex practices.

Unfortunately, little is known about the cult. They only lived briefly in the area before moving to Brown County. Their beliefs were a little on the odd side, taking biblical verses and interpreting them literally. For instance, there is a part in the Book of Revelation that mentions angels coming from the "four corners of the earth." This led to William Crabb, the group's leader, teaching his followers that the earth was square because the Bible spoke of four corners.

Their frenzied religious services included speaking in tongues, raucous music, and snake handling - another literal interpretation from the Bible that claims God's followers could take up serpents, and if they were bit, they would not die. Their gatherings drew a circus-like crowd that hoped to see someone get bit by a snake - or witness one of the orgies that the Crabbites became famous for.

According to a woman named June Fulford, her grandfather was instrumental in chasing the Crabbites out of the county. He served in some official capacity in the area and was called on to disperse, with a bullwhip, a group of Crabbites who were engaged in a sex ritual in Stepp Cemetery. They didn't stick around long after that, but they helped the cemetery earn a less than wholesome reputation from which it never really recovered.

The rural cemetery became a remote and isolated one in 1929 when it was swallowed up by the Morgan-Monroe State Forest. The isolation of the burial ground helped to create the lore. Once you added in the strange religious cult and teenagers in the car, you had all the ingredients for the spookiest legends you can imagine.

It's no coincidence that most of the ghost stories about Stepp Cemetery began in the 1950s. That was when teenagers started getting cars and started looking for places to get away. The cemetery's stories ratcheted up a notch into the 1960s and 1970s. Stepp became a favorite place for "beer blasts" and late-night get-togethers for young people in the area.

The kids came, and the stories grew.

The most well-known involves a ghostly woman in black, who, for decades, has roamed the cemetery. There are now several variations of the story, but the most detailed involved a couple who settled in the area after the husband got a job in a local quarry. They had a daughter and lived happily until the husband was killed in an explosion at the quarry. He was buried in Stepp Cemetery. After that, the daughter became her entire life. The little girl grew up, went to school, met a boy, got engaged - and then was killed in a car accident. The daughter was also buried in Stepp Cemetery, and her mother never recovered from this second tragic death.

She began to make daily trips to the cemetery, where she sat for hours and talked to her family as if they were still alive. There was an old tree stump near their graves, and she would sit there until it got dark. Locals who passed by often spoke of a woman in black who sat on the stump and wept, talking to herself. If anyone approached her, she would run away and hide in the woods and wouldn't return until they were gone. People began to avoid the graveyard, unwilling to bother with the woman who seemed to be insane.

Eventually, the woman died, and she was buried near her husband and daughter in Stepp Cemetery. But her spirit still watches over their graves. The legends say that her ghost can still be seen in the cemetery some night, seated on the old stump that someone dubbed the "Warlock's Chair."

The old stump that was dubbed the "Warlock's Chair," where the ghostly woman was so often reported.

Numerous sightings of the woman's spirit - dressed in black mourning clothes - occurred over the years. Many left the cemetery shaken after having seen the woman rise from her seat on the stump and turn in their direction. The descriptions of the woman in black were always the same. She wore a long dress, and her hair was long and white - not from old age but whitened from shock and grief.

Even those who didn't see her had tales to tell. Strange sounds often emanated from the burial grounds, and law enforcement officials and park rangers frequently received reports of a woman sobbing in the cemetery at night - a woman who isn't seen. When they have checked the cemetery to see if anyone is injured or ill, they find no one is there.

Over the years, the descriptions of the ghostly woman and her heartbreaking cries haven't changed much, but the origins of the specter often vary depending on who is telling the story.

One version of the story is dated to the 1950s and involves a young girl who was murdered in the area, and her body dumped at Stepp Cemetery. The crime was never solved, but her mother never gave up the search for the killer, even after death. Her spirit now watches over the graveyard in hopes that the killer might return, and she can have her revenge.

Another version tells the story of a child who was killed in an auto accident in the 1920s. Her mother blamed herself, and in a fit of grief, she exhumed the child's body, just so that she could hold her last time. A short time later, the mother committed suicide, and now her spirit returns to watch over the little girl's grave. She was frequently encountered sitting in the tree stump chair. To this day, cemetery visitors still leave toys at a grave that is located near the Warlock's Chair - or at least where it used to be. The tree stump chair is gone now, but its legend remains.

The story may have changed many times over the years, but it may just have a kernel of truth. As we know, legends are created to explain experiences that are difficult to understand. There have been so many first-hand accounts of encounters with the woman in black at Stepp Cemetery that it seems difficult to believe that none of them are true.

Even if only a small percentage of them are real, this still leaves an inordinate number of them unsolved.

Perhaps before we judge the veracity of the tale, it might be worth a trip to the depths of the Morgan-Monroe Forest and to that narrow dirt trail that leads back into the woods to the burial ground. Perhaps as we stand there among the stones, we might consider if we can believe in the ghost - or not.

The Legend of Stiffy Green

There's nothing usual about hearing a dog bark in a cemetery - unless you happened to be in Highland Lawn Cemetery in Terre Haute, Indiana. If you hear a dog barking there, it might not be a dog from this world. It might be the legendary bar of Stiffy Green, Indiana's favorite graveyard specter.

In the early 1900s, Stiffy was a familiar character around Terre Haute. The stubby little bulldog was the constant companion of John

John Heinl's mausoleum in Highland Lawn Cemetery

Heinl, a well-liked older gentleman in town. The two of them were familiar figures as they strolled about downtown each day. Stiffy had been named for his unusual, stiff-legged walk, and he was known for his startling green eyes. Both man and beast were well-liked, and Stiffy was loveable, yet fiercely protective of his master.

John Heinl passed away in 1920. While his death was a cause for sadness in the community, there was no person affected by it as much as his little dog. Stiffy was heartbroken by the loss, and he refused to leave John's side, even as the funeral services were taking place. He was there when his master was interred in the Heinl family mausoleum at Highland Lawn - and refused to leave. He laid down in front of the door as if waiting for John to come and take him for a walk.

As his health had declined, John had arranged for a friend and his wife to take care of Stiffy after he was gone. They gathered up the little bulldog and took him to his new home. Stiffy was listless, refusing to eat. He spent most of his time near the door, waiting for John to come and take him home.

A few days later, the couple awoke to find that Stiffy was missing. He was found a few hours later, outside the door of the mausoleum. John's friend took him home again, but less than a week later, Stiffy was missing once more. He continued to slip away from the house, over and over, and each time he would be found a few miles away at the cemetery. This soon became a routine. If the dog couldn't be found around the house somewhere, his new owners always knew where he was.

The afterlife of Stiffy Green

Eventually, they gave up and let Stiffy Green stay at the graveyard. They brought him food and water and did their best for him, but the bulldog refused to leave John's side. He stayed there in the rain and cold and never shirked what he felt was his duty - guarding his master's grave.

And it was on the cold stone step that the body was Stiffy Green was eventually found.

As word of the loyal little dog's death spread throughout the community, John's friends weren't sure what to with his remains. They certainly didn't want to simply dispose of their friend's constant companion, but they weren't certain he should be entombed as a human would be either. Finally, they reached a compromise. A fund was established, and the dog's body was taken to a local taxidermist. Stiffy was mounted into the sitting position that he had maintained outside of the tomb for so many months. His bright green eyes were replaced with glass orbs that managed to capture the gleam of the originals. When the task was completed, Stiffy Green was placed inside of the Heinl tomb, next to the crypt that held the remains of his beloved companion.

This should be the end of the story - but it's not.

Several months after Stiffy Green's death, a caretaker was leaving the cemetery on a warm evening. Just as he was opening the door to his car, he heard the bark of a dog from the direction of the Heinl mausoleum. Thinking that something about this seemed odd, he decided to go and have a look. As he neared the tomb, the sound got louder, and then he suddenly realized why the bark seemed so strange and so eerily familiar. He had heard this dog barking before.

It was the bark of Stiffy Green.

Of course, this was impossible since the poor animal had died many months before. He decided the bark must have been his imagination and walked back to his car. He would think no more about the incident until other people started to report the same barking from the area around the tomb. And that wasn't all.

The barking, which always comes from around the Heinl Mausoleum, is sometimes accompanied by the sight of an older man who strolls among the tombstones. Sometimes, he smokes a pipe and, at other times, just looks off into the distance. While his behavior sometimes varies, one thing always stays the same - he is always accompanied by a little bulldog with a stiff-legged walk and piercing green eyes.

Lights of the Old Miner's Cemetery

It's a ghost town now, but at one time, Dawson, New Mexico, was one of the rowdiest, toughest, wealthiest towns in the West. But life was cheap, death frequently came calling, and one disaster after another eventually brought an end to the town's prosperity. There is little left of it today, aside from some ramshackle, wind-blown old structures, but on the edge of town is a cemetery that is very much still alive.

And haunted.

In the 1880s, everyone thought J.B. Dawson was crazy when he started scraping coal from his farm and using it to provide heat for his house rather than wood. But they changed their minds once they tried it and realized how well it worked.

Dawson was a small rancher in New Mexico - one of many who were living on a few hundred acres that were part of the Maxwell Land Grant. The grant was the largest ever made in what would become the United States. In 1841, it had been given to Charles Beaubien and Guadalupe Miranda to encourage settlers from Mexico to come to the area and utilize its resources. Then along came Charles Lucien B. Maxwell, a fur trapper from Illinois, who was working as a guide in the area. His work often brought him to the Beaubien-Miranda ranch, where he met and married one of Beaubien's six daughters, Luz. In 1864, after the death of his father-in-law, Maxwell and his wife bought out the five other heirs and found himself in control of a massive piece of land. He developed towns, banks, and businesses on the land until he died in 1875.

J.B. Dawson was one of many ranchers who had bought their land from Lucien Maxwell himself. After the grant began to be sold and divided after Maxwell's death, the Maxwell Land Grant Company - a consortium from back east - began trying to move ranchers like Dawson off the property. But Dawson and the others weren't willing to go.

The company had never considered that ranchers might be living on the land and had no idea who was squatting and who was a legal owner. However, when they realized how much coal was on Dawson's land, they immediately sought to have him convicted - whether he owned the property or not. Dawson fought back and claimed that he had bought the land from Maxwell and had sealed the deal with a handshake - which turned out to be the truth. Dawson gathered as many friends as possible, and armed to the death, he planned to fight to the death to keep his ranch. In the end, he didn't have to. The company took him to court in 1893 and lost. Dawson's claims were legal, and he also found out that Maxwell had not sold him the 1,000 acres that he expected - he'd given Dawson 20,000 acres instead.

With legal matters settled, Dawson began marketing his coal. He sold off a large section to the Dawson Fuel Company and sold another

Dawson, New Mexico in its heyday as a coal mining community

section to be developed as a town. He kept 120 acres for himself, sat back, and watched a town named in his honor begin to grow.

The town was developed by C.B. Eddy, the president of the El Paso and Northeastern Railroad, and had plans to connect Dawson to other cities by a rail line. The first mine opened in the town in 1901, and a sawmill was started that same year. Lumber was soon being produced at a steady rate and used to build homes and businesses and to shore up the tunnels in the mine. By the end of its first year, Dawson was well on its way to becoming the largest coal mining operation in New Mexico.

A post office was established. It was followed by saloons, a bank, a church, hotel, school, doctor's office, and the Southwestern Mercantile Company general store. By 1902, the population had already reached 600, and the town was regarded as having a "fine, stimulating climate" with "plenty of work for everyone."

And then the first disaster occurred.

On September 14, 1903, a fire and explosion in Mine No. 1 killed three miners. The bodies of the men were quietly buried in a newly established town cemetery and largely forgotten. Everyone knew that coal mining was dangerous work. Accidents happened, and life went on - but there would be more to follow.

In 1905 and 1906, more businesses came to the region and brought more people with it. A newspaper was established, and the population of the town rose to more than 2,000 people. The mine expanded and then expanded again. New shafts were dug, more workers arrived, and Dawson gained the attention of the giant Phelps Dodge Corporation. They bought out the mining company and reorganized it as the Stag Canyon Fuel Company. With the mine under the new management, the town continued to grow. Phelps Dodge wanted to attract more workers to the remote location, so they built homes for the miners and invested in the community. They added a hospital, department store, swimming pool, golf course, and a palatial theater that was constructed at the cost of nearly $40,000. With these amenities, Phelps Dodge was able to maintain a stable employment rate - mostly with recent immigrants - despite the dangers of mining and the isolation of northern New Mexico.

Many of the men were single - helping the town's brothels do a steady business - but those with wives and children lived in a part of town called "Boarding House Row." They formed a close-knit community of families, most of whom spoke little English.

But that part of town would tragically be left without its husbands, fathers, and sons.

On October 22, 1913, a tremendous explosion rocked Mine No. 2. The explosion was felt two miles away in the town proper. Relief teams rushed in from surrounding communities and as far away as Pittsburg, Kansas, and Rock Springs, Wyoming. In the first few hours, 23 of the 286 men who arrived to work in the mine that day were found alive, bringing hope to the rescue crews. Phelps Dodge sent a special train from El Paso, Texas, with doctors and nurses, but as days passed, no other survivors were found.

The crews worked around the clock, and as the rows of the dead brought to the surface grew longer, distraught wives and family members impeded the operations at the entrance of the mine. It was not until two rescue workers were killed by falling debris that the families moved back to a safer distance.

It was later determined that the explosion was caused by a dynamite charge set off while the mine was in general operation,

The stark white crosses of the coal miner's cemetery - almost all that's left of Dawson today. There are many stories that say these miners don't rest in peace.

igniting coal dust in the mine. This was in violation of mining safety laws, but the laws were too late to help those who had perished.

Huge mass funerals were conducted for the victims, and the tiny cemetery in Dawson overflowed, making it necessary to extend the graveyard far up the hill. Funeral services went on for days, and the men were buried under identical rows of metal crosses. They were painted white, reflecting the harsh glare of the New Mexican sun.

Even after such a tragedy, life in Dawson went on. The town continued to prosper, and new safety measures were added at the mine. It was still a dangerous job, but there were fewer accidents and only a handful of fatalities.

But then on February 8, 1923, an explosion occurred at Stag Canyon Mine No. 1. A mine car derailed, knocking down timbers, and the electric trolley cable caused sparks that ignited coal dust in the mine. The explosion killed another 125 miners - many of whom were the sons of men who had died in 1913.

The cemetery was enlarged again, making room for more bodies and additional rows of bleak white crosses.

But Dawson did not become a ghost town until 1950 when the Phelps Dodge Corporation shut down the mines. At closure, Mine No. 6 was the largest producer, and several other mines had been previously closed because of declining demand. The mine had once had a 25-years contract with the Southern Pacific Railroad, but it had come to an end.

On April 20, the last mine was closed. By this time, many of the residents of Dawson had already departed. Windows without curtains stared out from vacant houses as the mine emptied for the last time, and the remaining workers packed up to leave town for good. In June, the mine was stripped of most of its machinery, and the town was sold or razed, with some of the miners' houses moved to other locations. A handful of structures remained for a cattle operation, and today they are just about all that's left of this once proud and prosperous boomtown.

And then there is the cemetery.

More than 350 white iron crosses mark the graves of those who perished in the mine disasters. These silent sentinels, some with individual names and some unmarked, are reminders of the lives of the victims. And of their tragic deaths, too.

According to the legends, the dead miners of Dawson refuse to go quietly into the night, forgotten, and unremembered. Witnesses say that eerie lights can often be seen dancing and flickering among these metal crosses in the darkness. These lights, they say, are the carbide lamps of the miner's helmets, still hoping they'll be rescued from the dark depths of the mine where they died.

A Spectral Reunion

For nearly a century and a half, people have gathered on the night of November 21 at the Reynolds Cemetery in Jackson, Michigan, in hopes of witnessing the ghostly reunion of two lost souls - two victims of one of the region's most infamous unsolved murders.

It was a dark and stormy night - seriously.

Thunder, lightning, high winds, and rain filled the night skies over Spring Arbor Township on the night of November 21, 1883. The storm hid the sounds of gunshots inside of a farmhouse owned by Jacob Crouch.

The dawn would lead to the discovery of the victims - Crouch, his daughter, Eunice White, who was eight months pregnant; her husband, Henry; and a Pennsylvania cattle buyer named Moses Polley.

Jacob Crouch's farmhouse on Horton Road

The murders were never solved, which only added to the local lore about the strange Crouch family.

Jacob Crouch had arrived in Jackson County from New York in 1830, and he settled on a farm along Horton Road. At the time of his death at age 74, he was a very wealthy man. He owned nearly 1,000 acres of land and had a valuable herd of cattle, along with more property, in Texas. He was also unfriendly, tight-fisted, and had a deep distrust of banks and lawyers.

Jacob and his wife, Anna, had five children, but Anna died in 1859, six days after their birth of their son, Judd. The boy ended up being raised by his sister, Susan, and her husband, Daniel Holcomb, on their nearby farm. He believed they were his parents until he was ten years old.

Against their father's wishes, sons Dayton and Byron, both moved to Texas to raise sheep after the Civil War. Dayton died mysteriously there in 1882.

Eunice - Jacob's favorite child - was a graduate of St. Mary's College at Notre Dame. She married Henry White, who was the bother of prominent physician and patent medicine salesman, George J. White. Eunice and Henry had been married for two years at the time of the murders and had been living with Jacob so that she could take of her aging father.

The only other people who were present at the house that night were Moses Polley, a business acquaintance; George Bolles, a 16-year-old black farmhand; and Julia Reese, the housekeeper. The staff lived in the Crouch home, which, despite Jacob's wealth, was an unpretentious, shabby farmhouse.

It was George Bolles who discovered the murders. He later stated that he had been awakened in the night by thunder and had looked out the window. He thought he saw a man with a lantern in the yard. Then, from downstairs, he heard what sounded like a heavy thud, followed by another and another and finally, a muffled scream. Terrified, he climbed into a

Victims of the unsolved Crouch murders

trunk and stayed there until morning. When he went downstairs and saw the blood and carnage, he ran to the home of the nearest neighbor, who called Sheriff Eugene D. Winney.

Jacob had been shot in the head. Polley was shot in the head and chest. Henry had a bullet hole in his abdomen and another in his neck. Eunice had been shot four times - twice in the right arm, once in the neck, and once in the head.

Julia Reese knew nothing of Bolles' gruesome discovery. She was in the kitchen preparing breakfast when neighbors burst into the house and frightened her.

Because they were the only two left alive in the house, Reese and Bolles were immediately arrested for the murders. They stayed in jail for less than a day before being released. There was no evidence against them, and neither had a motive.

Sheriff Winney began an investigation, but he was out of his element. The small-town sheriff had no experience with murders, and in those days, of course, no forensic evidence or fingerprints could be gathered. Winney was left to do anything that he could, including calling in an Ann Arbor photographer to photograph Eunice's eyes to see if the image of the killer was still reflected in them. He tried but said that too much time had passed for it to work.

Thousands of curiosity-seekers visited the Crouch farm. The Michigan Central Railroad reportedly halted trains there to accommodate those who wanted to see the scene of the crime.

This led to rampant speculation on the part of neighbors, townspeople, out-of-towners, and the general public. Some suggested that "gypsies" robbed the home, or that Polley, known for bragging about how much money he carried, was followed from the train to the farm by thieves. Others thought it might have been the revenge on the part of a farmhand Crouch had fired, but that list of suspects was long. There were also those who claimed that Byron had hired a band of Texas cowboys to kill his father to resolve a dispute over an inheritance.

Jackson County offered a $10,000 reward for information that led to the capture of the killer. A White relative offered $2,000 more.

This led to the involvement of Pinkerton Detective Agency and dozens of amateur detectives, who descended on Jackson after news spread about the murders - and the rewards. One of them was Daniel Holcomb's brother, Henry, who donned a disguise so that he could hang out in the seedier parts of Jackson to get information. One amateur detective, Galen E. Brown, a former policeman from Battle Creek, was shot in the chest while walking down the road near the Crouch farm one day. The person that shot him was never identified.

The first major arrest in the case was a man named Joseph Allen, a machinist who was arrested in Hamilton, Ontario, and charged with the murders on the testimony of Henry Holcomb. Allen had mortgages, deeds, land patents, and a letter that belonged to Jacob Crouch. However, charges were dismissed on May 6, 1884, when Allen was able to prove that the papers had been given to him by Henry White.

Holcomb seemed to have a good reason to want to throw suspicion on someone other than his brother. Rumors in Jackson claimed that Jacob Crouch had been planning to leave his substantial fortune to Eunice's unborn child and cut his son Judd and the Halcombs out of his will. The authorities took the rumors seriously - and perhaps someone else did as well.

On January 2, 1884, Susan Holcomb was found dead in her bed. She had died from poisoning. Some believed that she had been force-fed rat poison, but others said that she had killed herself because she was afraid of having to testify against her husband if he was arrested for murder. According to the coroner's report, though, her heart had simply "gave out."

Strange, but then things got stranger.

Two days later, the Holcombs' farmhand, James Foy, was found shot to death. He was found with a bullet in his head. It was said that Foy talked too freely about the Crouch murders in the local saloons and had even shot a Union City man who implied that Foy was involved in the murders. Foy's death was ruled a suicide.

A short time later, Judd Crouch and Daniel Holcomb were arrested and charged with the murders. Daniel's trial started on November 8, 1884. Prosecutor Frank Hewlett, who was in poor health,

Reynolds Cemetery, where Jacob Crouch is buried. It is here where the spectral reunion between Crouch and his daughter, Eunice, is supposed to take place each year.

called on Austin Blair, former Michigan governor, to serve as special counsel. Hewlett died a few days into the trial.

There were 145 witnesses called to testify, but they offered only circumstantial evidence, and none could say positively who killed Jacob Crouch, the Whites, and Moses Polley. Oddly, one of the witnesses at the trial, Mrs. Thomas Murphy, was killed by her insane ax-wielding husband during the trial.

On January 10, 1885, the jury returned a verdict of not guilty for Daniel Holcomb. They deliberated for less than an hour.

Judd Crouch was never brought to trial, and no one was ever arrested or charged in the case again.

In the aftermath of the case, Hudd moved to Indiana but quietly returned to Jackson in the early 1900s and made a living hauling scrap and doing landscaping work. He inherited his father's farm, estimated to be worth $50,000, but he later lost it to the bank. Judd died in 1946, and his father's house was destroyed in a suspected arson fire in 1947.

That would have brought an end to the story, if not for the haunting.

On the first anniversary of the murders, stories spread that a hazy white, could-like mist was seen traveling between St. John's

Cemetery in Jackson - where Eunice White was buried - to Reynolds Cemetery, which was five miles away. The glowing apparition would stop in front of the grave of Jacob Crouch and slowly disappear. Locals came to believe that it was the ghost of Eunice White, reuniting with her father, and at some point, a yearly vigil began to take place at Reynolds Cemetery, hoping that the ghostly reunion would again take place.

It continues to this day, although the police and neighbors have tried to keep people away from this spot-on November 21, so it's not advised to hang out there.

Believe me, though, if that spectral reunion is taking place, it's going to happen whether anyone is there to see it or not.

The Grave of A "Bookbinder"

A few miles outside of the city of Peoria, Illinois, on a bluff that overlooks the Illinois River, is the site of what was once the Peoria State Hospital. It was a place that was built with the best of intentions, and the asylum was filled with hope when the first patients arrived in 1902. By the time that it closed its doors in 1973, though, it had become a relic of the past and a sad reminder of the unrealized dreams of many of the people who had founded it more than 70 years before.

Before 1907, the people of the Peoria area took great pride in what was then called the "Illinois Asylum for the Incurable Insane at Bartonville." Their feelings did not change when the name was altered to the "Illinois General Hospital for the Insane" or, finally, the "Peoria State Hospital" in 1909.

Early in its history, and throughout most of its years of operation, the hospital and adjacent grounds were almost park-like in appearance. This is a far different scene than what can be found there today. For many years, the few original buildings that remained after 1973 were decrepit and badly in need of repair. Those who visited the site were drawn to the large, looming structures, but always with a sense of unease. Most are gone now, and the few that remain are unrecognizable from what they once were. The cottages and

The Peoria State Hospital in the early 1900s

outbuildings have been destroyed, and the grounds of the asylum on the hilltop have been filled with new buildings, industrial-type businesses, and garages.

For the most part, people don't come here today looking for the grand place that thousands of mentally ill men and women once called home - they come because of the ghosts. For well over a century, the Peoria State Hospital has almost become synonymous with ghost stories. It wouldn't be until the 1970s when the public would start to hear stories of the abandoned buildings being haunted. Since that time, countless tales of encounters with the spirit world have swirled about the old asylum. Prior to that - going back to the early days of the institution - the Peoria State Hospital was known to be home to a famous spirit.

He was called the "Bookbinder" when he was alive, and after all these years, his grave can still be found in the oldest cemetery that is located on the hospital's former grounds. He only made one appearance, but it was a sensational one that was witnessed by several hundred people, including the superintendent of the hospital himself.

But there is much more to the story of the Peoria State Hospital than just ghosts - and more to the ghost story that haunts it than most people probably realize.

Dr. George A. Zeller

The Peoria State Hospital - actually located in the small, nearby town of Bartonville but named for Peoria because it was the closest railroad station - got off to a rather inauspicious start. The original building that was built in 1896 had to be torn down just one year later after it was found to be collapsing into an abandoned coal mine. The asylum was started over from scratch and by that time, the Kirkbride Plan - an asylum that was one large building designed to let in sunlight to "cheer up" the mentally ill patients - had started to fall out of favor and had been replaced by the "Cottage Plan," which involved a large administration building and a number of smaller buildings spread throughout the property. These cottages bore little resemblance to the harsh and foreboding look of the original building. When the first patients arrived in February 1902, they found a new, modern facility waiting for them - and a new way of thinking regarding the treatment of mental health.

One doctor at the forefront of this new medicine was Dr. George A. Zeller, who was appointed as the first superintendent of the Peoria asylum in 1896, long before it had even been built. During the problems with construction, Dr. Zeller was serving with the military in the Philippines during the Spanish-American War. He did not return to Illinois until about eight months after the asylum opened when he took over from Dr. H.B. Cariel, who had been acting superintendent in his absence. Zeller's arrival in Bartonville began his 36-year connection to the Peoria State Hospital.

Dr. Zeller's initial impression of the hospital was not a favorable one. He even expressed his dislike for the name, feeling that it hearkened back to mental illness treatment of the past. In time, he would see the name changed, but this was not what displeased him the most. He felt that this hospital had been created not to help the mentally ill people who were languishing in the poor houses across the state, as had been intended, but built so that other facilities could simply send their problem patients there. Of the 690 patients that he had when he started, Dr. Zeller found that not a single inmate had come from a poor house. He knew the horrors that were being experienced by those patients and wanted to do all that he could to help them. They would become the focus of some of his initial changes at the hospital.

Other changes were physical. While Dr. Zeller was away serving the military, the state had installed heavy iron gratings and bars on the windows and doors. He discovered this when he returned, along with the addition of rooms designed to be seclusion rooms, with heavy doors and peepholes so the staff could monitor those restrained inside. This had been common practice for many state hospitals of the era, but it was unacceptable to Dr. Zeller. He immediately started to implement drastic changes, starting with the removal of the bars and grates from the windows and doors of as many cottages as possible. At first, the bars were only removed from the dining rooms, and once success had been determined, then from doors and windows of other cottages. Dr. Zeller believed this would contribute to the bucolic, peaceful atmosphere that he was trying to maintain at the asylum, and he was right. By October 1905, the last of the bars and guards were removed from all the buildings on the grounds.

Another of Dr. Zeller's programs involved the reduction and eventual banning of all forms of mechanical restraints. By June 1904, he wrote that all forms of straitjackets, chains, and shackles had fallen into disuse, except for rare cases with the most violent inmates. He believed that such restraints were more for the convenience of the attendants, rather than for the good of the patient.

Dr. Zeller also instituted an eight-hour workday for the staff at the hospital, which was revolutionary at the time. He believed that employees who were forced to work longer than eight hours were, in many cases, too exhausted to care for their charges properly. He worked hard to get this into the hospital's budget and still make sure that all the cottages were properly staffed. He solved that problem by having the hospital do a systematic reclassification of all the patients. Once this was accomplished, Dr. Zeller was generally able to reduce the number of attendants needed in some cottages. The excess attendants were now able to not only supplement the cottages that contained violent and destructive patients but to schedule more time off for the entire staff.

Once the news of Dr. Zeller's innovations started to emerge, a great deal of attention was focused on him and the hospital - not all of it favorable. Many believed that he had gone too far. They could not fathom how he could manage a facility with 1,800 patients without any sort of restraints, no cells, and no places of seclusion and confinement. They were even more puzzled by the lack of bars and grates on the doors and windows. In fact, many of the wards and cottages were unlocked day and night. Some of Dr. Zeller's detractors were so alarmed that they voiced their concerns to his superiors in the state capital. According to Dr. Zeller, they had reported, "that a reign of terror existed in our neighborhood and that our paroled patients were committing all sorts of depredations."

As a result - and unknown to Dr. Zeller and the staff - an investigator was sent to the hospital by the State Board. After spending three days visiting various homes and interviewing people who lived in the area, the investigator found that there was no basis for the complaints. In fact, quite the opposite was found. He found that the community supported not only Dr. Zeller but his new open-door policies as well. Due to the investigation, the board encouraged Dr. Zeller not only to continue what he had been doing but to expand on it however he wanted.

But Dr. Zeller knew his days at the asylum were numbered. He had been appointed as the asylum's superintendent in 1896, and his appointment, by his own admission, had been as the result of his political activities. In 1912, the general election saw the Republican Party's power and influence diminish both on a national and state level. As a result, Dr. Zeller was replaced as superintendent. He knew that no matter what he had accomplished at the hospital, politics would always get in the way. Dr. Zeller had been assured by many that his job was secure, but he knew otherwise, so he began lobbying for the position of state alienist. In those days, "alienist" was a term for a specialist in mental disease. He assumed that position on December 1, 1913, and was succeeded at Peoria State Hospital by Dr. Ralph T. Hinton.

The following year, Dr. Hinton began undoing many of the changes that Dr. Zeller had made over the last decade. His first order of business was to have the bars and restraints placed back on the wards and cottages. A zoo that Dr. Zeller had built for the patients using the metal bars that had once confined them in the buildings was shut down. Dr. Hinton remained as the superintendent until 1917 when he was replaced by Dr. Ralph Goodner.

It was during his tenure that the first staff member at the hospital died on the premises. She was a housekeeper named Anne M. Stuart, who had fallen ill while working. Soon after she was moved to her room, she slipped into a coma and died. Her death was never explained. And neither was the brutal beating of a patient in October 1903. Two attendants were accused of his murder, but they were never charged.

After his tenure as the state alienist, Dr. Zeller took over the position of superintendent at the state hospital in Alton, Illinois. He remained there for several years and then returned to Peoria State Hospital - although no one knew it right away. After hearing rumors of overall neglect and abuse at the asylum, he checked himself in as an inmate for three days, living on a different ward every night. He was so moved - and so sickened - by his experience that he ordered all the staff to serve an eight-hour shift as an inmate so they could see what the patients were forced to endure.

Once again, Dr. Zeller began implementing changes to the hospital. He reformed the nursing academy that had been allowed to fall apart during his absence, introduced new social services, and worked to bring the hospital back to its earlier standards. He was also active in social affairs in Peoria and bought the Jubilee College and grounds in 1933 and donated the grounds to the state of Illinois. His wife, Sophie, later donated the chapel. Dr. Zeller retired in 1935, and he and his wife continued to live in a home on the grounds of the Peoria State Hospital. He died on June 29, 1938, and his funeral was held at the hospital attended by friends, family, dignitaries, and former and current patients.

After the death of Dr. Zeller, the hospital remained in use for many years, adding buildings, patients, and care facilities for children and tuberculosis patients. But not all the advances that occurred in the modern era were positive ones, no matter how they might have seemed at the time. In October 1938, the hospital took a big step away from the hydrotherapy, color, and music treatments that had been instituted by Dr. Zeller. It was in that month that the first Insulin Therapies were introduced as "shock therapy." Lobotomies began being performed in the 1940s, and in September 1942, the first Electro Convulsive Therapy was introduced to treat epilepsy.

By the 1950s, the asylum's population had started to decline with the introduction of new drugs that could not only balance out the problems being experienced by many patients but make them capable of leaving to live in the community again. In the 1960s, reform laws prevented patients from working at the institution, which led to increased budgets and patient idleness. The activities that had been given to these lost souls had given them a feeling of worth and usefulness, but that was now lost to them. They were left to wander back and forth to the places where they had been working each day, only to be turned away from the tasks that made them feel useful.

By the 1960s, mental health treatment had changed from a pastoral community that cared for patients for decades to a quick turn-around, open-door treatment plan that fed the patients drugs and put them back out onto the street again. In 1965, the population of the Peoria State Hospital was at 2,300, and by the time it closed in 1973, there were only 280 remaining. Only five of the buildings were in use.

The final years of the hospital seem to have been a time of chaos and neglect. In 1967, a nurse was killed by one of the patients. He struck her in the head with a steel bar from a garbage can lid. In June 1972, patient Bernard Roe was struck in the head with a chair while standing in the line for lunch. He collapsed in the dining hall, did not receive treatment until the following day, and died a short time later. A few days later, another patient, Jerome Spence, was beaten to death by a fellow inmate. In August 1972, James Logan died from an untreated ear infection, which turned into spinal meningitis.

When the hospital finally closed, it was in deplorable condition. A report from the Illinois Investigating Commission on December 18, 1973, told of the shocking condition of the buildings and the last remaining patients. The buildings were filthy and falling apart, crumbling into a state of decay and disrepair. The odor of urine and filth filled the air. Blood and excrement had been smeared on the walls. The patients wandered the halls, naked, or in torn and soiled clothing. Most of them were filthy and had open sores and untreated physical illnesses. The heavy use of narcotics kept them in a constant stupor - and, of course, under control. The last remaining patients were transferred to the Galesburg State Research Hospital.

The city of Bartonville acquired the hospital land, intending to turn it into an industrial park. All the original buildings that formed the main part of the complex were left intact for a time, even though all of them were in various stages of decay, disrepair, and collapse. In time, most of them vanished altogether.

The end had come at last to what had once been one of the finest mental health facilities in the country.

After the hospital closed and the site was sold at auction in 1980, the doors were seemingly thrown open for every kind of trespasser, vandal, urban explorer, and ghost hunter imaginable. Many of these curiosity-seekers, drawn to the building because of its legends and ghosts, claimed to encounter some pretty frightening things in the remaining buildings, especially the old Bowen Administration building, which had been left largely intact.

The atmosphere of the place alone is more than enough to justify the reports of apparitions and strange energy. The impressions of the past would certainly be strong in a building where mentally ill people were housed and where "psychic disturbances" would be common. And then, of course, there are the spirits who simply don't want to depart. The hospital was the only home that many of the patients knew and, even after death, there was no reason for them to leave.

Even before the hospital closed its doors for the final time, rumors spread about disturbing sights and sounds inside of the asylum buildings. There were reports of strange lights, footsteps, eerie sounds, disembodied voices, and doors that opened and closed on their own. The stories continued after the hospital was abandoned, and curiosity-seekers began making their journeys into the crumbling building. Some reported seeing shadows that flickered past doorways and darted around corners. They would walk into freezing blasts of cold air that seemed to come from nowhere, without explanation, and then fade away.

But there is no story as famous as the one attached to the asylum's original cemetery.

When the hospital closed in 1973, there had been more than 4,000 patients buried in the asylum's four cemeteries, most of them in unmarked graves in the two oldest burial grounds. Dr. Zeller developed a numbering system for the cemeteries, and that system - as well as all the names that went with each number - has never been publicly disclosed.

The cemeteries remain today, still hidden among the trees and behind the buildings that have been constructed on the hilltop over the years.

They are still there - as so is the legend of "A. Bookbinder."

The first patients arrived by train to the Peoria State Hospital on February 10, 1902, and by June 30, of that same year, there had already been 22 deaths among them. Such numbers would not change much through the asylum's history, largely due to the poor health conditions often faced by the patients who came from terrible circumstances to find a new home at the hospital. They were quite literally killed by their pasts.

The Peoria State Hospital was in operation for a period of 72 years - 1902 to 1973. It was over this relatively short span of time that

4,132 patients died and were interred on the hospital grounds. This did not include those who died and then were taken to be buried elsewhere. The early reports gave numbers as to how many deaths occurred each year, but the later reports did not offer such detailed statistics. This makes it impossible to know just how many patients perished during those 72 years.

Dr. Zeller was aware of the fact that deaths would occur at the Peoria State Hospital and that not all of the deceased would be claimed by family and friends. He later wrote, "I recognized that along with the problem of the living, the disposal of the dead was one that must also have its share of attention. We buried the bodies of the friendless and unclaimed, as the remains of the well-to-do were shipped at the expense of friends and relatives to such points as they designated."

Dr. Zeller supervised the creation of cemeteries, where the bodies of unknown and forgotten patients could be buried. The burial grounds would eventually spread into four separate cemeteries. From the very beginning, every attempt was made by Dr. Zeller to show proper respect for those unfortunates that were interred at Peoria State Hospital. Dr. Zeller's sense of propriety when dealing with the deceased came about partially as a result of his military service, which left a lasting impression on him. He also believed any disrespect for the dead would inevitably lead to disregard and unconcern for the living. With this in mind, Dr. Zeller instituted a short burial service for the staff to perform at the grave of the dead. For the first few years, he personally presided over the services.

It would be Dr. Zeller's close connection with the burial of the dead at the asylum that would lead to the telling of the very first ghost story associated with the hospital. And this was no mere rumor or folk story, but a documented account of a supernatural event - told by Dr. Zeller himself in his autobiography.

Shortly after organizing the cemeteries for the hospital, Dr. Zeller also put together a burial corps to deal with the disposal of the bodies of patients who died. The corps always consisted of a staff member and several of the patients. While these men were still disturbed, all of them were competent enough to take part in the digging of graves. Of all the gravediggers, the most unusual man, according to Dr. Zeller, was a fellow that he dubbed in his writings as "A. Bookbinder."

This man had been sent to the hospital from a county poorhouse. He had suffered a mental breakdown while working in a printing house in Chicago, and his illness had left him incapable of coherent speech. The officer who had taken him into custody had noted in his report that the man had been employed as "a bookbinder." A court clerk inadvertently listed this as the man's name instead of his occupation, and he was sent to the hospital as "A. Bookbinder."

Dr. Zeller described the man as being strong and healthy, although completely uncommunicative. He was attached to the burial corps, and soon, attendants realized that "Old Book," as he was affectionately called, was especially suited to the work. Ordinarily, as the coffin was lowered at the end of the funeral, the gravediggers would stand back out of the way until the service ended. Nearly every patient at the hospital was unknown to the staff, so services were performed out of respect for the deceased and not because of some personal attachment. Because of this, everyone was surprised during the first internment attended by Old Book when he removed his cap and began to weep loudly for the dead man.

"The first few times he did this," Dr. Zeller wrote, "his emotion became contagious and there were many moist eyes at the graveside but when at each succeeding burial, his feelings overcame him, it was realized that Old Book possessed a mania that manifested itself in uncontrollable grief."

It was soon learned that Old Book had no favorites among the dead. He would do the same thing at each service, and as his grief reached its peak, he would go and lean against an old elm tree that stood in the center of the cemetery, and there he would sob loudly.

Time passed, and eventually, Old Book also passed away. Word spread among the employees, and since the man was so well-liked, everyone decided they would attend his funeral. Dr. Zeller wrote that more than 100 uniformed nurses attended, along with male staff members and several hundred patients.

Dr. Zeller officiated at the service. Old Book's casket was placed on two cross beams above his empty grave, and four men stood by to lower it into the ground at the end of the service. As the last hymn was sung, the men grabbed hold of the ropes. "The men stooped forward," Dr. Zeller wrote, "and with a powerful, muscular effort, prepared to lift the coffin, in order to permit the removal of the crossbeams and allow it to descend into the grave gently. At a given signal, they heaved away the ropes and the next instant, all four lay on their backs. For the coffin, instead of offering resistance, bounded into the air like an eggshell, as if it were empty!"

Needless to say, the spectators were a little shocked at this turn of events, and the nurses were reported to have shrieked, half of them running away and the other half coming closer to the grave to see what was happening.

"In the midst of the commotion," Dr. Zeller continued, "a wailing voice was heard, and every eye turned toward the Graveyard Elm from whence it emanated. Every man and woman stood transfixed, for there, just as had always been the case, stood Old Book, weeping and moaning with an earnestness that outrivaled anything he had ever shown before."

Dr. Zeller was amazed at what he observed but did not doubt that he actually saw it. "I, along with the other bystanders, stood transfixed at the sight of this apparition... it was broad daylight, and there could be no deception."

After a few moments, the doctor summoned some men to remove the lid of the coffin, convinced that it must be empty and that Old Book could not be inside of it. The lid was lifted, and as soon as it was the wailing sound came to an end. Inside of the casket lay the body of Old Book, unquestionably dead. It was said that every eye in the cemetery looked upon the still corpse and then over to the elm tree in the center of the burial ground. The specter had vanished.

"It was awful, but it was real," Dr. Zeller concluded. "I saw it, 100 nurses saw it, and 300 spectators saw it." But if it was anything other than the ghost of Old Book, Dr. Zeller had no idea what it could have been.

A few days after the funeral, the Graveyard Elm began to wither and lose its leaves. Despite efforts to save it, the tree declined over the next year and then died. Later, after the dead limbs had dropped, workmen tried to remove the rest of the tree, but stopped

The grave of "A. Bookbinder"

after the first cut of the ax caused the tree to emanate what was said to be "an agonized, despairing cry of pain." After that, Dr. Zeller suggested that the tree be burned. However, as soon as the flames started around the tree's base, the workers quickly put them out. They later told Dr. Zeller they had heard a sobbing and crying sound coming from it. "In the clouds of smoke that curved upward," the workman said, "he could plainly outline the features of our departed mourner."

Eventually, the tree fell in a storm, taking with it the lingering memories of a mournful man known as "Old Book."

The tale of the "Bookbinder" has been told so many times over the years that it has - and rightfully so - taken on the status of legend. For many, it seems hard to believe that Dr. Zeller would have confessed to witnessing a ghost in the cemetery that day. Surely the story was merely a tall tale, embellished by the superintendent to make his autobiography more interesting. Zeller also wrote fiction, it's been claimed, based on his life at the asylum. He must have invented the character of "Old Book" for pure entertainment. Right?

We shouldn't be too quick to dismiss the story because, as has been proven time and again, almost every legend contains at least a kernel of truth. In this case, records show that the "Bookbinder" really did exist.

In 1974, a newspaper reporter decided to track down the story of the Bookbinder and discovered that there really had been a patient at the asylum who had been dubbed "Manual Bookbinder," which would have been a description of his duties at the bookbindery where he worked. Dr. Zeller did slightly alter his name in the story. Bookbinder was a native of Austria who had been admitted to the asylum in 1904. According to additional records, he died during an outbreak of pellagra in 1910.

Pellagra was a vitamin deficiency disease most frequently caused by a chronic lack of niacin in the diet. It's classically described by "the three Ds": diarrhea, dermatitis, and dementia, but makes its physical presence known by red skin lesions on the hands, hair loss, insomnia, mental confusion, and aggression. During the 1909-1910 outbreak, Dr. Zeller estimated that at least 500 patients were afflicted with the disease, and this resulted in the death of 150 of them.

There is no direct reference to this man being "Old Book," and the character was never mentioned in any of the asylum's annual reports. However, in the statistical tables of the "Sixth Biennial Report of the Commissioner, Superintendent, and Treasurer of the Illinois Asylum for the Incurable Insane at Peoria," on page 32, listed under the "Nativity of All Patients Present June 30, 1906," there are six male patients from Austria. The "Eighth Biennial Report" contains a report dealing with the outbreak of pellagra, noting that there were 38 male deaths from the disease. One could say that this substantiates at least some of the findings of the reporter.

The most reliable evidence that "Old Book" really did exist was found in a 1905 Supervisor's Journal. This ledger contains the clothing accounts of the patients at the hospital, and on pages 2 and 24, there are entries that state that "Bookbinder, M." received six handkerchiefs with a total value of 12-cents.

Does this mean that there really was a "Bookbinder" at the Peoria State Hospital? Yes, it does. But it's up to the reader to decide if the story of his ghost actually occurred or if one of the most respected doctors in the history of Illinois' treatment of mental illness simply made up the story because he wanted to concoct a spooky tale. We'll likely never know for sure, but there is no question that the legend of "Old Book" will make sure that the Peoria Asylum is never forgotten.

Cities of the Dead

There are 38 cemeteries in New Orleans. The traditions of death, burials, and boneyards in the city are unlike anything you'll find in other American cities.

It was Mark Twain who first praised the uniqueness of New Orleans' cemeteries. He wrote: "Our cities of the dead look just like our cities of the living - long narrow houses, housing multi-generations of the same family with above-ground basements."

Twain had always intended to buy a house in New Orleans, but he never did. He died in Redding, Connecticut, and his funeral was held in a Presbyterian Church in Manhattan. My guess is that he would have preferred a send-off in New Orleans instead of the dignified service that he got in New York.

The graveyards of New Orleans are much like the city itself. They are a mirror to its greatness. They are beautiful and in ruin, at the same time. And like the city, they hold many secrets.

New Orleans is the most unique city in America. Its way of death is the most distinctive part of its culture. For more than 200 years, the people of New Orleans have housed their dead in small, above-ground tombs. They are built along streets in miniature cities of the gone and the forgotten. These cities of the dead provide hours of discovery for the intrepid tourist and sometimes, for the brave of heart.

New Orleans is a city that has known death. Just a few short years after the colony was founded, it was flattened by a hurricane, bringing ruin and destruction. Fire, epidemics, and hardship claimed more lives, and there was always a need for a way to dispose of the dead.

The city was - and continues to be - wet. The water table is located just below the soil. The colonists searched for higher ground for their burials and found it along the banks of the Mississippi. But during the frequent floods, the bodies of the dead would wash out of their muddy graves and come floating through the streets of the town.

The first public cemetery in New Orleans was created on St. Peter Street in 1721. It was officially outside the town limits at the time. This was not done for aesthetic reasons but for health. It was commonly believed that graveyards exuded a noxious odor that carried disease. They didn't, but it seemed like a good idea in a town that had already seen more than its share of epidemics.

Those early burials were all below ground. Plots were reserved for the clergy and the wealthy and distinguished of the city, but it was a shabby and dirty place that only operated until 1788. It was closed, but not because of bodies that kept popping up out of the ground, but because this was the year of the great fire that burned down most of the city and killed more than 1,200 people. The St. Peter Cemetery couldn't handle the overflow of bodies, so they had to be taken and buried in the cypress swamp that is now located where Basin Street exists between Conti and St. Louis Streets.

St. Louis Cemetery No. 1 took its place. The new cemetery was a walled enclosure with its main entrance off Rampart Street. The poor were buried in unmarked graves until the middle 1800s, and as available space filled, the level of the soil began to sink. Contracts for dirt were frequently bid upon, and city chain gangs shoveled it evenly throughout the graveyard, making room for more bodies. It is believed that beneath the grounds of the cemetery, there are layers of bones several feet thick.

For all but the indigent, though, above-ground tombs were the rule. There were several reasons for this - not the least of which was the wet soil. As graves were dug, they often filled with water. Coffins floated out of the holes, despite gravediggers placing heavy stones or bricks on the lids. Such conditions made funerals a somewhat terrifying affair. Caskets were often lowered into gurgling pools of water and oozing mud. As often as not, the coffin would capsize as the water began to leak in, causing newly buried and half-decomposed cadavers to float to the surface of the grave --- to the horror of those attending the funeral, of course.

St. Louis Cemetery No. 1 in New Orleans

Another reason for the above-ground tombs was fashion, of all things. During this same period - back home in Paris - the French were creating the first garden cemeteries outside of the city. Pere Lachaise Cemetery was the first City of the Dead, with above-ground mausoleums and tombs with space for multiple bodies in the same small stone house. It became the final resting place of France's most famous citizens, and the style spread to other places, including New Orleans.

And then, of course, there is the Catholic Church, which helped spread the stories of dead people popping up out of the ground every time it rained. They used the stories as a sales pitch to guilt their parishioners into buying the more expensive above-ground tombs that were owned by, sold by, and filled the pockets of the New Orleans archdiocese.

The burial plots in the cemetery were sold to families, and they constructed tombs to suit their purposes on the land. Most of the tombs had two vaults, and the top vault is used first. By law, you could only inter two fresh bodies at a time. After that, you were cut off. Once occupied, the burial houses were sealed and had to remain sealed for one year and one day. This was a rule that came along during the days of the yellow fever epidemics in New Orleans when it was worried - incorrectly - that the disease could be caught from a dead body.

The real advantage to the year and a day rule is that the body would be inside the tomb over an entire New Orleans summer. When it's 110 degrees outside on a hot August day, it's well above 300 degrees inside the tomb. The body is cooked and naturally cremated. At the end of the 366 days, the vault is opened, and the remains are moved into the *caveau* - a chamber in the tomb's foundation - to make room for the next occupant.

If more than two members of your family died during that 366 days, they were out of luck. The law prohibits the tomb from being opened. But there's an option available in the cemetery wall. Each cemetery is outfitted with dozens of vaults that look like brick pizza ovens. They are rental properties for when a family member dies while the tomb is still sealed. They can be used for 366 days, and then they are scooped and bagged, making room for more of the recently dead to fill the slots.

If you failed to pay the rent on the oven vault, though, you'd get evicted, just like when you don't pay your rent on a living space. A cemetery employee would use a long pole to push the remains to the back of the oven, where an opening in the floor allowed them to be dumped to the bottom of the vault and mix with the ashes of the other people who didn't pay rent over the years.

Obviously, not having money could be an issue when it came to your funeral. So, many in New Orleans started to build monuments that were dedicated to an association or group, rather than just to a family. Many poor immigrants could not afford funeral expenses or a personal tomb. Benevolent societies formed, allowing members to pool their money and build society vaults in the city's cemeteries.

The tallest monument in St. Louis Cemetery No. 1 is the Italian Mutual Benevolent Society tomb. It has space for more than 1,000 remains. Many film buffs will recognize it as the background in the

LSD trip scene from *Easy Rider*, where Peter Fonda climbed all over the monument, and Dennis Hopper allegedly tore the head off one of the statues. By the way, that scene was filmed there without permission from the archdiocese, which led to a permanent ban on all Hollywood productions in the cemetery.

At the end of Canal Street, where New Orleans becomes Metairie, are the Cypress Grove and Greenwood Cemeteries, both built by the Firemen's Charitable and Benevolent Societies. It was founded in 1834 to arrange burials and help the families of nearly impoverished, all-volunteer firefighters lost their lives in the line of duty. There's also a Police Mutual Benevolent Association, a Confederate monument, and the Benevolent and Protective Order of the Elks.

And while the societies to help bury European immigrants are largely a thing of the past, another New Orleans custom continues today - the Second Line.

The origins of the Second Line procession come from West Africa. During a traditional African circle dance, adults formed the inner circle, and children assembled around the outside. They brought those traditions with them when they arrived in America as slaves. Their music and burial traditions continued in New Orleans mostly because the French and Spanish allowed the slaves to express their music and dance heritage every Sunday - the slave's one free day from work - in Congo Square. The tradition of the Second Line grew out of this.

In the New Orleans Second Line parade, the family of the deceased forms the first line; the second line are the friends and more distant relatives, with lots of room for people who didn't even know the deceased but want to join the party.

Brass bands accompany the funeral party from the church to the gravesite, playing traditional slow spiritual hymns like "Just a Closer Walk with Thee" and "Amazing Grace." Leaving the cemetery, though, the tunes become lively and upbeat. Handkerchiefs that had been used for tears become waving flags, and everyone dances to the Second Line songs that are a celebration of the life that was.

Historically, Second Lines occurred in predominantly African American communities like Treme, but today, they can be found pretty much all over the city and not just for funerals. There are Second Lines staged for weddings and even store openings.

Call me a traditionalist, but I think Second Line parades should only be used in the way they were intended - to bury the dead and celebrate the way they lived their life.

Obviously, I love cemeteries. I love the artwork, the symbols, the atmosphere - and especially the history. Many people laugh when I talk about the most popular cemetery for tourists to visit - but these are special kinds of tourists who understand that graveyards are not just for those with a gruesome or macabre frame of mind.

You know, like the person reading this book.

You understand that visiting the dead is a way of reliving the history of a place. Most of the most famous people in New Orleans can *only* be found in the cemetery. That's the only way that we now have of paying them the respect they deserve.

We talked about Metairie Cemetery earlier in the book, in the section about Josie Arlington and her "flaming tomb," but there are plenty of well-known occupants in other graveyards in the city, too.

St. Louis Cemetery No. 2 is now home to Dominique You, a lieutenant of pirate Jean Lafitte, and to New Orleans mayor Nicholas Girod, who once famously offered his home to Napoleon Bonaparte to live in New Orleans in exile. Musicians Earl King and Ernie K-Doe - most famous for the song "Mother-in-Law" - are buried here. Ernie was supposed to be buried in a family plot outside the city, but his wife, Antoinette, stepped in, saying, "If you're from New Orleans, you want to be buried in New Orleans."

St. Louis Cemetery No. 3 has a chef's corner with adjacent family tombs that belong to the restaurant families of Prudhomme, Galitoire, and others.

E.J. Belloq is also buried here. The weird loner and photographer became famous after death for his private photographic collection of the prostitutes who worked in Storyville. If you haven't seen these photos, seek them out. They are a time capsule of the heyday of one of New Orleans' most notorious spots.

Holt Cemetery was originally a potter's field, holding the remains of those who couldn't afford to pay for a burial. Somewhere on the grounds is the final resting place of Buddy Bolden, the man who invented jazz. He became a victim of acute alcohol psychosis and spent the last 24 years of his life in an asylum. When the most important man in the history of New Orleans music died, he was buried here - but no one knows where.

Some charred bits of Cecil Ingram Conor III are in a grave at Garden of Memories Cemetery. You might know him by better by his professional name of Gram Parsons. A pivotal member in such bands as the Byrds and the Flying Burrito Brothers. He died at the age of 26 from an overdose of alcohol and morphine. His stepfather overruled his wish to be cremated at California's Joshua Tree National Park. His body was on its way to New Orleans when it was intercepted by some pals, who drove his coffin to Joshua Tree, doused it in gasoline, and set it on fire. The resulting fireball alerted the police and led to a high-speed chase and a $700 fine. What was left of Gram was buried in New Orleans.

Mount Olivet Cemetery holds the remains of Henry Roeland Byrd, who was better known as Professor Longhair, the Rock and Roll Hall of Fame member who is also known as the "Picasso of Keyboard Funk."

But our journey through New Orleans cemeteries eventually brings us back around to where we began - at St. Louis Cemetery No. 1. This cemetery is also home to many names from the city's past, and it's also the future resting place of actor Nicholas Cage, who will be someday interred in an oversized and gaudy Egyptian pyramid that is usually covered in lipstick prints left by adoring female fans.

Among the crypts, you'll find the monument of Renest "Dutch" Morial, New Orleans' first black mayor and ardent civil rights activist. He was buried here for years, and while the monument in his honor remains, his body was recently moved to St. Louis Cemetery No. 2.

Benjamin Latrobe - the man called the Father of American Architecture - is buried here. He is most famous for designing the Capitol Building in Washington, D.C., and in New Orleans, he completed the tower of the St. Louis Cathedral and the U.S. Customs Building before dying from yellow fever.

Homer Plessy is also interred here. He was "Rosa Parks" more than 50 years before Rosa Parks. He was of mixed race, which made him African American in the eyes of the law. He purposely sat in a whites-only railroad car intending to be arrested. Plessy took his case all the way to the U.S. Supreme Court. In May 1896, the court issued its infamous "separate but equal" ruling that legalized segregation - like the Jim Crow laws - in America for decades to come.

The cemetery's Protestant Section also holds the remains of many of the city's well-known residents. After the Louisiana Purchase, Americans flooded into the city, and many of them eventually needed a place to be buried. That place is now the low-rent section of St. Louis Cemetery No. 1, a section without vaults, in the far back left corner. The newly arrived Protestants had no interest in being buried above ground, even though this part of the cemetery is below sea level.

Because of this, you can see the double layers of brick and large slabs that have been designed to hold the water-logged coffins below the surface. Legend has it that in the 1800s, visitors to this section of the cemetery often reported the sounds of the coffins knocking and thumping against the undersides of the below-ground tombs.

Later, many of these bodies were moved to other parts of the city, like the first Protestant Cemetery on Girod Street, which was started in 1822 and then closed in 1957. All the bodies were supposed to be moved out at that time - but we know how that goes.

The Superdome now stands atop these old burial grounds, and some football fans that suffered through the first 43 seasons with the Saints claimed they were so terrible because they were playing on an old cemetery.

One of the notables allegedly buried in the Protestant section of the cemetery is William C.C. Claiborne, the first American governor of Louisiana. As an American, Claiborne wasn't a popular politician with the local Creole merchants and families, so after his first wife died, he remarried a Creole woman named Clarisse Durand, hoping to win some favor. After only two years of marriage, though, Clarisse died. When Claiborne died, he was not permitted to be placed in a tomb with his wife because he was not a Catholic. He was buried in the Protestant section instead - but is he still there?

Who knows? There is also a Claiborne family vault at Metairie Cemetery. His remains may have been moved there, or they might be mixed in with the bodies that were taken to Girod Cemetery. No one really knows.

One thing we do know, of course, is that St. Louis Cemetery No. 1 is the final resting place of Voodoo queen Marie Laveau.

Ask any tourist - or anyone who watched a season of *American Horror Story* - and they can tell you that Marie Laveau is the undisputed Queen of Voodoo in New Orleans. Voodoo is as big a part of New Orleans as jazz, gumbo, and Mardi Gras. Most tourists, even after seeing the voodoo shops in the French Quarter, assume that voodoo is a thing of the past - but they couldn't be more wrong. The religious faith is very much alive today, and it's taken just as seriously now as it was in the days of Marie Laveau.

Voodoo came to New Orleans from Africa, mostly by way of the Caribbean islands. Slaves in Louisiana began arriving in 1719. Most enslaved Africans that ended up in New Orleans came directly from West Africa, bringing with them their language and religious beliefs, which were rooted in spirit and ancestor worship. In the Fon language of West Africa, *Vodun* means spirit - an invisible and mysterious force that can intervene in human affairs.

One reason that voodoo developed in New Orleans more than in other parts of America is largely because the French - then the Spanish, then the French again - colonized Louisiana. They were far more tolerant of the practices and the faiths of the slave population than were the British - the people who came to America for religious freedom and then suppressed the faiths of anyone who didn't agree with them.

Another reason was because of the sheer numbers. Thousands of slaves were brought to Louisiana. In fact, according to the census of 1732, the ration of slaves to French settlers was two to one. The white minority would have had a hard time suppressing the voodoo faith, so they mostly didn't bother.

However, some worries popped up here and there. The first reference to voodoo in official documents appeared in 1782 when the Spanish were in charge. In a document about imports to the colony, there is a terse line regarding black slaves from the island of Martinique. Governor Galvez wrote: "These Negroes are too much given to voodooism and make the lives of the citizens unsafe."

But I think the governor was less worried about voodoo and more worried about rebellious slaves. A series of slave revolts had rocked Haiti and other islands in the Caribbean, and each time, French colonists were driven from those lands and ended up in New Orleans. When they arrived, they brought their slaves with them - slaves who not only practiced voodoo but who also may have been recently involved in uprisings.

New Orleans-style voodoo evolved just like the food in New Orleans did - as a blend of different cultures. One of the most important cultures was Catholicism. Some people feel those who practiced voodoo started using Catholic saints, holy water, and the Lord's Prayer in their ceremonies so they could hide voodoo in plain sight. It's been suggested that slaves were forbidden to practice their religion, so they used Catholic saints and icons as stand-ins for important voodoo deities.

But this may not be true. More likely, there was a conscious decision to integrate Catholicism into voodoo because the white man's magic did seem to have some power, as shown by the fact that the white man had a better life as a slave owner instead of as a slave.

For others, the blending of voodoo and Catholicism was simply a natural course of events. After many years and generations away from their homeland, slaves slowly lost their old beliefs, and the predominant Catholicism of New Orleans bled into their practices.

Regardless, if you go into an authentic voodoo shop today, you'll find - in addition to charms, roots, potions, and powders - icons of Catholic saints, statues, and prayer candles, all of which are used in the ceremonies and practices of the faith.

Voodoo in New Orleans grew to be quite a bit different than what is practiced in Haiti and other places. The evolution of the faith in New Orleans created many new practices that most of us associate with some of the basics of voodoo, including voodoo dolls, *gris-gris* -

which are small bags filled with magic items to bring good luck or protect us from evil - and voodoo queens. In Africa, voodoo is a male-dominated faith, but it was the opposite in New Orleans. The slaves gave credit to a female spirit, Aida Wedo, for allowing them to survive the ocean crossing to the New World. This was the beginning of women having central importance in New Orleans-style voodoo.

Marie Laveau is, of course, the most famous voodoo queen in the city's history, but she was not the first. Sanite Dede was an early voodoo practitioner in the city. She was a young woman from Haiti who held rituals in her courtyard at Dumaine and Chartres Street, just a few blocks from the St. Louis Cathedral. The local newspaper printed sensational stories about her rituals, described "wild, uncontrolled orgies" and "serpent worship."

It was the newspaper stories that first upset the white colonists. Whether it was the drums that could be heard during Mass or the supposed orgies, the Church managed to push through an ordinance in 1817 that stated that Catholicism was the only recognized faith in New Orleans - making it illegal to practice any others. Soon after, the police arrested 400 women for allegedly dancing naked in Sanite's courtyard.

The charges were later dropped for lack of evidence, which turned out to be almost as bad as if they had been sent to jail. Rumors spread that voodoo spells had either erased the evidence or clouded the minds of the judges and prosecutors. White residents feared that the religion - practiced by slaves and free people of color - was so powerful that it could entice followers to commit any crime or deed. Supernatural powers and secret drugs made voodoo a force to be reckoned with. Slaves owners began to fear poison in their food. Men and women were convinced they could be forced to fall in love with anyone, just because of a sprinkle of magic powder. Even death could be held in check using "zombie drugs."

The message was clear - voodoo was not welcome in New Orleans. To avoid harassment in the city, voodoo practitioners moved outside the city limits to the swamp of Bayou St. John, near what is now the City Park.

But the fears and prejudices of the white residents of the city did not drive voodoo out of New Orleans altogether. The next leader of voodoo in the city was John Montent, a heavily tattooed voodoo priest known better as Dr. John. He was a well-respected free person of color who sometimes claimed to have once been an African prince. He had several beautiful wives and mistresses, with whom he had over 50 children. In addition to what must have been a busy love life, he was also famous for predicting the future, casting spells, making gris-gris bags, and reading minds.

And if his name sounds familiar, it's likely because you've heard his music. Well, not the original Dr. John, but the music of Mac Rebennack, who took the stage name of Dr. John as an homage to the nineteenth-century voodoo man.

Dr. John was the first in New Orleans to use voodoo for profit. He charged fees to mix potions and make *gris-gris* bags and was happy to sell them to whoever wanted to pay - black or white. He was the mentor, teacher, and some even say the power behind Marie Laveau. She eventually decided to break away from Dr. John and set up her own practice.

Marie Laveau became for voodoo what Louis Armstrong is for jazz. By that, I mean that there are a lot of people who claim to have invented jazz, from Buddy Bolden to Jelly Roll Morton - but it was Louis Armstrong who made it internationally famous. Marie Laveau may have come later than Sanite Dede and Dr. John, but she was the one who made it notorious and the reason that we still talk about it today.

Marie Laveau was born in New Orleans - or maybe in Haiti - in 1794, or maybe not. Her father was a white plantation owner, and her mother was one of his slaves. The first official record of her appeared in 1819 when she married Jacque Paris, another free person of color. She was soon abandoned or maybe widowed, no one knows. At some point in 1825, she began a second, common-law marriage to Christophe de Glapion, another free person of color with whom she would have 15 children. It seems hard to believe that she had time for making potions, holding voodoo ceremonies, and doing hair.

Marie Laveau was a hairdresser. She learned all the latest styles and cared for the most affluent ladies of New Orleans. This allowed her access to the most fashionable homes in the city, gathering gossip

Artist's rendering of Marie Laveau

and information during every appointment. Her clients talked to her about anything and everything, from childbirths to scandals, and she created a network of intelligence by recruiting cooks, maids, and domestic workers as her informants.

In this way, when she told fortunes, she was remarkably well-informed, presenting information that she couldn't possibly know - or so it seemed to her clients. Her reputation became well-known throughout the city. To visit Marie for a reading became the latest craze throughout the city. Politicians paid her as much as $1,000 for help in winning elections. The cost of her love potions soared to $10. As a lifelong Catholic, she has been credited for introducing the Virgin Mary as a central figure of worship in voodoo, attracting even more followers. She dealt in spells and charms, for both white and black customers, and produced cures for their ailments. Marie was a clever and astute businesswoman who knew how to use her beliefs - and the beliefs and fears of others - to the advantage of herself and her clients.

One tale of Marie Laveau has reached legendary status in New Orleans. A young man from a wealthy family was arrested and charged with a series of crimes. While the young man himself was innocent, the true perpetrators had been several of his friends, and they had let the blame fall upon their unlucky pal. His grief-stricken father sought out the assistance of Marie and explained the circumstances of the case to her. He promised a handsome reward if she would use her powers to obtain his son's release. When the day of the trial arrived, Marie placed three peppers into her mouth and went into the St. Louis Cathedral to pray. She remained at the altar for some time and then managed to get into the courtroom where the trial was going to be held. Before the proceedings could start, she took the three peppers from her mouth and put them under the judge's chair. None of the spectators could see them - but there was no way that the judge could miss them as he walked to his chair. We can only imagine what he must have thought after seeing the peppers and then looking out and seeing Marie Laveau sitting behind the defendant in his courtroom.

The trial began, and the prosecutor presented hours of unfavorable evidence against the young man. But after lengthy deliberation, the judge returned to the courtroom and pronounced the young man "not guilty."

Magic? Probably not. More likely, it was the power of suggestion and the worries of the judge about what might happen to him if the young man went to prison. Marie possessed the secrets of the most influential people in the city - probably including the judge.

The father of the young man was thrilled with the verdict, and in return for her help, he gave Marie the deed to a cottage at 1020 St. Anne Street, between Rampart and Burgundy. It remained her home until her death many years later.

Above and beyond her network of spies and her potions and charms, Marie had great showmanship. She knew how to take money from the white man's pockets so that he could watch her rituals. Men and women danced wildly after drinking rum and seemed to become possessed by various gods. Seated on her throne, Marie directed the action, or she danced with a large snake in honor of Damballah, the Sky Father, and the creator of all life.

Once each year, Marie presided over the ritual of St. John's Eve, beginning at dusk on June 23 and ending at dawn the next day. St. John's is the most sacred of holy days in the voodoo faith. Hundreds attended each year, including reporters and curious white onlookers, each of whom was charged a sizable admission. Drum beating, bonfires, animal sacrifice, and nude women dancing were all part of the all-night ritual - which, of course, created lurid stories for newspapers and magazines across the country.

But Marie knew what she was doing. She was a mother, a voodoo queen, and a hairdresser, but she also probably should have started New Orleans's first tourism bureau. One of the reporters who attended Marie's was a writer named Lafcadio Hearn. The quiet, scrawny, bug-eyed, weak-chinned, bird-legged writer was a reporter in Cincinnati before moving to New Orleans in 1877. He'd been fired from his job at a Cincinnati because he'd married an African American woman, which was against Ohio law at the time. He spent the next ten years in New Orleans, writing pieces about the city for national magazines like *Scribner's* and *Harper's Weekly*. His articles created the popular reputation of New Orleans as a place that was more like Europe or the Caribbean than like the rest of the United States. Essentially, he put the city of New Orleans on the tourist map.

He also wrote a lot about voodoo, and while not completely accurate in his reporting, he certainly made it seem like something every adventurous traveler of the nineteenth century should see. Most of his articles portrayed voodoo rituals as snake handling, bourbon drinking, nude dancing, chicken killing affairs that ended with people sticking pins into dolls.

It's a reputation that has endured for a century and a half - all thanks to Lafcadio Hearn and, by extension, the showmanship of Marie Laveau, the voodoo queen who laughed all the way to the bank.

But make no mistake, she also helped a lot of people along the way. She has become a woman known for two identities. She was feared by some and beloved by others. While she charged uptown ladies and politicians hefty fees, she provided many services for free when she cared for the sick during yellow fever outbreaks, ministered to inmates in jail, or just helped those in need who had no money.

Marie died in June 1881 - maybe - but whenever it was, many people didn't realize she was gone. One of her daughters, also using the name Marie Laveau, stepped in and took her place and continued her traditions for some time to come.

But the golden age of voodoo in New Orleans was not destined to last. By the 1930s, tourism had become the foundation of the city's economy. City leaders didn't want to frighten away visitors with the sensationalized version of voodoo that had been created by Hollywood movies like *White Zombie* and best-selling books like *The Magic Island* by William Seabrook. Most of the publications about voodoo in New Orleans or Marie Laveau printed in the 1930s, '40s, and '50s are always sensationalized and usually inherently racist.

Voodoo today is making something of a comeback in New Orleans. There's the touristy voodoo rebirth - which means you'll find about a dozen shops selling *gris-gris* bags and pin dolls in the French Quarter - and then there's the real embrace of the religion. People today are hungry for spiritual fulfillment, and voodoo offers a direct experience that appeals to people. What's happening is very apparent in New Orleans, which has always been the center for these beliefs. The main focus of voodoo today is to serve others and to influence the outcome of life events through a connection with nature, spirits, and ancestors. Most rituals are held behind closed doors since public shows are considered disrespectful to the spirits. Voodoo practices include readings, prayer, and personal ceremony and is often used to cure depression, loneliness, anxiety, depression, and other ailments. It also tries to help the poor, the hungry, and the sick, just as Marie Laveau once did.

But attitudes are slow to change. There is still fear among many people as to what voodoo is and how it works. They dismiss it as superstitious nonsense, but there's no denying that they are afraid of it, too. It's impossible to deny the fear and racism that lurks behind statements made by people like evangelist Pat Robertson, who, after the massive earthquake that occurred in Haiti a few years ago, stated that the Haitians deserved the death and destruction because, in following voodoo, "they made a pact with the Devil."

You won't find the Devil mixed up in voodoo, but you will find some strange stories of spirits that have lingered in New Orleans after all these years.

Marie Laveau allegedly died in 1881, but based on the tales that have been told for years, her spirit may not rest in peace. Some believe that Marie returns to life once each year to lead the faithful on St. John's Eve.

It is also said that Marie haunts the site of her former home at 1020 St. Ann Street. The original house was torn down in 1903, and a new structure was built on the same foundation, which is why many believe her spirit still calls this place home. People have claimed to have seen her walking down St. Ann Street wearing a long white dress, her trademark *tignon*, or headdress, which she knotted seven times to represent a crown. Marie's spirit and those of her followers are said to still perform rituals at the site of her old house.

There is another house also that may harbor Marie's ghost, located on Chartres Street. It was built in 1807, and according to legend, Marie lived there for a time. Residents of the house once said that an apparition appeared in the house and hovered near the fireplace. They claimed that it was the ghost of Marie Laveau.

But the most famous place connected to the spirit of Marie Laveau is her tomb in St. Louis Cemetery No. 1. Thousands of people come here every year in search of her crypt. The tomb looks like so many others in the cemetery until you notice all the things that have been left in front of it. You'll find coins, pieces of herb, bottles of rum, beans, bones, bags, flowers, tokens, and just about anything else you can imagine left behind as an offering for the good luck and blessings of the Voodoo Queen.

If you visit the tomb and don't leave anything, legend has it that your teeth will fall out. I don't know if this is true, but there are supposed to be bad things that happen to those who cross Marie Laveau. In late 2013, someone climbed over the cemetery wall at night and painted Marie's famous vault with pink latex paint. Latex paint, which traps in moisture and does not breathe, can ruin brick and mortar tombs. It required months of work and over $10,000 to repair. I don't know if anything bad happened to this person, but I hope it did.

But not all the damage that has been done to her tomb is quite so dramatic. In fact, most of it is done out of ignorance. You see, in addition to the offerings, you will also find thousands of markings and X's covering the tomb. The tomb is often repainted, but the marks come back. There's nothing supernatural about this - it's done by stupid people. The origins of what some claim is a voodoo practice are unclear but, despite what some people may claim, it's *not* an old tradition. The

X's that are found on the tomb have been left by tour groups and uneducated guides, who instruct the tourists to leave three X's inscribed on the tomb in hopes of good luck.

If visiting St. Louis Cemetery No. 1, think twice before leaving your own X's on the tomb. The Glapion family - who owns the tomb - does not consider this voodoo, but vandalism. If you are hoping to get on the good side of Marie Laveau, leave an offering instead.

Over the years, Marie's ghost has been seen many times in the cemetery along with the ghost of Zombi, Marie's large black pet snake. Legends say that she has sometimes been seen walking the cemetery's narrow paths. One man even claimed to have been slapped by her spirit after making a disparaging remark at her tomb one day.

The tomb of Marie Laveau - whatever you do, don't vandalize it. Leave an offering for good luck instead.

Another story, which was popular in the 1930s, involved a drifter who decided to sleep in the cemetery one night. He slept fitfully for several hours before being awakened by a strange sound. Thinking that perhaps vandals or grave robbers might injure him, he decided to make his escape to the streets. As he rounded the corner of a row of tombs, he saw a terrible sight. Positioned in front of Marie's tomb was a glowing, nude woman with her body entwined by a huge snake. Surrounding her were the ghostly forms of men and women, who were dancing to music only they could hear. Needless to say, the drifter fled for his life.

Perhaps the most unusual sighting of Marie's spirit took place when a man was in a drug store near St. Louis Cemetery No. 1 one afternoon. He was speaking to the druggist when an older woman in a white dress and a blue turban came and stood next to him. Suddenly, the druggist was no longer listening to him, but looking in terrible fear at the older woman instead. Then, he turned and ran to the back of the store. The man turned and looked at the older woman, and she started laughing. He thought that perhaps the druggist had been frightened of a "crazy woman" who lived in the neighborhood.

Finally, the woman looked at the man and asked if he knew her. He replied that he didn't, and she laughed some more. Then, she turned and looked behind the counter and demanded to know where the druggist had gone. She had stopped laughing and seemed truly angry.

The man shrugged, and she suddenly slapped him across the face. Moments later, she turned and ran out the door and, to his shock and surprise, vanished over the cemetery wall. Stunned, the man then stated that he "passed out cold."

When he woke up, the druggist was pouring whiskey down his throat. "You know who that was?" he asked the dazed and confused young man. "That was Marie Laveau. She been dead for years and years but every once in a while, people around here see her."

And then he added, "Son, you've just been slapped by the Queen of Voodoo!"

But Marie's ghost is not the only spirit that is believed to haunt this cemetery.

Another resident spirit is said to be that of Henry Vignes, a sailor who lived in the nineteenth century and roamed all over the world. The closest place that he had to a home was a New Orleans boarding house, where he stored the personal belongings that he didn't carry with him and all his private papers, including the title to his plot at St. Louis Cemetery No. 1. He had left his papers in the care of the boarding house's proprietor in case anything ever happened to him at sea. But once when Henry was away for an extended time, the proprietor sold his plot in the cemetery to the highest bidder. When Henry returned, he was never able to remedy the situation, and when he later fell ill and died, he had no place to be buried. His remains were sent to a potter's field, but his spirit remained in St. Louis Cemetery No. 1. He still walks there today. Visitors sometimes claim they have encountered a thin, pale man with blue eyes who asks them where the Vignes tomb is located.

Another lingering ghost is that of a man known only as Alphonse. Legend has it that he was murdered, but no one knows for sure, and there are no clues to his identity, other than when visitors get too close to the Pinead family tomb; they are told to stay away. Aside from that, Alphonse is not threatening. Instead, he has been known to stop visitors on the narrow paths between the tombs, take them by the hand, and ask them to take him home with them.

The ghost of Paul Morphy has also been encountered in the graveyard. Morphy was the greatest chess player in the world in his day. He became the international chess champion at age 19 but got bored traveling to Europe and Russia and winning every match. He returned to New Orleans in 1859 and retired at age 23. He planned to become a lawyer but instead mostly lounged around his family's home on Royal Street for the rest of his life. At some point, Morphy started living in his own reality. He feared being poisoned and would only eat food prepared by his mother and sister. He also claimed he was

Paul Morphy, chess champion - and weirdo.

being watched while, at the same time, he was following women around the city and spying on them as a voyeur. In the late 1870s, he ran through the streets of the French Quarter one night, completely naked and waving an ax, threatening to kill anyone who tried to stop him.

Morphy was found dead in his bathtub in 1884. He was only 43. The official cause of death was cardiac arrest - some say from jumping into a very cold bath on an extremely hot day - but the official report made no mention of the collection of ladies' shoes that encircled his bathtub.

And a haunted cemetery would not be complete without a classic graveyard tale:

It was said that in the 1930s, New Orleans taxi drivers avoided St. Louis Cemetery No. 1 whenever possible. If they did drive past, they allegedly refused to pick up any young woman in white who hailed them from the graveyard's entrance.

Rumor had it that one driver had picked up such a young girl one night and drove her to the address that she gave him. Once they arrived, she asked him to go up and ring the bell, then inquire for the man who lived there. The man came out, but when the driver told him of the girl waiting in the cab, he immediately asked for her description. When the driver told him what the girl looked like, the man shook his head sadly. This was obviously not the first time that a driver had appeared on his doorstep. The young girl, he explained to the taxi driver, was his wife, but she had died many years ago and had been interred wearing her bridal gown at St. Louis Cemetery No. 1.

That was when the driver suddenly realized the white gown the woman was wearing had been a wedding dress.

He raced back to the cab and jerked open the door, but the woman was gone. The driver fainted away on the spot. After that, young women in white stood little chance of hailing a cab near the entrance to St. Louis Cemetery No. 1.

This was a fitting story with which to end this part of the book. We have one final section of the graveyard to explore now - a tale of another vanishing hitchhiker.

But this is no legend.

This vanishing hitchhiker was - and is - very real.

5. THE GIRL BY THE SIDE OF THE ROAD

The True Story of Resurrection Mary

For many who know me, my endless fascination with the famous Chicago ghost known as "Resurrection Mary" is often a source of amusement. I've talked about her for nearly three decades in lectures, presentations, and even in casual conversation. I've created bus tours that visit the places where she's been encountered and where her legend began. I've searched through newspaper files and old records and interviewed dozens of people who have claimed to see her over the years.

It's undoubtedly an obsession, but I know exactly how it began - with a box of cereal.

 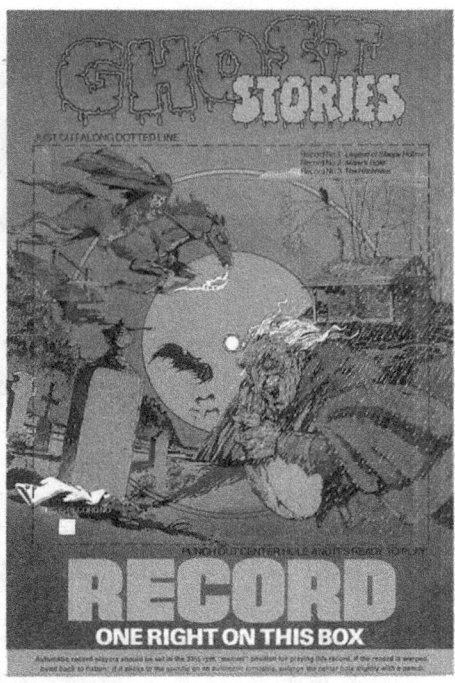

The Honeycomb cereal box record that started my search for vanishing hitchhikers and Resurrection Mary

One Halloween season in the late 1970s, my mother purchased a box of Honeycomb cereal at the grocery store. That October, the cereal maker decided to manufacture boxes with three different 45-rpm records pressed into the cardboard. Each of the records had a different story on it, and once you finished eating all the cereal, you could cut it out of the box and play it on your record player. I don't remember what one of the stories - "The Miser's Gold" - was about, but I do remember the second one was a dramatized version of "The Legend of Sleepy Hollow."

The other one was "The Vanishing Hitchhiker."

I remember sitting transfixed in front of the record player in our basement, listening to the scratchy sounds of the story on the record. The quality was not great - what do you want from a record that used to be part of a cereal box? - but I can remember my hair standing on end when the narrator went out to the cemetery the next morning and found...

Well, I won't ruin the story for you, but let me just say that this record probably had a greater impact on me than years of wandering around so-called haunted houses and sitting for hours in dark graveyards at night.

That was when my obsession with vanishing hitchhikers began, and I started collecting every story, legend, and book that even mentioned the subject that I could find. Then, when I was in high school, I started hearing stories about a Chicago ghost that was hitching rides along Archer Avenue on the South Side of the city. I convinced a librarian to get copies of the Chicago newspapers for me, and I began following the exploits of a specter they were called "Resurrection Mary."

And I never forgot her. Years later, when I started making my living writing about ghosts and creating tours of haunted places, Resurrection Mary became a favorite subject of mine. She ended up in many of my books and in the lectures I gave for libraries, private functions, and conferences.

And there were not just lectures in Illinois or Chicago. I talked about her all over the country. Often, people in other states or distant parts of the country would tell me: "Oh, I've heard that one already." Then, they would tell me their own vanishing hitchhiker stories about beautiful young girls who hitched rides along deserted highways and then mysteriously vanished from the automobiles that picked them up. Each story was basically like the last one I'd heard, but the location was always different. The stories were similar but were never quite the same as the story of Mary.

I had to explain to people that Resurrection Mary is no ordinary "vanishing hitchhiker" story - it was "*THE* vanishing hitchhiker story. Mary is the phantom who has inspired countless other legends and boasts one of the rare stories that did not take place on some forgotten highway somewhere, at some distant time, vanishing from the company of some nameless driver who was "a friend of a friend of mine's cousin." The story of Resurrection Mary is filled with real dates, real people, along a real highway, and is one of the only ghosts who has left physical evidence of her presence behind.

The story of Resurrection Mary is not a piece of "urban folklore." To the people who have encountered her, she is quite real. She is not as elusive as she once seemed either - I know her identity, although it's much more complicated than we ever would have dreamed.

The Vanishing Hitchhiker

But before we get to the origins of "Resurrection Mary," I should note that while Mary may be the most famous roadway ghost, she is certainly not the only one. The "vanishing hitchhiker" is undoubtedly one of the greatest stories in American ghost lore. There is not a single part of the country that does not boast at least one tale about a pale young girl who gets a ride with a stranger, only to vanish from the car before they reach their destination.

Stories like this have been a part of American lore for many years and tales of spectral passengers --usually young women - are often attached to bridges, dangerous hills, intersections, and especially to graveyards. Folklorists have called the vanishing hitchhiker "the classic automobile legend," but stories of these spirits date back as far as the mid-nineteenth century when men told stories of ghostly women who appeared on the back of their horses. These spectral riders always disappeared when they reached their destination and would often prove to be the deceased daughters of local farmers. Not much has changed in the stories that are still told today, outside of the preferred method of transportation.

In modern times, such tales are usually referred to as "urban legends" - stories that have been told and re-told over the years and, in almost every case, have been experienced by the proverbial "friend of a friend." In most cases, such tales have little or no basis in fact, but occasionally, we discover that such stories have gotten started for a reason. We're back to that kernel of truth at the heart of the story that turns be more shocking than the legend that grows from it.

There are numerous variations on the "classic" vanishing hitchhiker story. Here is one of the basic - and most popular - versions of the story, which incidentally has its origins on Route 40 in Maryland during the 1950s:

On a cold and rainy night, a young man was on his way to a party at a local dance hall and he offered a ride to an attractive young woman who agreed to go with him to the dance. Everyone at the party found her to be very charming and after the dance was over, the young man offered to drive her home as the night had turned quite chilly. She accepted and because it was so cold out, he gave her his coat to wear.

He asked for her address and she gave it to him and a short time later, they pulled into the driveway of the house where the girl said that she lived. When the driver turned to tell her that they had arrived, he was astonished to find she was gone. The passenger seat of the car was empty, although the door had never opened. The girl had simply vanished.

Not knowing what else to do, the man went up to the door and knocked. An elderly woman answered the door and he explained to her what had happened. Right away, she seemed to know exactly what he was talking about. The young girl he had taken to the dance was her daughter - but she had died ten years before in an auto accident.

The horrified young man didn't believe her, even though the name of the girl he had taken to the dance and the woman's daughter were the same. To convince him, the old woman told him where to find the dead girl's grave in the local cemetery. The young man quickly drove there and following the directions he had been given, found the stone with the girl's name on it. Folded neatly over the top of the marker was the coat that the girl had borrowed to ward off the night chill.

Another basic version of the vanishing hitchhiker story was told in the 1940s:

One evening, a man was driving through the country and spotted a young woman hitchhiking along the road. He stopped and offered her a ride and the girl climbed into the passenger seat. As she did, she explained that she lived in a house about five miles further up the road.

She didn't really speak after that, but simply sat and stared out the window. When the man saw the house, he turned to the girl to tell her that they arrived, but she was gone.

Stunned, he decided to go knock on the door of the house and tell the residents what had happened. An older man and woman told him that they had once had a daughter who looked much like the girl he described, but she had disappeared some years ago. She had last been seen hitchhiking on the same road where he claimed to have picked her up --- and today would have been her birthday.

One story, which comes from Los Angeles around 1940, involves a girl who was picked up in a downtown "beer joint."

One night, two young men were drinking in a downtown Los Angeles tavern and they met a girl there. She asked if they would give her a lift home to an address in the Belvedere Gardens neighborhood.

The two fellows agreed, and they went outside to the car. The girl climbed into the back seat and one of the men was kind enough to lend her his overcoat. It was a very chilly evening, especially for Southern California.

They drove along until they passed Evergreen Cemetery. At that point, the girl asked the driver to stop for a moment and let her out. The driver pulled to the side of the road and they watched as she climbed out of the backseat. They waited several minutes and when she didn't come back, they thought she had stolen the overcoat. Aggravated, the two men drove home but went out the next morning to the address that she had given them.

When they arrived there, an old man came to the door and after hearing the story said that the girl had been his daughter. She had been murdered a few years before and was buried in Evergreen Cemetery. The two men went to the gravesite the girl's father had directed them to and there, they found the "stolen" overcoat draped over a tombstone.

While those are the classic versions of the story, many from around the country purport to be true - Like "Lydia," who has been haunting U.S. Highway 70 near Greensboro, North Carolina, since 1923. She appears in a white evening gown and waves frantically for someone to stop and pick her up. Those travelers who do so are directed to an address in High Point. On the way, she tells the driver that she has spent the evening at a dance in Raleigh and is anxious to get home but had some car trouble on the way.

Just as the driver approaches the house, the girl always vanishes from their car. The door never opens, and she never gets out. She is simply there one minute and then gone the next. The stories say that those drivers who go on to inquire at the house are always told that Lydia died in a car wreck many years ago - as she was coming home from a dance in Raleigh.

Highway 365 in Arkansas, just south of Little Rock, has several different vanishing hitchhiker stories connected to it. One story from near Woodson involves a young woman who manages to catch a ride every year on the anniversary of her death. A similar story involves a coat, but not the coat of the driver - a coat that is left behind in the car by the hitchhiker. When the driver reaches the address given to him by his vanishing passenger, the mother of the dead girl identifies the coat as belonging to her daughter.

Another tale involves a bridge near Batesville and a young woman who was first picked up there in 1973. The girl was bruised and battered, with a cut above her eye, and she told the driver she had been in an accident. He gave her a ride home, and when he turned to speak to her, she had vanished from his car. He went to the door and the man who opened it told him that his daughter had died just one month before on that same bridge. It was not the first time that someone had brought her home - and it wouldn't be the last. The stories say she is still hitching rides today.

Reeder Road runs between Merrillville and Griffith in Northwest Indiana and is frequented by a mysterious young woman who hitches rides with unsuspecting male motorists - and, of course, disappears. Drivers who try and track her down from the address she gives them discovers that she died in a car accident in the late 1950s and has been trying to get home ever since.

Other vanishing hitchhikers in Chicago are an enigmatic bunch. Their stories are not always like those heard around the country. For instance, in December 1941, a cab driver picked up a nun who asked to be taken to an address in the city. As they drove, they listened to the radio, which had news about the attack on Pearl Harbor a short time before, as well as America's preparation for war.

The nun suddenly spoke up from the back seat. "It won't last more than four months," she said and then didn't speak again for the rest of the ride.

When the cabbie reached the address, he got out to open the door for the sister but found she was no longer in the back seat. Concerned that the elderly nun had forgotten to pay her fare, the driver climbed the steps of the address she had given him and discovered that it was a convent. He knocked on the door and was brought to the Mother Superior. He explained his predicament to her, but she told him that none of the sisters had been downtown that day. She asked the driver what the nun had looked like.

As the driver began to describe her, he happened to look up at a portrait that was hanging on the wall behind the Mother Superior's desk. He pointed to the picture and, in an excited voice, told her that the woman in the portrait was the nun he had brought to the convent house. He probably thought that he was going to get his fare after all - but he couldn't have been more wrong.

The Mother Superior smiled and quietly said: "But she has been dead for ten years."

Another passenger from the Windy City had her own strange prediction to make. During Chicago's Century of Progress Exposition in 1933, a group of people in an automobile told of a strange encounter. They were traveling along Lake Shore Drive when a woman with a suitcase, standing by the roadside, hailed them. They invited her to ride along with them, and she climbed in.

As they drove along, they got into a conversation about the Exposition, and the mysterious woman oddly told them: "The fair is going to slide off into Lake Michigan in September." She then gave them her address in Chicago and invited them to call on her anytime.

When they turn around to speak to her about her doom-filled warning, they discovered that she had disappeared.

Unnerved, they decided to go to the address the woman gave them, and when they did, a man answered the door. They explained to him why they had come to the house, and he merely nodded his head. He told them: "Yes, that was my wife. She died four years ago."

Another ghostly hitchhiker haunts the roadways between the site of the old Melody Mill Ballroom and Waldheim Cemetery, which is located at 1800 South Harlem Avenue. The cemetery, once known as Jewish Waldheim, is one of the more peaceful and attractive graveyards in the area. There is nothing out of the ordinary about it, aside from the stories of the "Flapper Ghost," as she has been called.

Although her identity has never been discovered, this restless spirit is said to have been a young Jewish girl who attended dances at the Melody Mill Ballroom, which was once located on Des Plaines Avenue. During its heyday, the ballroom was one of the city's favorite venues for ballroom dancing and played host to dozens of popular big bands from the 1920s to the middle 1980s. The brick building was topped with a miniature windmill, the ballroom's trademark.

She was an attractive brunette with bobbed hair and dressed in the style of the 1920s, which is where she earned her "flapper nickname." According to the stories, she was a regular at the Melody Mill until she died from peritonitis, the result of a burst appendix.

The girl was buried at Jewish Waldheim, and she likely would have been forgotten, to rest in peace, if strange things had not started to happen a few months later. The events began as staff members at the Melody Mill began to see a young woman who looked just like the deceased girl appearing at dances at the ballroom. Several different men claimed to meet the girl here - after her death - and offered her a ride home. During the journey, the young woman always vanished.

She was also known to try and hitch rides on Des Plains Avenue - outside the ballroom - and was sometimes spotted near the cemetery gates.

Although recent sightings have been few, the ghost was most active in 1933, during the Century of Progress Exhibition. She became

The Melody Mill Ballroom -- once the favorite dance venue of the hitchhiking spirit known as the "Flapper Ghost."

active again 40 years later, during the early 1970s, and stayed active for nearly a decade. Since that time, sightings of the "Flapper" have been few, and this may be because the old Melody Mill is no more. The days of jazz and big bands were gone by the 1980s, and attendance on weekend evenings continued to slip until the place was closed in 1985. It was later demolished, and a new building was put up in its place two years later.

Has the Flapper Ghost simply moved on to the other side since her favorite dance spot has disappeared? Perhaps - and perhaps she is still kicking up her heels on a dance floor in another time and place, where it's 1933 every day.

Another phantom hitcher haunts the roadways near Evergreen Cemetery in Evergreen Park, a Chicago suburb. For more than two decades, an attractive girl who has been described as a young teenager has been venturing out beyond the confines of the cemetery in search of a ride. In the 1980s, there were more than a dozen drivers who reported picking her up. She always asked for a ride to a location in Evergreen Park and then mysteriously vanished from the vehicle at the cemetery.

According to the legends, she is the spirit of a child buried within the cemetery, but there is no real folklore to explain why she leaves her grave in search of travelers to bring her back home again

She also doesn't just travel by car - she also likes to climb aboard Chicago Transit Authority buses. One evening, a young girl was waiting at a bus stop near the cemetery. She climbed aboard a bus and breezed right past the driver without paying the fare. She walked to the back portion of the vehicle and sat down, seemingly without a care in the world. Irritated, the driver called out to her, but she didn't answer. Finally, he stood up and walked back toward where she was seating. She had to pay the fare or get off the bus, he told her. But before he could reach her seat, she vanished in front of his eyes.

According to reports, other shaken drivers have had the same eerie experience at this bus stop. They have also seen this young girl, and all of them have seen her disappear.

And there are others, like the "Kennedy Road Phantom," that was seen in 1980 around Byron, Illinois. She attracted a lot of attention at the time because she as spotted wearing nothing but her underwear, no matter what the weather was like.

And there's "Chicago Avenue Mary," a pale woman wearing clothing from the late nineteenth century who began wandering the roadways in Naperville, Illinois, in the 1980s.

Another lingering spirit of the Chicagoland roadways is believed to be that of Marion Lambert, a young Lake Forest girl who was found dead in the woods in February 1916. She died from a deadly dose of poison, but whether her death was caused by suicide or murder remains a mystery. This may be why she has appeared along the road near where she died for almost a century. There have been dozens of a rain-soaked, barefoot girl in a blue dress on the side of the road, desperately trying to flag down a ride. When drivers stop for her, she disappears.

Archer Avenue

The story of Resurrection Mary is a part of Illinois and Chicago history --- but she is also an essential part of Archer Avenue history,

Old Archer Avenue bridge

too. This ghost would likely not exist without Archer Avenue, and it's unlikely that this haunted highway would have found its fame without Mary.

Archer Avenue, which runs along the southwest side of Chicago, following the route of the old Illinois & Michigan Canal, seems to be the perfect place for a haunting. It isn't just Resurrection Mary who prowls the shadowy sections of this highway. There are many locations along this road --- from homes to cemeteries to businesses - that boast more than their share of ghosts.

But what makes Archer Avenue so haunted?

In the early days of Chicago, the road was an Indian trail that stretched all the way from Fort Dearborn and the old mouth of the Chicago River to what is now the southwest suburbs. The pathway linked to the Saucunasi Trail that led south to the Joliet Trail that led to the southwest. An Indian village was located just north of the trail's end, across from what would be the Illinois & Michigan Canal and along Mud Lake. Some have suggested that the original inhabitants forged a path here because of some mystical, magnetic force that connected it to the next world. Others believe that the area is so haunted because Archer Avenue is nearly surrounded by water sources like the Cal-Sag Channel, the Des Plaines River, the Illinois and Michigan Canal, the Chicago Sanitary and Shipping Canal, and even Maple Lake, where mysterious ghost lights have been seen for many decades.

I believe that Archer Avenue is haunted because of the history that has taken place along it. Archer is one of Chicago's most historic roads, and it was used as a trail by Native Americans long before the first explorers and settlers came to the region. It was turned into a road to follow Illinois and Michigan Canal, becoming the way that men and materials were brought to the construction site. After that, it was known as one of the best roads for

Building the Illinois and Michigan Canal

travelers to come into Chicago from the southwest. The road has seen hundreds of thousands of travelers during its centuries of use and that history seems to have left some of itself behind as a myriad of hauntings.

There was death on the road, as well as hardship, starvation, and disease. The canal workers who used Archer Road were largely Irish and German immigrants. They lived and worked along the path of the canal, often under horrible conditions. They labored hard all day and slept in drafty, poorly heated shanties at night. Disease was common, and scores of men died from illness, dehydration, dirty water, bad food, and violence. When the canal was finished, many of the workers settled in the towns that had formed along the canal.

After the canal was finished, Archer Road began to be developed into a real highway - one that could be used to transport goods and to bring people back and forth to Chicago. The muddy track was grated and covered with planks to assist in travel during the rainy season. It passed through miles of open prairie and dense forest, making it a place where theft and robbery were common. An unknown number of travelers fell victim to violence along Archer Road in the middle nineteenth century.

A lot has changed since then. The road - now called Archer Avenue - still travels from Chicago's South Loop to the Southwest Side, but over time it lost its importance. Smaller highways like this have been replaced by the interstates, which can take travelers to the suburbs at a much faster pace than the men who built Archer could have ever imagine.

Archer Avenue - when it comes to the hauntings - is linked by Chicago's Chinatown on one end and the St. James-Sag Church on the other. It travels through Bridgeport and through Summit, where many of the homes, banks, gas stations, and grocery stores disappear and are replaced by vintage roadhouses, forest preserves, and dance halls that are part of the legends that haunt this roadway.

This is a sampling of just some of the hauntings that haunt Archer Avenue. This isn't all of them, but even with this number, you can understand why this is perhaps the most haunted roadway in America.

Chinatown Hauntings

Chicago's Chinatown was established around 1910. As it grew, it began to extend down Wentworth Avenue from Cermak to 26th Street, spreading out to run alongside the diagonal line of Archer Avenue.

There are several hauntings reported in Chinatown, some of which may be connected to the Native American burial ground that was destroyed nearby when the original trail was turned into the canal road. There are several haunted houses - plagued by poltergeist activity and mysterious fires - in the 200 block of West 22nd Place and a haunted restaurant called the Triple Crown. The former restaurant was in a converted apartment house where a suicide occurred many years ago. Apparently, the man's ghost never left.

The Devil in the Dance Hall

Along Archer Avenue in Bridgeport is Kaiser Hall, a former butcher shop, residence, and ballroom, which was located on the third floor. According to legend, the Devil himself dropped in at a dance in the early 1900s. An Irish girl who made the mistake of dancing with the handsome stranger almost lost her life. When some neighborhood men intervened, the stranger jumped out the high window to the sidewalk below and ran away. The story claimed that he left hoof prints in the pavement that remained for many years.

Bethania Cemetery

There are many haunted cemeteries along Archer Avenue, including this small cemetery, which is located between 79th and 84th Streets. At least two ghosts have been widely seen - an older man who is spotted raking leaves during the early morning hours and a man who runs across the roadway, covered in blood as if he were just in an accident. Each of the ghosts vanishes without a trace when approached by passersby.

Archer Woods Cemetery

Not far from Bethania Cemetery, located in the woods near where Kean Avenue comes to a dead-end just south of Archer, is another cemetery with a long connection to the supernatural. This secluded - and rather foreboding - burial ground

315 | IN THE BONEYARD

is called Mount Glenwood Memory Gardens West, but most people know it by its original name of Archer Woods Cemetery.

For many years, a female phantom has been reported along the edge of the grounds, wandering near Kean Avenue. She doesn't try to flag down passing motorists, though. She is usually encountered by people driving by the cemetery at night, who say they are spooked by the sound of a woman loudly weeping in despair. The gut-wrenching wails are followed by the sighting of a woman in white. She is only glimpsed for a moment, and then she disappears. Her identity is a mystery. One story suggested that she was a suicide victim that was connected to a small roadhouse that once operated directly across the road from the cemetery's entrance, but there's nothing to substantiate the tale.

The weeping woman is not the only specter connected to the cemetery. A much older story tells of an old-fashioned phantom hearse that emerges from the graveyard and travels the roads throughout the area. This hearse, which is made from black oak and glass and carries the coffin of a child as its cargo, is said to be driverless and pulled by a team of crazed black horses.

The origins of the hearse vary, but many believe that it may be connected to the story of a black coach that was first reported along Archer Avenue in 1897. This "phantom hearse" sighting was a single incident that occurred in the fall of 1897 and was reported in the *Chicago Tribune*. According to the account, a fundraising dance was held at the St. James-Sag Church, also located along Archer Avenue. The church had a community center and dance hall of sorts in a stone building near the

The community hall at St. James-Sag Church and Cemetery, where the two musicians encountered the phantom coach.

entrance gates for the church and adjacent cemetery. The church's pastor, Father Bollman, hired two Chicago musicians - William Looney and John Kelly - to provide accompaniment for the dance. The exciting event extended into the night, and rather than risk the long drive back into the city, the exhausted men decided to spend the night at the community hall. In the middle of the night, the musicians were awakened by a sound outside and looked out to see a woman in white being picked up by an empty carriage pulled by a team of black horses. It started down Archer Avenue and then vanished.

Some legends maintain that the eerie scene the musicians witnessed that night was a ghostly re-enactment of an attempted elopement that ended in tragedy. According to the story, a young assistant pastor at St. James fell in love with a housekeeper in the 1880s. The couple decided to run away and get married. Late one night, the young man was supposed to meet his fiancée on the drive near the community hall. He hitched a carriage to a team of horses and started down the hill toward the road. Suddenly, the horses bolted, and the carriage went careening down the hill. It overturned just where the young woman was waiting, and both were killed in the horrific crash. They are now buried in an unmarked grave in the cemetery, and, on certain nights, witnesses may catch a glimpse of their failed attempt at happiness as it repeats itself.

Maple Lake

In 1924, the Cook County Forest Preserve created Maple Lake as a recreational area for fishing and swimming. Although swimming was banned in 1939, the lake area continues to be used by fishermen, boaters, hikers, and outdoor enthusiasts. Although closed at night, it's after dark that the lake sees some of its largest crowds, as people come searching for the "spook light" that is said to appear along the edge of the lake.

Numerous stories have been created to explain the eerie light, from beheaded Indian chiefs to a farmer who perished looking for his lost children, leaving the light of his lantern to haunt the lake after he was gone. Skeptics call it "marsh gas" or the reflection of headlights on a distant highway. To date, the mystery of the light's appearance remains unsolved.

Irish Legend

This Irish pub began as the Oh Henry Roadhouse back in the 1930s. Although connected to South Side mobsters, the roadhouse opened long after Al Capone was sent to prison, and his brother, Frank, was killed, even though both men have been erroneously connected to the place over the years. In recent times, the location operated as a pizza place and an Italian restaurant before its current incarnation as an Irish pub.

In addition to its history as a roadhouse for hard-drinkers during the heyday of a ballroom located across the road, the place also boasted a brothel on the upper floor - evidence of this remains - and a gambling parlor in the basement. During renovations in the 1990s, owners uncovered a room filled with gambling devices that had been hidden away. There were also rumors of tunnels that stretched under the road to the ballroom and a nearby cemetery.

It's believed that the building's violent past has left a haunting that lingers behind. In addition to the bloodstains and bullet holes that can still be found in the pub, current and past staff members have spoken of the resident ghosts. They have been seen and heard on numerous occasions and seem to have no interest in leaving.

St. James-Sag Church and Burial Ground

Further south on Archer Avenue is the Irish Catholic church and a burial ground that began serving parishioners during the days of the building of the Illinois and Michigan Canal. The first church was constructed at the site in 1833 and was replaced by the current one in 1850 when it was built using local Lemont limestone. Over the years, the church and burial ground have attracted many ghost stories, from the phantom coach mentioned previously to the mysterious black "monks" that were spotted in the graveyard in 1977 by a Cook County Sheriff's Police Officer. He passed by the cemetery one night, and in his headlights saw nine hooded figures on the road, heading toward the rectory. He warned them that they were trespassing, but the figures ignored him and continued up the road.

He chased after them into the cemetery. He pursued what he first thought were pranksters into the graveyard, but while he stumbled and fell over the uneven ground and tombstones, the monk-like figures eerily glided past without effort. He said that he nearly caught up with them when "they vanished without a trace." He searched the area but found no one.

Archer Avenue has long been plagued by ghosts - from haunted buildings to ghostly graveyards - but there is one story, of course, that rises above all the others. The story of Resurrection Mary is unquestionably the most famous ghost in the region.

Although stories of "vanishing hitchhikers" in Chicago date back to the horse and buggy days, Mary's tale begins in the 1930s, it was during this time that drivers along Archer Avenue started reporting strange encounters with a young woman who appeared along the side of the road. She seemed to be real - until she inexplicably vanished. The reports of this girl began in the middle 1930s when motorists passing by Resurrection Cemetery began claiming that a young woman was attempting to jump onto the running boards of their automobiles.

Not long after, the woman became more mysterious and much more alluring. The strange encounters began to move further away from the graveyard and closer to the Oh Henry Ballroom, which later became known as the Willowbrook. She was often reported on Archer Avenue and sometimes, inside of the ballroom itself. On many occasions, young men would meet a girl at the ballroom, dance with her, and then offer her a ride home at the end of the evening. She would always accept and would offer vague directions that would lead north along the roadway. When the car reached the gates of Resurrection Cemetery, the young woman vanished.

Just as common were the claims of motorists who saw the girl walking along the road, they offered her a ride, and then they also witnessed her vanishing from their car. These drivers described the girl in detail and, while those descriptions sometimes varied, they were always adamant about the fact that she existed.

Others had even more harrowing experiences. Rather than encountering the girl who vanished from their car, they actually ran her down in the street. They saw a woman in a white dress bolt in front of their car near the cemetery and felt the sickening thud as they hit her with their car. When they stopped and went to her aid, the girl was gone. Some said they didn't hit her, but their automobiles passed directly through the girl. At that point, she turned and disappeared through the cemetery gates.

Bewildered and shaken drivers appeared routinely at nearby businesses - and even at the local police station - telling strange and frightening stories. Sometimes they were believed, and sometimes they weren't. Regardless, the legend of the vanishing girl began to grow, and eventually, she became "Resurrection Mary."

Who was this unnerving ghost - and perhaps more importantly, who was she when she was alive? That's not a simple question, and it doesn't have a simple answer. But I can say that, unlike so many other ghosts that have been dismissed as mere legends, Mary has a real-life counterpart.

In fact, she has more than one, which is why what has always seemed to be a simple ghost story turns out not to be simple at all.

The "Birth" of Resurrection Mary

The legend of "Resurrection Mary" was born on August 10, 1976.

Around 10:30 p.m., a driver was passing by the front gates of Resurrection Cemetery in Justice, Illinois. As he traveled along Archer Avenue, he happened to glance over and see a girl standing on the other side of the gates. He said that when he saw her, she was wearing a light-colored dress and was grasping the iron bars of the gate. The driver was considerate enough to stop down the street at the Justice police station and alert them to the fact that someone had been accidentally locked in the cemetery at closing time.

A patrolman named Pat Homa responded to the call, but when he arrived at the cemetery gates, he couldn't find anyone there. He called out with his loudspeaker and looked for her with his spotlight, but there was no one to be seen. He finally got out of his patrol car and walked up to the gates for one last look. As far as he could tell, the cemetery was dark and deserted, and there was no sign of any girl. It had apparently been a crank report of some kind.

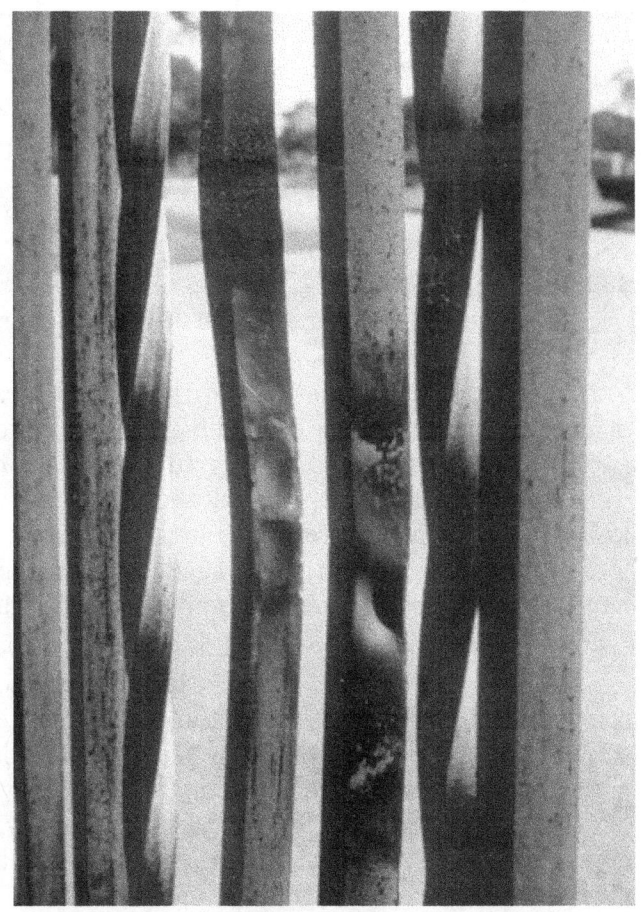

The burned and twisted bars discovered in the front gates to Resurrection Cemetery in August 1976.

Courtesy of Jim Graczyk

But his inspection of the gates, where the girl had been seen standing, did reveal something unusual. What he saw there chilled him

The front entrance gates of Resurrection Cemetery

to the bone. He found that two of the bronze bars in the gate had been blackened, burned, and - well, pulverized. It looked as though someone had taken two of the green-colored bars in his or her hands and had somehow squashed and twisted them. Within the marks was what looked to be skin texture prints and handprints that had been seared into the metal with incredible heat. The temperature - which had to have been intense - blackened and burned the bars at just about the spot where a small woman's hands would have been.

The police officer didn't keep the story to himself. In fact, the story of the handprints made the newspapers and curiosity-seekers came from all over the area to see them. Trying to discourage the crowds, cemetery officials attempted to remove the marks with a blowtorch, making them look even worse. Finally, they cut the bars out of the gate and installed a wire fence until the two bars could be straightened or replaced.

The furor over the mysterious handprints eventually died down, and the cemetery has always emphatically denied the supernatural version of what had happened to the bars. In fact, in 1992, they offered an alternate explanation. Officials claimed that a truck backed into the gates while doing sewer work at the cemetery and that grounds workers tried to fix the bars by heating them with a blowtorch and bending them. The imprint in the metal, they said, was from a workman trying to push them together again. While this explanation was convenient, it didn't explain why the marks of small fingers were clearly visible in the metal, why the bronze never reverted back to its green, oxidized state - or why a witness had seen a woman standing at that exact spot in the gate.

The bars were removed to discourage onlookers, but taking them out had the opposite effect. Soon, people began asking what the cemetery had to hide. The events allegedly embarrassed local officials, so they demanded that the bars be put back into place. Once they were returned to the gate, they were straightened and left alone so that the blackened area would oxidize to match the other bars. Unfortunately, though, the scorched areas continued to defy nature, and the twisted spots where the handprints had been impressed remained obvious until the late 1990s when the bars were finally removed permanently. At great expense, Resurrection Cemetery replaced the entire front gates, and the notorious bars vanished for good.

But by then, it was too late - a legend had already been created.

The incident in 1976 wasn't the first encounter with what the newspapers would soon call "Resurrection Mary," but it would become the first widely reported one. Soon after, the number of "Mary sightings" began to increase. People from many different walks of life - from cab drivers to clergy - claimed they picked her up and gave her rides. They encountered her in local nightspots and saw her vanish from the passenger seats of their automobiles.

Around this time, Mary was said to have shown up at least twice at a nightclub called Harlow's, which was located at 8058 South Cicero Avenue, almost directly east of Resurrection Cemetery. Bob Main was the night manager at Harlow's at the time, and he is perhaps the only person ever to encounter Resurrection Mary on two different occasions. He saw her on a Friday night that spring and then saw her again about two weeks later, on a Saturday.

He described her: "She was about 24 to 30 years old, five foot eight or nine, slender with yellow-blond hair to the shoulders that she wore in these big spooly curls coming down from a high forehead. She was really pale, like she powdered her face and her body. She had on this old dress that was yellowed, like a wedding dress left in the sun. She sat right next to the dance floor and she wouldn't talk to anyone. She danced all by herself, this pirouette-type dance. People were saying, 'Who is this bizarre chick?'"

When Main and some of the other staff members tried to talk to the young woman to make sure that she was okay, the woman only shook her head. Main said she "seemed to look right through you."

Bob had no idea who the woman might have been, and while he doesn't dismiss the idea that it could have been some sort of prank, or just a person who was mentally disturbed, he did add something rather disconcerting to the story: "The strangest thing was, even though we carded everyone who came in there - I worked the door, and there were waitresses and bartenders and people there - nobody, either night, ever saw her come in and never saw her leave."

He added that he would never have assumed the woman was "Resurrection Mary" until he read a newspaper article about her a few years later. After that, it was the only explanation that really made sense.

Other types of accounts began to surface around this same time, too. In these stories, Mary was running out into the middle of Archer Avenue and being struck by passing cars. These reports, although unknown to most of those who submitted them, were almost identical to accounts that dated back to the middle 1930s - a fact that would later become apparent.

In these mid-1970s accounts, drivers reported a young woman with brown hair, wearing a light-colored dress, who ran out in the front of their automobiles. Sometimes, the girl would vanish just before colliding with the car, and at other times, they would feel the impact and see her crumple and fall to the road as if seriously injured. When the motorist stopped and went to help the girl, she would either disappear before their eyes or no sign of her body would be found.

On August 12, 1976, Cook County Sheriff's officers investigated an emergency call about an apparent hit and run victim near the intersection of 76th Street and Roberts Road. The officers found a young female motorist in tears at the scene, and they asked her about the body that she had reporting finding on the side of the road. She pointed to a wet grassy area. There was no body there, although the officers could plainly see a depression in the grass that was in the shape of a human body. The girl said that just as the police car approached the scene, the body on the side of the road vanished.

In May 1978, a young couple - Shawn and Gerry Cape - was driving north on Archer Avenue when a girl wearing a long white gown suddenly darted into the road in front of their car. The driver swerved off the road to avoid hitting her but knew when he hit the brakes that it was too late. As they braced for impact, the car passed right through the girl. She then turned and ran into Resurrection Cemetery, melting right past the bars in the gate.

Later that same month, a man was on his way to work in the early morning hours and spotted the body of a young girl lying directly in front of the cemetery gates. He stopped his truck and got out and found the woman was apparently severely injured, but still alive. He jumped into his truck and sped to the nearby police station, where he summoned an ambulance and then hurried back to the cemetery. When he got there, the woman was gone. However, the outline of her body was still visible on the dew-covered pavement

In October 1979, two women were driving past Resurrection Cemetery when a girl in a light-colored dress ran out in front of their car. The driver slammed on the brakes, sure that she was going to hit the woman, but there was no impact. Neither of the women could explain where the apparition had disappeared to. They had seen the young girl clearly and described her as having brown, curly hair.

Just a few minutes after midnight, in the early morning hours of Friday, January 12, 1979, a taxicab driver had an unsettling experience with "Resurrection Mary." It would be this encounter that would finally reveal the mystery of Mary to the world.

It was a cold winter's night, and at the time the driver picked up his unusual passenger, a major blizzard was just hours away from hitting Chicago's Southwest side. As he traveled along Archer Avenue, rain and sleet pelted the windshield. The driver - who gave a newspaper interview on the condition of anonymity and called himself "Ralph" - was returning to the city after dropping off a fare in Palos Hills. His route took him past the Old Willow Shopping Center, located at the intersection of Archer Avenue and Willow Springs Road. As he passed the collection of stores at the shopping center, a pale figure, blurry through the wet and icy glass of the window, appeared along the road. The driver craned his neck and saw a woman standing there. He later

The Old Willow Shopping Center, located at the intersection of Archer Avenue and La Grange Road - where the cab driver "Ralph" picked up Mary on a winter's night in early 1979.

recalled: "She was a looker. A blond. I didn't have any ideas or anything like that. She was young enough to be my daughter."

The young woman was strangely dressed for such a cold and wet night. She was wearing only a thin white cocktail dress. She never stuck out her thumb or gestured for the cab to stop. She just stood there, looking at the cab, but she looked so lonely that Ralph decided to stop. The girl stumbled as she walked toward him, and he rolled down the window to speak to her. She was wet and cold.

Ralph asked the woman where she was going, and she replied that she "had to get home."

He invited her into the cab, and she opened the rear passenger door and slid into the seat. The cabbie looked over at her and asked her what was wrong. Had she had car trouble or something? The girl didn't answer. He thought she seemed tired, drunk, or simply "fuzzy." Ralph told her that the ride was free and that he'd get her home. It was the least he could do in such lousy weather.

She didn't say much after that. She only nodded when the driver asked her if he was just supposed to keep going up Archer. As they drove, he commented on the weather, making conversation, but she didn't answer him at first. She stared out the window in such a vacant way. Finally, she answered him, although her voice wavered, and she sounded almost fearful. The driver was unsure if her whispered words were directed to him or if she was speaking to herself. She murmured: "The snow came early this year." After that, she was silent again.

Ralph agreed with her and attempted to make small talk, but he soon realized the lovely young girl was not interested in conversation. He said: "Her mind was a million miles away."

Finally, the girl spoke, but when she did, she shouted at him, "Here! Here!"

The startled driver jerked the steering wheel to the right and stopped in an open area in front of two large metal gates. He looked across the road, searching for a house or a business where his strange passenger might need to go. He knew there was nothing on the right. She couldn't get out there; it was a cemetery.

"Where?" he finally asked her.

She stuck her arm out the window and said, "There!"

He looked back at the girl to tell her that she shouldn't get out, and he realized that she was gone. The backseat of the car was empty. "Vanished!" he later said. "And that car door never opened. May the good Lord strike me dead, it never opened."

The beautiful young girl had simply disappeared.

At the time of this encounter, the driver - who described himself as an ordinary 52-year-old working guy who was a father, a veteran, a church-goer, and a Little League coach - had no idea that he had just had a brush with the region's most enigmatic ghost. He wouldn't find out until a friend put him in touch with a newspaper columnist, who had started looking into the story. And with the publication of the resulting article, all of Chicago - and beyond - was introduced to "Resurrection Mary."

When the reporter started delving into the legend, he found that, despite the recent sightings and encounters, the story of Mary - the girl by the side of the road - was nothing new. People on the Southwest Side of Chicago were already familiar with it. They had been telling the story since the 1930s.

The Willowbrook Ballroom - located on Archer Avenue - became an integral part of the "Resurrection Mary" story, starting in the 1930s. The ballroom is gone now, destroyed by fire in 2016.

It was a dark and stormy night.

It actually wasn't - it was a cold and icy one instead.

The legend of Resurrection Mary began at the Oh Henry Ballroom, a rambling, Tudor-style building at 8900 Archer Avenue that was a popular place for swing and big-band dancing during the middle 1930s. In those days, the ballroom was located on a secluded stretch of Archer Avenue in unincorporated Willow Springs, a town with a "wide open" reputation for booze, gambling, and prostitution. Young people from all over Chicago's Southwest Side came to the Oh Henry Ballroom for music and dancing because owner John Verderbar was known for booking the hottest bands in the area and the biggest acts that traveled around the country.

The story goes that Mary came to the Oh Henry one night with a boyfriend, and they spent the evening dancing and drinking. At some point, they got into an argument, and Mary stormed out of the place. Even though it was a cold winter's night, she decided that she would rather face a cold walk home than spend another minute with her obnoxious boyfriend. She left the ballroom and started walking up Archer Avenue. She had not gotten far when she was struck and killed by a passing automobile. The driver fled the scene, and Mary was left there to die.

Her grieving parents buried her in Resurrection Cemetery, wearing her favorite party dress and her dancing shoes. Since that time, her spirit has been seen along Archer Avenue, perhaps trying to return to her grave after one last night among the living. Motorists started picking up a young woman on Archer Avenue. Once she was in the car, she offered them vague directions toward home - but then she vanished from the automobile at the gates to Resurrection Cemetery.

Or so the story went.

The rumors led the reporter to the Oh Henry Ballroom, which had since been renamed the Willowbrook. He discovered that "Ralph" the cab driver had picked up the young girl just a few blocks from the Willowbrook on Archer Avenue. A coincidence? The reporter didn't think so, especially based on the strange occurrences connected to Mary that had taken place at the Willowbrook Ballroom over the years.

The site of the ballroom in Willow Springs, right on Archer Avenue, started as a beer hall that was operated by the Verderbar family in 1920. In 1929, the original structure burned down and was replaced by an elaborate ballroom. They called it the Oh Henry, but the name was later changed to the Willowbrook. In the 1930s, the ballroom gained a reputation as one of the best dance clubs in Illinois and attracted customers from all over the area.

The Willowbrook developed a strong following and survived time and changing musical tastes until it was destroyed by fire in 2016. It was a tragic loss, not only to the legend of Resurrection Mary but to the history, as well.

A visit to the Willowbrook was like taking a trip back in time. The old dance floor, the tables, the cocktail bar, and even the restrooms were just as they were in the days when Mary danced there. It was a place where the big band sound could still be heard and was a time capsule of another era. I always used to say that it was impossible to truly comprehend the legend of Resurrection Mary without at least one visit to the Willowbrook Ballroom. I walked on that dance floor when the ballroom was empty and when it was filled with partygoers, dancing to the sounds of a swing band. At moments like those, it was not hard to imagine how customers and staff members encountered Mary there over the years.

Of course, it's gone now, but the legend of Resurrection Mary - and the Willowbrook Ballroom - lives on.

Starting in the 1930s, Mary began to be encountered at the ballroom - in the bathrooms, on the dance floor, and at the bar - by customers and employees alike. Reports usually told of an attractive young woman in a white party dress who was seen from the opposite side of the ballroom. Occasionally, she was dancing, and at other times, she was just standing at the edge of the dancing floor, watching people with a slight smile on her face. Sometimes she vanished without warning, and, on other occasions, she disappeared whenever someone tried to approach her.

But at the time of the sightings in the 1970s and early 1980s, people were seeking out Mary at the Willowbrook - not yet anyway. There were still many other sightings that took place first. This period became one of the most prolific periods for Mary encounters - and one of the last highly active ones.

On August 14, 1980, a Brookfield man named Nick Muros was driving north on Archer Avenue from the Holy Cross Hellenic Church, where he had been working until after midnight, cleaning up from the church's annual picnic. Although tired, Muros maintained that he was completely alert as he drove along the dark stretch of Archer Avenue, adjacent to Resurrection Cemetery. He said that when he reached the main gates, he noticed an object in the road, just out of the view of his headlights. As he got closer, somewhere about halfway between the gates and the large mausoleum that was alongside the road, his lights illuminated the object, and he realized that it was a girl in a white dress.

Muros recalled after the encounter: "She walked right up to the end of the road. Then she just walked right into the middle of my lane. I could see her clearly; she was walking very slowly, and I took my foot off the pedal, and the car began to slow."

Nick guessed that he was driving at about 35-miles-per-hour when he saw the figure and estimated that she was probably in his line of sight for about 10 seconds, possibly more. She moved across in front of his car and then stopped in the median of the road. Nick said: "She had her palms kind of turned up and I don't think she was wearing any shoes. At first, I thought it was a kid, pulling a prank. But it was so dark and so desolate with nobody else on the road. She just walked right out there in the middle, a short-haired blond girl, with this flowing white dress, her hands outstretched like that. It was creepy."

Muros said that he knew nothing about the story of Resurrection Mary until he started telling people about his unnerving encounter. At that time, she was still not widely known. He didn't know the particulars of her story, but he became convinced that he had encountered a ghost.

As he passed by her, she turned away and simply disappeared. She walked right out of sight. He later said in an interview: "I've never been one to say I saw a ghost, but it was a warm night, a full moon. I had my windows down, and I could see her profile, and it was a young, blond-haired girl."

During the last weekend of August 1980, Mary was seen by dozens of people, including the Deacon of the Greek Orthodox Church on Archer Avenue. Many of the witnesses contacted the Justice Police Department about their sightings. Squad cars were dispatched, and although the police could not explain the mass sightings of a young woman who was not present when they arrived, they did find the witnesses themselves. Many of them flagged down the officers to tell them what they had just seen.

On September 5, a young man was driving on Archer Avenue after leaving a softball game. As he passed the Red Barrel Restaurant, he spotted a young woman in a white dress

The iconic Red Barrel Restaurant on Archer Avenue

standing on the side of the road. He stopped the car and asked if she needed a ride. She accepted and then asked him to continue on Archer. He tried to draw her into a conversation, even joking that she looked like "Resurrection Mary," but she was not interested in talking. He tried several times to get her to stop for a drink, but she never replied. He was driving past the cemetery - he never stopped or slowed down - and looked over to see the girl was gone from the car. She had simply vanished.

On September 7, Claire Lopez Rudnicki was traveling with her boyfriend, Mark, and another couple along Archer Avenue when they saw a girl walking along the side of the road outside of Resurrection Cemetery. According to the four witnesses, the girl was wearing a white dress, but there was something very peculiar about her. She seemed to give off a sort of glow as if a fluorescent light was shining from under her dress - or from her skin. The young woman walked along very slowly, and Claire later recalled that she was terrified when she saw her. As they passed by, she could feel her stomach clench with fear. Her boyfriend, however, wanted to turn around and drive past the woman again.

As they drove slowly past where the girl was walking, Mark leaned over and tried to get a close look at her. He wanted to see her face so he could tell others what she looked like. He was stunned! He later swore that the girl had no face - only emptiness, a black void, where her face should have been. The group quickly turned the car around and went back to take another look, but the young woman was gone. She had simply vanished, even though there was no place that she could have gone.

On October 23, two couples who were driving on Archer Avenue spotted what appeared to be a woman in a light-colored dress just outside of the gates of Resurrection Cemetery. According to their account, she was walking quickly from the edge of the road, directly toward the gates. It was late at night, just a little before midnight, and the cemetery was definitely not open. One of the women in the car later stated that the girl just seemed to sort of appear in the middle of the roadway and then walk briskly toward the gates. She could not be sure that the woman had not come from the other side of the street, but she didn't think that she had. When the car reached the entryway in front of the gates, there was no one there. The mysterious young woman had vanished.

On November 6, two young men were driving south on Archer Avenue toward Willow Springs to visit some friends. It was early in the evening, around 7:30 p.m., and they had both recently gotten off work. As they passed Roberts Road, just north of Resurrection Cemetery, they saw a girl in a white dress appear from the edge of the road. There were several trees and some bushes on the side of the cemetery, but they didn't think that she had come out of the woods. If she had, she would have needed to scale a chain-link fence before she could get to the roadway, and the witnesses were sure that they would have seen this, even on the darkened street.

The young woman lurched forward quickly as if she had started to run or had stumbled, and the driver slammed on the brakes. Convinced they were going to hit the girl - who was now in the middle of the road - they braced for the impact. It never came. The young man in the passenger's seat said that he closed his eyes just before he expected the car to hit the girl and when he opened them, she wasn't there.

He asked his friend what had happened - had they hit the girl? His friend, shaken and out of breath, could barely reply: "We never hit her. She just wasn't there anymore. I never saw anything like it. She just disappeared."

The last Mary sighting for 1980 occurred just before Christmas. Two men saw a woman dancing in the middle of Archer, just east of Harlem Avenue, and they immediately knew there was something odd going on. They watched the girl dance past them, even though other people who were around never seemed to notice that she was there. As strangely as she had come, the girl simply disappeared. Later that evening, they described the girl and the strange incident to the father of one of the young men. Neither of the boys was familiar with the story of Resurrection Mary, but the older man was, and he was convinced they had encountered the legendary phantom. He found out that, one week before the boys encountered her, Mary had been seen dancing outside the fence of Resurrection Cemetery.

During the weekend of May 22, 1983, at least five different people saw Mary on Archer Avenue, near the Willowbrook Ballroom. One of them, a bartender at Johnny's Route 83, was traveling home after work on Friday night - actually, early Saturday morning - when she spotted a woman in a white dress. She was passing by Fairmont Hills Cemetery, just a little south of the ballroom when she saw the woman dancing on the side of the road. There was really nothing too unusual about it, she later said. It was as if this young girl were listening to music that only she could hear. But what would a young woman be doing out on such a lonely stretch of road so late at night? The bartender drove past the girl and then turned around for another look. In the matter of seconds that it took for her to turn her head, the girl in the white dress had vanished.

Another sighting that occurred that weekend took place closer to the ballroom. At that time, there was a bar located directly across the street, which was open until the early morning hours. According to a bar customer named Bill Hanning, he was leaving the place just after midnight on Saturday when he saw a girl in a white dress on the other side of Archer Avenue. He saw her hurry across the street from the Willowbrook and then start walking north up Archer Avenue. Wondering what a young girl would be doing walking by herself so late at night, Bill recalled that he walked to the edge of the parking lot and leaned out to watch her walk away. He remembered, "I had just watched her run across the street but in the few seconds that it took me to walk from my motorcycle to the edge of the road and look after her, she was gone. The side of the road was empty."

Bill was not familiar with the story of Resurrection Mary at that time but was sure that he had experienced something strange. He later heard about the stories when he mentioned the encounter to some friends. Many years later, he would recount this incident to me after hearing me speak about Mary at a local library. He vividly remembered the date of the sighting and was surprised when I told him that he was not the only one to see Mary around the Willowbrook Ballroom that weekend.

The next possible sighting occurred on an early Sunday morning in October 1983. Nancy Buck, a staff member at the Willowbrook Ballroom, had just gotten off work at about 1:30 a.m., and she and two co-workers walked out into the parking lot that adjoined the dance hall. They spotted a young, "strangely dressed" woman, who appeared to be in her early 20s, with blond hair, walking north along Archer Avenue. Whoever the woman was, she simply vanished without a trace.

Was this Resurrection Mary or simply some young woman out for the night around Halloween? None of the Willowbrook staff members could say for sure, but this was not the first time that employees had experienced a similar incident. Two years before, also in mid-October, two of the waitresses at the ballroom saw a strange woman walking north on Archer Avenue. In that situation, the woman was dressed all in white and disappeared while the women were watching her. Staff members admitted that they had been on the lookout for the ghost ever since but had never really expected to see her.

And yet, there she was.

There is another location besides the Willowbrook Ballroom that has become linked to the story of Resurrection Mary over the years - Chet's Melody Lounge. Located just across the road and a little south of the Resurrection Cemetery gates, the tavern opened around 1900 and, for years, served food and drinks for those who came to bury their dead. In 1965, it was purchased by Chet and Clara Prusinski and, since that time, has earned its place in the legend of Resurrection Mary. Because the bar remains open into the early morning hours - one of the only places on this stretch of road that does - it is often the first place where late-night drivers come to look for the young woman who vanished from their car as they drove past on Archer Avenue.

Chet's Melody Lounge on Archer Avenue - and across the road from Resurrection Cemetery. It's location - and its late-night hours - have made it a popular spot for "Mary" reports.

Many of these shaken drivers have stumbled into the bar after their strange encounters. One of them was a cab driver who came in one night in 1973. He claimed that a young woman had jumped out of the back seat of his cab without paying. She ran off, and he came into Chet's because it was the only spot that was open and the closest place which she could have gone. He told the bartender that she was an attractive blond and that he was sure that she had come into the tavern. Staff members and customers assured the man that no one had come inside, but he didn't believe them. To placate the man, Chet allowed him to search the restrooms and the rest of the bar, but there was simply no one fitting the girl's description in the place. Embarrassed and irritated, the man finally left.

In the fall of 1996, I had the chance to visit with Chet, and he recalled many incidents like the one experienced by the cab driver. He told me that quite a few people had come in looking for a young woman that they claimed had vanished on the road. Some had been in cars; others had vanished after running out into the roadway. He remembered, "We had a guy who came in here one time who wanted to know what happened to the girl in the white dress that he dropped off across the street. He was so sure that she had walked in here, but I was alone that night. There wasn't another person in the place."

Another eerie encounter took place in the summer of 1996, a couple of months before I met Chet. He told me that he was leaving the bar one morning, just after 4:00 a.m., when a man came running inside, insisting that he needed to use the telephone. Chet recalled, "I asked him what was wrong, and he told me, very excited, that he had run over a girl on Archer Avenue, and now he couldn't find her body."

Chet admitted that he was skeptical about the man's story until a truck driver came in and confirmed the incident. He had witnessed the accident and saw the man's car strike the girl. But he also added that the girl had then vanished "like a ghost." Chet called the police, and officers came to investigate but - surprise - they found no trace of her.

I asked Chet if he was a believer in Resurrection Mary or whether he just liked being a part of the story. He chuckled, "I don't know if I believe in ghosts, I guess I would just have to see her for myself. But I have to say, some people around here have had some pretty strange things happen. So, who am I to say they're not telling the truth?"

Chet Prusinski passed away years ago, but his namesake tavern remains alive and well. His son, Rich, still runs the bar in much the same way that his father did. Not much has changed here since the first time that I walked into the place, and it's unlikely that anything ever will. Two songs about Resurrection Mary are still on the jukebox, and occasionally, someone will still leave a Bloody Mary down at the end of the bar in hopes that Mary herself will walk through the door and tip her glass.

I have to say it's a good feeling to still see Chet's Melody Lounge along Archer Avenue at night, its lights burning long after other places on the roadway have gone dark. Those lights shine as an open invitation --- perhaps even a safe haven --- for a restless ghost and for the unwitting travelers who encounter her.

By the middle 1980s, the sightings began to fade. The stories were suddenly less frequent than they had once been, and Mary was no longer being seen in the bars and dance halls along Archer Avenue. She no longer danced by the side of the road or ran out in front of passing cars. Yes, there were still encounters with a mysterious figure into the 1990 - and sometimes even today - but authentic encounters with the spirit have become few and far between.
Strangely, this is not the first time that Mary has disappeared from our consciousness. It happened before, back in the 1940s, and that time, she stayed away for more than three decades.
Are we due for her return?

The "Real" Resurrection Mary

I have been researching Resurrection Mary for a little more than 30 years now. For me, she has gone from being a legendary story and an elusive spirit to something tangible and likely, quite real. People who have encountered Mary over the years have taken her as seriously as I do, and many of them have even believed that they knew her in life, not only in death.

I have discovered that the first reports of Resurrection Mary came from the late spring of 1934. It was at this time that motorists on Archer Avenue, passing in front of Resurrection Cemetery, began describing how a young woman would appear on the roadway as if trying to hitch a ride. On some occasions, she became frantic as cars passed her by. Motorists told of a woman running toward them across the road, trying to climb onto the running boards of their automobiles and sometimes, even trying to climb into open back windows. They all described her in the same way - wearing a light-colored dress and having curly, brown hair that didn't quite reach her shoulders.

This was frightening enough, but what made it more unnerving was that many of the people in those automobiles - all residents of the Southwest Side - recognized the woman! Her name was Marie Bregovy, and some of the motorists were her friends. They laughed with her, drank with her, and often danced with her at their favorite spot, the Oh Henry Ballroom.

But that had been in the past.

When these motorists started seeing Marie on Archer Avenue, trying to flag them down for a ride, she had been dead for several weeks.

I believe that Marie Bregovy was the original "Resurrection Mary."

There have been other suggestions as to the famous ghost's living identity, of course. I have collected dozens of believable sightings of Resurrection Mary over the years, but one thing that I can count on is that they are rarely *exactly* the same. They are often confusing and often contradictory. In one account, Mary would be a beautiful blond and, in another, would be a pretty, curly-haired brunette. Assuming that Mary was not a client at some otherworldly beauty salon, what was going on here? Could some of these people be mistaken? Was it really Mary they were encountering or some other ghost entirely?

The more that I researched the history of the case, the more convinced that I became that these motorists and witnesses really were encountering *the* Resurrection Mary. The problem was, I eventually realized, "Resurrection Mary" was more than one ghost. I believe that this famous legend has been created from the lives of two - perhaps even more - young women.

Over the years, there have been many who have searched for the earthly counterpart of Resurrection Mary, and several candidates have emerged. Some are more likely than others.

One of the options is Mary Duranski, who was killed in an auto accident in 1934. There's also a Mary Dorencz, who died in 1938. She was 30 years old when she died, which makes her a little older than the other candidates. There's also a girl named Anna Norkus, who was killed in a car accident in 1936. However, Anna was only 12 years old

Mrs. Mary Bojacz, dead.

Mary Bojacz, from the accident report in the *Chicago Tribune*

when she died, which makes her a little too young to match the descriptions of witnesses.

Another interesting candidate is Mary Bojacz, who died in a terrible train wreck on her way to a funeral at Resurrection Cemetery. There were two cars in the funeral party that day. The first made it to the cemetery without incident, but the second car, which contained a dozen people, was hit head-on by a train, instantly killing all but one of the passengers - including Mary.

There are other stories that are a little more vague. In one case, a farm truck collided with an automobile, and three of the four passengers in the sedan were killed. One of the victims, a young woman, may have become Resurrection Mary. Others believe Mary can be traced to an incident near Resurrection Cemetery that occurred in the 1940s. In this case, a young Polish girl had taken her father's car to meet her boyfriend in the early morning hours. She died in an accident and was buried in the nearby cemetery. Most believe this to be little more than a neighborhood cautionary tale told by protective parents, but it certainly adds another element to the legend.

It's possible that any one of these young women could still haunt Archer Avenue and may have contributed to the Resurrection Mary legend. However, I believe there that many of the sightings that have occurred can be connected to one woman. The rest? I don't know. But it is interesting that at least two the candidates lived only a few blocks away from one another in life.

Marie Bregovy was 21 years old in March 1934. She had been born on April 7, 1912, and attended St. Michael's Grammar School, a short distance from her home. She lived in a small house at 4611 South

Damen Avenue, which was in the Back of the Yards neighborhood of Bridgeport. She was of Polish descent and was employed at a local factory, where she worked hard to help support her mother, father, and two younger brothers - Steve and Joseph - during the early days of the Great Depression.

The old Goldblatt's Department store at 47th and Ashland, where Marie and Vern spent their last day together.

Friends later remembered Marie as a fun and exciting girl who loved to go to parties and go out dancing, especially to the Oh Henry Ballroom, which was her favorite place. Her friend LaVern Rutkowski - who grew up with Marie and lived just two houses away from her - recalled in a 1984 interview, "She was personality plus. She always had a smile, and you never saw her unhappy." Even in the only photograph that still exists of Marie, you can see a bright smile on her face.

Mrs. Rutkowski, or "Vern," as she was commonly known, spent Marie's final day with her on March 10, 1934. The two of them were together all the time, and Vern later recalled the many nights the two of them went out to the dance halls all over the Southwest Side. Ironically, Marie's parents had forbidden her to go out on the night of March 10, and Marie might have listened to them if she and Vern had not met a couple of young men earlier that day. These two men - John Reiker and John Thoel - were in the car that night when Marie was killed.

Marie and Vern spent Saturday afternoon shopping at 47th Street and Ashland Avenue, and it was in one of the stores located at the busy intersection where they met the two boys. They seemed nice and asked the girls if they wanted to go out dancing with them that

This is a restored version of the only known photograph of Marie Bregovy in existence. She is the young woman on the right side of the photo.

This photo was given to my Kathleen Buchanan in 2017. The woman on the left was her grandmother, who grew up in the Back of the Yards neighborhood and was friends with Marie Bregovy.

On the next page is a closer-up of Marie, taken from the original image, as well as the back of the photograph, which confirms her identity.

Photo courtesy of Kathleen Buchanan

Restored by Jennifer Jarrell from Ginger Ale Pictures

night. Marie hesitated but then agreed. Vern wasn't so sure, and after she got into their car with them to go for a ride, she was convinced she wanted nothing to do with them.

 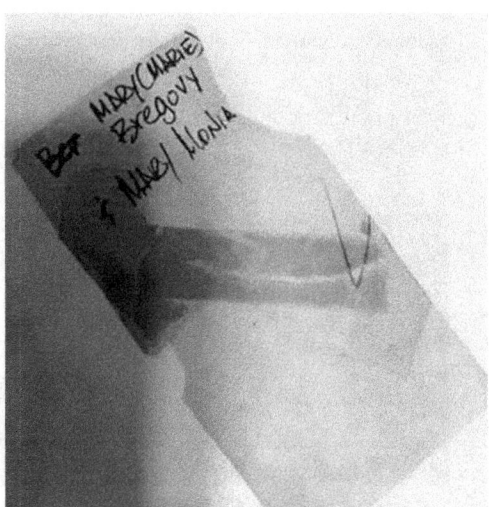

The original photo that was restoring, showing Marie Bregovy and Kathleen's grandmother, Mary Nonia - as well as the note on the back of the photo, which was written with a fountain pen.

She later said, "They looked like wild boys, and for some reason, I just didn't like them." Vern was frightened because they drove recklessly, turning corners on two wheels and speeding down narrow streets. Finally, she demanded to be let out of the car a few blocks from home. She asked Marie if she planned to go out with the young men that night and Marie said that she did. Vern urged her to reconsider, not only because she didn't like the boys but also because Marie's parents had already told her that she needed to stay home. Marie shrugged off her friend's warning and said, "You never like anyone I introduce you to."

Vern stood watching on the street corner as Marie and the young men roared away in the car. It was the last time that she would see her friend alive.

No one knows how Marie Bregovy spent the rest of the day, but a few clues have emerged from family members over the years. The wife of Marie's younger brother, Steve, reported in 1985 that she had received a letter from a friend of Marie's years before that said Marie had attended a novena at church before she went out dancing that night. The Bregovys were devout Catholics, and this would not have

South Damen Avenue in the Back of the Yards Neighborhood where the Bregovy family lived.

been out of the ordinary for Marie to do. She also said that she believed Marie had been going to the Oh Henry Ballroom that night.

But did she ever arrive there? No one knows for sure, but tradition holds that Marie and her new group of friends - which now also included a young woman named Virginia Rozanski - did go dancing at the Oh Henry that night. After the ballroom closed, they drove into the city, where most of the clubs stayed open much later. In the early morning hours, they left downtown Chicago and were driving down Wacker Drive, along the Chicago River, when the accident occurred. There's no information to corroborate it, but it's possible that alcohol and the reckless driving described by Vern Rutkowski combined to cause the crash.

A short piece in the March 11, 1934, edition of the *Chicago Tribune* described the accident:

Girl Killed in Crash

Miss Marie Bregovy, 21 years old, of 4611 South Damen Avenue, was killed last night when the automobile in which she was riding cracked up at Lake Street and Wacker Drive. John Reiker, 23, of 15 North Knight Street, Park Ridge, suffered a possible skull fracture and is in the county hospital. John Thoel, 25, 5216 Loomis Street, driver of the car, and Miss Virginia Rozanski, 22, of 4849 South Lincoln Street, were shaken up and scratched. The scene of the accident is known to police as a danger spot. Thoel told police he did not see the "L" substructure.

The accident occurred along Wacker Drive, just as it curves to the south and away from the river. At the point where Wacker crosses Lake Street, there is a large, metal support for the elevated tracks overhead. If a driver were coming along Wacker too quickly, it was easy not to make a complete turn and collide with the support column, which is almost in a straight line around the curve. This is apparently what happened to John Thoel that night.

The image that appeared in the *Chicago Tribune* of Marie Bregovy after the accident.

When the automobile collided with the metal column, Marie was thrown through the windshield and instantly killed. Her body was badly cut up by the glass. Before her funeral, the undertaker had to sew up a gash that extended all the way across the front of her throat and up to her right ear. Tragically, Marie was not even supposed to be sitting in the front seat when the accident occurred. Her parents would later learn that she had switched places with Virginia Rozanski because Virginia didn't like John Thoel, who she had been sitting next to in the passenger's seat. She had asked Marie to sit in front with Thoel and Marie had agreed. Unfortunately, her good-natured personality would turn out to be fatal for her.

Vern Rutkowski accompanied Marie's mother and her brother, Joseph, to the morgue to identify the body. Marie was taken to the Satala Funeral Home, located just a few blocks from the Bregovy home,

The Satala Funeral Home, located on South Damen Avenue, just a few blocks from Marie Bregovy's home. This location is no longer in operation.

to be prepared for burial. The owner at the time, John Satala, easily remembered Marie. In 1985, he recalled, "She was a hell of a nice girl. Very pretty. She was buried in an orchid dress. I remember having to sew up the side of her face."

Marie was buried in Resurrection Cemetery, and there is some confusion about this. According to records, she was buried in Section MM, Site 9819. There is a Mary Bregovy - not *Marie* Bregovy - buried here, but this is a different woman. Mary Bregovy was a 34-year-old woman who was born in 1888 and died in 1922. This was not the girl who died in a car accident in 1934.

Family members of Marie Bregovy said that Marie was actually buried in a term grave and never moved. After World War II, when space was needed for more burial sites at Resurrection Cemetery, some of the term graves were moved, but others, like Marie's, were simply covered over. For this reason, according to Mrs. Steve Bregovy, the location of Marie's grave is unknown.

Marie was buried, but she did not in peace.

Stories about Marie Bregovy's ghost began a short time after her death. In April 1934, a caretaker at Resurrection Cemetery telephoned funeral home director John Satala and told him that he had seen the barefooted ghost of a young girl walking around the cemetery. She was a lovely girl with light brown hair, and she was wearing a pale, orchid-colored dress. The caretaker was positive that the ghost was the woman that Satala had recently buried. Satala later said that he recognized the description of the girl as Marie Bregovy.

Soon after, other stories began to circulate, claiming that motorists on Archer Avenue in front of Resurrection Cemetery were encountering a frantic woman who tried to hitch a ride with them. These Archer Avenue sightings also included reports from people who recognized the ghost as Marie Bregovy.

I'm convinced that these reports were the beginning of the Resurrection Mary legend. These were the first stories of a young woman hitching rides on Archer Avenue and thanks to the destination of many of these motorists - combined with the fact that the Oh Henry Ballroom was Marie's favorite dance spot - the story began to grow. I believe that many of the reports of a ghostly woman being seen around Resurrection Cemetery can be traced to Marie Bregovy - the "original Resurrection Mary."

But I've also come to believe that Marie Bregovy does not haunt Archer Avenue alone.

Marie may be the source of the legend of Resurrection Mary, but as you may have realized already, she doesn't fit the description of the spirit that may have reported. Marie had naturally curly, brown hair, so she was not the blond spirit that so many people had picked up or spotted on the side of the road. So, who was that ghost?

In 2005, I received a letter that answered the question of who the blond woman had been in life and how she managed to contribute to the legend of Resurrection Mary.

Maybe.

Anyway, aside from motorists who encountered Mary along Archer Avenue in the 1930s, there were also those who came face-to-face with her under other conditions. One of them was a young man named Jerry Palus, whose experience with Mary took place in 1939 and was so vivid that he never forgot it. When he died in 1992, he still insisted that his story was true. He was an unshakable witness and eventually appeared on several television shows to discuss the night with Resurrection Mary. Other than that, he never became famous for his encounter. He had little to gain from his story and no reason to lie.

He never once doubted that he spent the evening with a ghost.

Jerry Palus - years after his encounter with the young woman he dropped off at Resurrection Cemetery

Jerry met a young woman - an extremely attractive blond - at the Liberty Grove and Hall; a music, dance, and "jumping" spot that was near 47th Street and Mozart in the Brighton Park neighborhood on Chicago's Southwest Side. He got the courage to ask her to dance, and although he had been watching her for some time that evening, he admitted in later interviews that he never saw her come into the place. She spent a couple of hours sitting by herself, since she didn't seem to know anyone, and Jerry finally asked to take her out onto the dance floor. The girl accepted his invitation, and they spent several hours together. Strangely, though, she seemed a little distant and Palus also noticed that her skin was very cold, almost icy to the touch. When he later kissed her, he found her lips were also cold and clammy.

At the end of the evening, the young woman asked Jerry for a ride home. He readily agreed to give her a lift. When they got to his automobile, she explained that she lived on South Damen Avenue but that she wanted to take a ride down Archer Avenue first. Jerry shrugged and told her that he would be happy to take her wherever she wanted. By this time, he was infatuated with the girl and likely wanted to extend the night for as long as he could. He knew that it would be quite a bit out of the way to drive down Archer Avenue, but he didn't mind. He put his car into gear and drove off.

To reach Archer Avenue from the Liberty Grove and Hall, Jerry only had to travel west on 47th Street. Once he made it to the old roadway, they traveled southwest to Summit and then on toward Justice. It was a dark, dimly lit road in those days, but Jerry was somewhat familiar with the area, so he just followed the course of the road, heading eventually, he thought, towards Willow Springs.

But as they approached the gates to Resurrection Cemetery, the girl asked him to pull over. She had to get out here, she told him. Jerry was confused, unable to understand why she would want to get out at such a spot, but he pulled the car to the side of the road anyway. He agreed that he would let her out, but only if she allowed him to walk her to wherever she was going. There was a row of houses to Jerry's right, about a block off Archer Avenue, and he assumed that she was going to one of them. He wanted to be sure that she made it there safely.

The beautiful young girl refused to allow this, though. She turned in her seat and faced Palus. She spoke softly, "This is where I have to get out, but where I'm going, you can't follow."

Jerry was bewildered by this statement, but before he could respond, the girl got out of the car and ran not in the direction of the houses but across Archer Avenue toward the gates of Resurrection Cemetery. She vanished before she reached them - right before Jerry's eyes. That was the moment when he knew that he had danced with a specter.

Determined to find out what was going on, Jerry went looking for the girl's house the next day. She had given him her address. When a woman answered the door, Jerry saw a photograph in the living room of the girl he'd met the night before. When he told the woman about the evening, though, she told him that it was impossible - the girl in the photograph was her daughter, but she had been dead for years.

Jerry was stunned by this revelation, but apparently, the address and identity of the woman were forgotten over the years. Many years later, when Jerry was contacted again about his story - after the passing of time had renewed interest in the ghost - Jerry was unable to remember where he had gone on the morning after his encounter. Despite this memory lapse, Jerry's story remains one of the most credible of all the Resurrection Mary encounters.

But who was the woman Jerry danced with that night?

In July 2005, I received a vague letter from a woman who promised me information about Resurrection Mary, claiming that the real-life counterpart of Mary had once been her mother's babysitter when she was a child. If I were interested, I could call her and get more information. Her mother was still alive and would be happy to speak with me about it.

I read the letter with interest but with a lot of skepticism, too. This was not the first time that I'd received a letter of this sort, but, out of curiosity, I decided to give the woman a call. She gave me a few details of the story and then gave me the telephone number of her mother, who was 85 years old and urged me to contact her. The next afternoon, I called the number and was soon speaking with Mrs. Martha Litak, who grew up on South Damen Avenue in the Back of the Yards Neighborhood. I told her why I was calling and asked her what she could tell me about the story of Resurrection Mary.

Her answer surprised me. She laughed and said, "Resurrection Mary was my babysitter!"

According to Mrs. Litak, a young woman named Mary Miskowski had lived down the street from her family when she was a child. The Miskowski house was located at 4924 South Damen Avenue - interestingly, just three blocks away from Marie Bregovy's home, so it seems possible these two women could have known one another - and Mary often babysat for neighborhood children to earn extra money. Mrs. Litak was not sure if Mary had a regular job or not. She lived with her parents, she recalled, but Mary was old enough to be out of school.

Martha remembered her very well. She said, "She was a very pretty girl. She had light blond hair with just a little bit of curl to it. It was cut short, just a little below her ears. All the boys in the neighborhood were in love with her. I do remember that she liked to go on dates, but I don't recall that she had any one boyfriend in particular."

Martha remembered that her cousins told her that Mary loved to go out dancing, including to the Oh Henry Ballroom, which had opened in 1921. Her favorite place, though, was the Liberty Grove and Hall, which was located about 12 blocks from her home. It seemed possible that Mary Miskowski - if she were one of the spirits that created the "Resurrection Mary" legend - could have been the blond that Jerry Palus met on the night of his encounter. She might also be the blond that so many other people claim they have encountered over the years, too.

But Mary's favorite dancing spot was not the only convincing part of the story.

Martha told me that she had spoken with her younger brother, Frank after her daughter told her that I might get in touch. She had asked him if he could remember anything about their old babysitter, Mary Miskowski. Frank was only seven years old when Mary died, but he did recall what she looked like.

The Miskowski home on South Damen Avenue

In fact, he remembered her very well because Frank believed that he saw Mary one night many years after she died!

He was a young man at the time and had just returned home from the Army, where he had served during World War II. He was out for a drive one night on Archer Avenue, and while traveling north, he saw a woman standing on the side of the road. He slowed down to look at her, and as he did, the woman turned in his direction. He was stunned when he saw her face - it was his dead babysitter, Mary Miskowski! Frank slammed on his brakes and pulled over to the side of the road. He looked frantically backward, but the woman was gone. In a matter of seconds, she had simply vanished. Frank was so shaken by the encounter that he didn't drive that particular stretch of Archer Avenue again for years.

According to Martha, Mary Miskowski had been killed by a hit and run driver in October 1930. A car had struck her as she was crossing 47th Street and had sped away. Whoever the driver was, he was never caught. Martha surmised that perhaps this incident was how the story got started about Resurrection Mary being run over by a car and left for dead on Archer Avenue. With the Willowbrook Ballroom tied so closely to the legend, she was not surprised that the accident had been moved to a location that was closer to the dance hall. Mrs. Litak also told me that Mary had been on her way to a costume party that night. She had been dressed as a bride, wearing her mother's old wedding dress. Martha didn't know what Mary had been buried in, but she did believe that perhaps the white dress she was wearing her when she died explained the sightings of a woman in white on the side of the road.

Mrs. Litak also told me that she believed Mary had also been buried in Resurrection Cemetery. I have been unable to confirm this, but Martha and Frank were both sure this was the case. They told me that she had been buried in a term grave - just like Marie Bregovy - but she did not know the ultimate location of the site.

This all started to make sense to me after I spoke with Martha and Frank. It might explain why Resurrection Mary encounters don't always physically match and why the ghost seems to behave in different ways. Mary Miskowski might be the pretty blond who hangs out in dance halls and vanishes from cars, while Marie Bregovy might be the ghost who tried to hitch rides from her old friends in front of Resurrection Cemetery.

But then, a few years later, I hit a snag. Mary Miskowski, according to the story, had died around Halloween 1930 when she was probably 18- or 19-years-old. At least part of that was accurate. She had lived at 4924 South Damen Avenue in 1930, and she was 19 years old. The problem was verifying her death because there were no records or newspaper reports. It turned out that Mary - who got married and was no longer using her maiden name - died in 1956. She was 45 years old at the time. So, this was apparently not the same girl that Martha and Frank said had died in 1930. Had they been confused? Was Mary their babysitter, or was it someone else who lived on the block?

Unfortunately, at this point, both have passed away, so I have no way to ask them. I find it hard to believe that an 85-year-old woman and her elderly brother would come up with an elaborate prank about their old babysitter and Resurrection Mary, but it's possible, I suppose.

Unlikely, but still possible. What is more likely is that they confused some names, and while they knew Mary Miskowski, she didn't die in 1930. Someone they knew did die, though, and whoever that young woman was just might be one of the ghosts who went on to create a legend.

And whoever she was, I'll bet she was a blond.

It's a good story. And it seems possible. But who knows? Mary Miskowski was certainly not the only blond who *might* be Resurrection Mary. And she certainly wasn't the only young woman named "Mary" to be thrown in the mix. There are a lot of them because it was a very common name, especially among the first- and second-generation immigrant families who lived in the Back of the Yards.

And who says her name had to be "Mary?" Even Mary Bregovy's name wasn't Mary. She went by Marie - probably because there were too many Mary's in the neighborhood. There was even an older woman named "Mary Bregovy" who had a daughter named "Mary Bregovy!"

But even if Mary Miskowski turns out to be a dead end, I will say that it was Martha's story that prompted my theory that "Resurrection Mary" is not one ghost, but two, or maybe even more.

This still leaves us with another question, though: Why do encounters with Mary fade in the 1940s, only to return with such intensity three decades later? In the 1970s, Resurrection Cemetery began undergoing major renovations, including the movement of the term graves that had been in place for many years. Some of the graves were moved to other locations, while others - according to relatives who have loved ones buried in the cemetery - were reportedly bulldozed under the earth. It's believed that this disturbance may have been what caused Mary sightings to increase so dramatically in the 1970s and early 1980s. But once the work was finished, the sightings began to fade away again, just as they had done many years before.

So, finally, we ask - does this vanishing hitchhiker really exist?

She does, and she's real. She was a real person - or perhaps more than one - who lived and died and created a legend.

There are still many who doubt her existence, but I've never felt their skepticism really matters. Whether the doubters believe in her or not, people saw - and sometimes still see - Mary walking along Archer Avenue at night. Motorists stopped to pick up a forlorn young woman who seemed inadequately dressed on cold winter nights. Even today, curiosity-seekers still come to see the gates where the twisted and burned bars once were, and some even roam the graveyard, hoping to stumble across the place where Mary's body was laid to rest.

We may never truly know who she was in life, but that has not stopped the stories or the songs about her. She remains an enigma, and her legend continues, not content to vanish - as Mary does when she reaches the gates to Resurrection Cemetery.

Our individual belief - or disbelief - does not really matter. Mary lives on regardless, always as a mysterious, elusive, and romantic spirit of the graveyard.

BIBLIOGRAPHY

Bell, Michael - *Food for the Dead*, Middletown, CT, Wesleyan University Press, 2014

Bernstein, Joanna, Editor - *Death: A Graveside Companion*, London, Thames and Hudson, 2017

Bielski, Ursula - *Haunted Bachelor's Grove*, Charleston, SC, History Press, 2016

Bolte, Mary and Mary Eastman - *Haunted New England*, Weathervane Books, 1972

Bondeson, Jan - *Buried Alive*, New York, NY, W.W. Norton, 2001

Brown, John Gary - *Soul in Stone*, University Press of Kansas, 1994

Brunvand, Jan Harold - *The Vanishing Hitchhiker*, New York, NY, W.W. Norton, 1981

Citro, Joe - *Passing Strange*, Shelburne, VT, Chapters Publishing, 1996

D'Agostino, Thomas - *History of the Vampires of New England*, Charleston, SC, History Press, 2010

Davies, Rodney - *The Lazarus Syndrome*, London, Robert Hales LTD, 1998

Doughty, Caitlin - *From Here to Eternity*, New York, NY, W.W. Norton, 2017

Garner, Nicole - "How One Widow's Grief Turned a Small Town into a Roadside Attraction," *Mental Floss*, November 2017

Hammond, Amberrose - *Ghosts and Legends of Michigan's West Coast*, Charleston, SC, History Press, 2009

Johnson, Brenda - "Black Hope horror doesn't haunt this hood," *Houston Chronicle*, October 24, 2007

Keister, Douglas - *Stories in Stone,* Salt Lake City, UT, Gibbs Smith, 2004

Murphy, Michael - *Fear Dat*, New York, NY, W.W. Norton, 2015

My Haunted Library - "Grave Robbers & Ghosts: Haunted Cheesman Park," April 2, 2017

Ogden, Tom - *Haunted Cemeteries*, Lanha, MD, Globe Pequot, 2010

Pickover, Clifford A. - *Death and the Afterlife*, New York, NY, Sterling, 2015

Selzer, Adam - *Ghosts of Chicago*, Woodbury, MN, Llewellyn Publications, 2017

Smith, Leanne - "Crouch murders still captivating 127 years after infamous night", *Michigan Live*, November 20, 2010

Slaughter, April and Troy Taylor - *Disconnected from Death*, Jacksonville, IL, American Hauntings Ink, 2018

Taylor, Troy - *Beyond the Grave*, Alton, IL, Whitechapel Press, 2001
--------- - *Resurrection Mary*, Decatur, IL, Whitechapel Press, 2006

Thanatos. Archive - *Beyond the Dark Veil*, Fullerton, CA, California State University, Fullerton, 2017

Wolf, Christopher - *Haunted Highways and Ghostly Travelers*, Atglen, PA, Schiffer, 2011

Special Thanks to:
April Slaughter: Cover Design and Artwork
Becky Ray: Editing and Proofreading
Lisa Taylor Horton and Lux
Kathleen Buchanan
Lois Taylor
Orrin Taylor
Rene Kruse
Rachael Horath
Elyse and Thomas Reihner
Bethany Horath
John Winterbauer
Kaylan Schardan
Maggie Walsh
Cody Beck
Tom and Michelle Bonadurer
Susan Kelly and Amy Bouyear
And the entire crew of American Hauntings

ABOUT THE AUTHOR

Troy Taylor is the author of books on ghosts, hauntings, true crime, the unexplained, and the supernatural in America. He is also the founder of American Hauntings Ink, which offers books, ghost tours, events, and weekend excursions. He was born and raised in the Midwest and currently divides his time between Illinois and the far-flung reaches of America.

www.ingramcontent.com/pod-product-compliance
Lightning Source LLC
Chambersburg PA
CBHW070959160426
43193CB00012B/1834